# The Poor Clares in Belfast

## 1924–2012

Martin J Magill

For permissions, or to purchase copies of the book, please contact the author at: m.magill@downandconnor.org

Cover design: David-Lee Badger
Typesetting and layout: Shanway Press
Printed by Shanway Press

Material from the Order of the Poor Clares is reproduced with the kind permission of Sr Paschal and Sr Mary in the Poor Clare Monastery, Carlow and Mother Brigid in St Damian's Monastery, Dublin.

ISBN: 978-1-910044-19-3

Front cover depicts Sr Mary at prayer (image courtesy of Brendan Murphy).

In memory and gratitude for

the Poor Clares

in Belfast

1924–2012

# Contents

Foreword                                                          vii

Preface                                                          viii

Acknowledgements                                                    x

Introduction                                                     xiii

**Setting up in Belfast**                                           1

    Request to set up a foundation in Belfast     4

    Why Belfast?                                  11

    Prayer and reparation                         14

**The Move to the Antrim Road**                                    17

    Ascension Thursday, 29 May 1924               24

**Growing and Building**                                           29

    Solitude – a good place for contemplation     32

**'How We Prayed that Night!' – The Belfast Blitz**                41

**From Autonomy to Federation**                                    63

    The Federation of the Poor Clares of Ireland  68

    Vatican II                                    71

**Solace and Survival in the Seventies**                           73

    Ministry of listening                         78

    The Troubles close by                         83

    Continuing unrest                             87

**Living with Uncertainty**                                        97

    Peace prayers                                101

    Concern for suffering                        104

    Signs of hope                                107

**The Dark Night**                                                113

    A decision to rebuild                        118

    Support from far and wide                    124

    Monastery complete                           131

**The Long Struggle to Keep Going** 137

 The first Filipino nuns 142

 Under pressure 144

 An appeal for help abroad 147

 A re-foundation 150

 A Filipino Poor Clare community 153

 The decision to close 159

**The World Outside** 167

 Visitors from other denominations 177

 Franciscan visitors 182

 Watching the world 186

**The World Inside** 193

 The influence of St Clare 195

 Sacrifice 197

 Fun and humour 197

 Community life 205

**Resting in Peace** 211

 Sr Mary O'Connor 213

 Sr Paschal Hughes 214

 Sr Patricia Ward 215

 Sr Magdalen Power 216

 Mother Colette Egan 218

 Sr Oliver Feeney 219

 Mother Paul Hobbins 220

 Sr Malachy McHenry 221

 Sr Francis Bryce 222

 Sr Anthony Lloyd 223

Sr Clare Gaynor                              224

Sr Joseph Grogan                            225

Sr Bernadette McGrenra                      226

Mother Michael Sheridan                     227

Sr Thérèse Hoey                             228

Sr Assisi O'Neill                           229

Sr Catherine Fagan                          230

Sr Assumpta Horner                          232

Sr John Heaney                              234

Sr Petronilla Murtagh                       234

Sr Helena Forsythe                          236

Sr Gertrude Woods                           237

**Timeline for the Poor Clares in Belfast**     239

**Bibliography**                                242

**Glossary**                                    245

About the author                            248

# Foreword

Time is always in the hands of the Lord, yet it is hard to believe the Poor Clare community finally left Belfast just six years ago.

In that period, we have lived very happily as members of the Poor Clare community in Carlow, near the banks of the River Barrow. However, we will always look back on our time on the Cliftonville Road with immense fondness. Our years of contemplative life in the monastery brought deep joy, and we remember with much appreciation the many neighbours, friends, clergy, religious and family who came to see and support us during that time.

During our years in Belfast we had the privilege to meet, listen to and pray with a great many amazing people and it was a special blessing to be able to talk to some of the mothers who had suffered so much during the Troubles. Naturally, it was a very sad occasion when we had to leave our many friends behind, though we are glad that many still keep in touch and visit us here in Carlow.

In perusing Fr Martin's book, it is humbling to see how the Poor Clares were welcomed to the city in 1924 and to recollect how much support we received until the point we had to say goodbye. We hope that those who read this book will come to understand in some way what the people of Belfast meant to the Poor Clares in Belfast, in Ireland, and indeed well beyond our shores.

We are very grateful to Fr Martin Magill for the time he has spent in writing *The Poor Clares in Belfast 1924-2012*. Indeed, we are honoured that he has told our story in Belfast.

It strikes us that the city our sisters left in 2012 was very different to the one in which the foundation was first established. We therefore give thanks to God for the countless blessings he showered upon the monastery over 88 years of Poor Clare life in the city of Belfast.

*Sr Paschal McNeel and Sr Mary McGann*

# Preface

In May 2016, I found myself agreeing to chair a presentation on the Poor Clare nuns at the Duncairn Centre for Culture and Arts in North Belfast, an event that was part of a lecture series entitled 'The Many Faces of North Belfast,' organised by historian and playwright Philip Orr. Philip had asked me to find someone to talk about the history of the Poor Clares in Belfast. Something I had thought would be easy was however proving difficult, and in the end I stepped in myself to give the talk.

My reason for doing so was that I had learned from my, by then, three-year spell in Sacred Heart Parish, where I was Parish Priest, that this religious community had found a special place in the hearts of so many people – and not just Catholics – in the city of Belfast. Time and again in my work in Sacred Heart, the parish the Poor Clare community had been based in for most of their years in Belfast, I had come across the affection, esteem and respect in which this enclosed community of nuns were held, and I wanted to tell their story.

Through my research for the talk, I became even more interested in what the Poor Clares represented and what they had brought to the people of North Belfast and beyond. I was particularly captivated by the decision to set up a foundation in 1924 in a city that had endured two years of civil strife and which left 500 people dead. That decision could only be understood from a spiritual perspective. I also wanted to find a way to consider more fully the impact this small community had made in the life of the city from the time they arrived right up to their sad departure.

Subsequently, I was given access to the journals and records the nuns had kept of what they called the 'principal events' in the life of the community. In reading and studying these documents I found it very exciting, for example, to hear how a contemplative Poor Clare nun experienced the Belfast Blitz of 1941, which came very close to the community and indeed damaged parts of their monastery. So, the idea for this book was born and I began to research further, and I began to write. You are reading the outcome of my endeavours. It has been, as they say, a real 'labour of love.'

As I wrote this book I wanted to include the wider context of what was going on in the city of Belfast as well showing the importance of the spirituality of the Order of Poor Clares. In addition, regarding relationships and attitudes among Christians of different denominations, I believe it is possible to trace the change of spirit from when the first nuns arrived in 1924 until the closure of the monastery 2012. The regular contact with and appreciation of Christians of other denominations in the final years of the community's existence in Belfast give some idea of the improving ecumenical relationships.

I trust you will find this book not just a history of the time the Poor Clare nuns spent in Belfast, but also a sense of what they experienced inside their monastery, what they felt about their North Belfast neighbourhood and how they viewed the Church, the world, friends, visitors and indeed life and death from inside the cloisters of their enclosed community. More than that, I hope the book will honour the Poor Clares and stand as a testament to everything they represented during their time in the city of Belfast.

Something I was always conscious of as I wrote was that the Poor Clares' compassionate presence reached well outside of Catholic circles and into those of other faiths and even those with none. It is my wish that this book will do the same.

# Acknowledgements

A great many people gave of their time, assistance and expertise during my research and the compilation of this book, and I would like to acknowledge in particular the help I received from them.

I express first of all my profound gratitude to several nuns from the Order of Poor Clares, very particularly Sr Paschal and Sr Mary who were members of the Belfast community for over 50 years and at the time of writing are in the Poor Clare Monastery, Carlow. Without their assistance, guidance and support, this book would not exist.

I am also very grateful to Mother Rosario from St Clare's Monastery in Carlow and Mother Brigid from St Damian's Monastery in Dublin who graciously supported my efforts.

I thank people from the parishes of Sacred Heart, Ballyclare and Ballygowan and St John the Evangelist for their encouragement, understanding and support. I am also very grateful to Bishop Noel Treanor, Bishop of Down and Connor for his assistance in helping this book become a reality.

Thanks are also due to the priests of St Malachy's Seminary (which replaced the monastery) for their assistance at various stages of the production of this book: Fr Gerard Fox, Fr Eddie McGee and Fr Michael Spence.

The following people were very helpful at various stages throughout the writing:

Brian Barton, author *The Belfast Blitz. The City in the War Years*
Niall Cunningham, Assistant Professor in the Department of Geography, Durham University
Rev Rachel Creighton, former Rector, Parish of Holy Trinity, St Silas with Immanuel, Ardoyne, Belfast
Jim Deeds, Living Church Office, Down and Connor, author and poet
Frances Doran, Diocesan Office, Down and Connor

Helen Doran, Office Manager, Franciscan Missionary Union, Dublin

Hugh Dougal, O'Kane's Funeral Directors

Sr Marie Doyle, OSC, Belfast

Jenny Haslett, Museum Manager, Northern Ireland War Memorial

Roddy Hegarty, Cardinal Tomás Ó Fiaich Memorial Library & Archive, Armagh

Fr Brendan Hickland, Parish Priest, St Teresa's, Belfast

Caroline Hicks, Ara Coeli, Diocesan Office, Armagh

Liam Horner, The Horner Gallery

Seamus Kelters, Editor of *Lost Lives* (died September 2017)

Michael Kelly, Editor, *Irish Catholic*

Gerard Lawlor, Cliftonville FC

Mary McAleese, former President of Ireland

Fr Liam McCarthy OFM, Franciscan Friary, Killarney

Crawford McCully, Cliftonville Cricket Club

Jim McDermott, Author Northern Divisions

Fr Thomas McGlynn, Parish Priest, St Agnes', Belfast

Fr Aidan McGrath OFM, Minister Provincial of the Irish Franciscans

Michael McKernon, Multimedia Heritage

Denis Moloney, Donnelly & Wall Solicitors

David Nixon, O.D. Cars Ltd.

Philip Orr, author and playwright

Darren O'Reilly, Koinonia John the Baptist Community

Trevor Parkhill, author *A Nurse in the Belfast Blitz, The Diary of Emma Duffin 1939-1942*

Dr Eamon Phoenix, historian and author

Agnes Sheppard, secretary, Ballyclare and Ballygowan Parish

Joe and Peter Treacy, Tracey Architects, Derry

Paul Treanor, Cliftonville FC

Rev William Taggart, Rector, St Katherine Parish, Belfast

Bishop Patrick Walsh, Bishop Emeritus, Down and Connor

I am very grateful to the following for their practical help and/or guidance: Emma Graham, for typing several sections; Bernie Hughes for her guidance; John Leonard, for proof reading and editorial suggestions; Anne Magill, for additional research and proof reading; Fr Brendan McManus SJ for his advice and companionship; Josephine O'Neill, for transcribing some of the letters written at the time of the Blitz and also assistance in shaping the book; and Fr Paul Symonds for his assistance in visiting the Poor Clares in Carlow.

I also acknowledge the assistance I received from the Deputy Keeper of Records and members of staff in the Public Record Office of Northern Ireland (PRONI) as well as staff from Belfast Central Library and from the National Museums NI.

I am indebted to several people who helped me with the photographs and illustrations used in this book, in particular retired *Irish News* photographer Brendan Murphy, Mal McCann a current photographer with the *Irish News*, Peter Rainey the picture editor of the *Belfast Telegraph*, Thomas McMullan from the *North Belfast News* and Rev Elizabeth Hanna, Rector of St Nicholas' Church, Belfast.

I have made every possible attempt to contact the copyright holders and seek the relevant permission for each and every photograph, and the relevant credits appear alongside each image.

Sincere thanks to John Monaghan at Shanway Press, who has been very helpful over the last two years from my very first phone call to him in May 2016. I appreciate his time during many phone calls and emails. Thanks also to David-Lee Badger for the creative way he has designed this book.

Finally, I thank very specially the editor of this book, Michael Johnston from Editorial Solutions Ltd. Michael's professionalism, attention to detail and encouragement has made an enormous contribution towards making this book a reality.

Martin J Magill

# Introduction

As I was preparing to give my talk on the history of the Poor Clares in Belfast I became fascinated with the question of why the Poor Clare community in St Damian's Monastery in Dublin decided to establish a new foundation in Belfast in the first place. During a visit to St Damian's I was shown the community journal, which I quote from and refer to in this book. As we shall see, this journal and the journal kept by the nuns in Belfast helped to provide the answer to my question. I was however unable to locate any correspondence between Mother Genevieve, the abbess in Dublin and the bishop of the diocese at the time, Bishop MacRory. An exchange of letters would have been normal Church protocol and would have been expected in terms of seeking permission for the Poor Clares to set up in Belfast.

Down and Connor archivist Fr Thomas McGlynn explained that there was very little material from Bishop MacRory's time in the diocesan files. Noted historian and academic, Dr Eamon Phoenix, explained in a conversation with me that owing to the tensions of the times Bishop MacRory was concerned about his house being raided by the police or military and that the bishop had burned some of the papers from his files. This may possibly explain the non-existence of Mother Genevieve's letter or letters. Whatever about the dearth of material to trace the decision to establish a monastery in Belfast, suffice to say there certainly would have been correspondence and at least one meeting took place between members of the order and the bishop to agree the details of the move to Belfast.

Thankfully, however, when the Belfast monastery was established in 1924 different members of the Poor Clare community kept journals and notebooks over the years. One was called: *Principal Events. Poor Clare Colettine Convent Our Lady and St Michael's*, Cliftonville Road, Belfast which I refer to throughout as *Journal One*. It details events from the time the Order of the Poor Clares first contacted Bishop MacRory until the start of 1991. A second journal, *Journal Two*, begins in 1989 and continues until 1995. A file containing the most important community correspondence was also kept.

I was able to compile the last years of the nuns' story, from 1995 until 2012, using this community correspondence and various issues of an annual Poor Clare newsletter called *Tel-A-Vision*. I also had access to additional records and correspondence in St Damian's Monastery in Dublin.

From these sources I have chosen to write this book as much as possible using the Poor Clares' own words. When I quote the content of the journals – which appear in italics throughout the book – I have transcribed the notes and journal entries almost exactly as they were written. Minor errors such as the odd spelling mistake have been corrected. Where a word had been written twice by accident, this has also been corrected. Where words have been omitted, the necessary word has been added. I have at times added in some brief comments in parenthesis to clarify a point and tidied up some of the punctuation style. Otherwise the nuns' story and commentary is completely their own.

At the start of each chapter, I have used a direct quotation from one of the journals or the annual newsletter to give a flavour of what is to follow.

I should explain that in the Catholic Church, a 'sister' in a religious order is a woman who lives, ministers, and prays within the 'world.' A sister's life is often labelled 'active' or 'apostolic' because she is engaged in works of mercy and other ministries that take the Gospel to others where they are. Women, like the Poor Clares, who live contemplative lives in a monastery, which is usually enclosed, are called 'nuns' and I have used this term when talking about the Poor Clares throughout, even though they occasionally refer to themselves as 'sisters'.

# Chapter One

## Setting up in Belfast

Mother Genevieve, known as Mother Foundress of the Poor Clare foundation in Belfast

> ***The need was great for prayer and reparation*** "

In the journals, records and correspondence of the Order of the Poor Clares in Belfast, there are countless references to 'Our Holy Mother Saint Clare.' To fully appreciate the nuns' way of life and their presence in the city, it therefore helps to understand their religious order and at least some details about their founder, St Clare of Assisi.

Clare was born in Assisi in Italy on July 16, 1194, the eldest daughter of wealthy aristocratic parents. In 1212, aged 18, she heard a preacher during a Lenten service. It was Francis, who in 1208 had founded the Franciscan Order. Clare then made a radical decision to leave her wealthy family, asking Francis to help her live the Gospel more fully. As outward signs of her new way of life, Clare's hair was cut off and she was given a plain robe and veil in exchange for her rich gown. Francis arranged for Clare to join a monastery of Benedictine nuns at San Paolo delle Abbadesse, near Assisi. When her father found her there, he attempted to force her back into his home. She refused and professed that she would have 'no other husband than Jesus Christ.' To give her the greater solitude she desired, Francis sent Clare to another monastery of Benedictine nuns.

Over time other women joined Clare, including her sister, all wanting to be 'brides of Jesus' and to live with no money or property. The phrase 'without anything of one's own' was lived out by Clare and her sisters in religion. These women became known as the 'Poor Ladies of San Damiano.' They lived a life of austerity, seclusion from the world and poverty, according to a rule which Francis gave them. St Clare and her sisters wore no shoes, ate no meat, lived in a poor house and kept silence most of the time. Their lives consisted of manual labour and prayer. Despite such conditions, they were known for their joy.

Clare placed a great importance on poverty or 'holy poverty' as she called it. Her inspiration for living this way comes from St Francis who had already rejected all material goods and had chosen the way of poverty. She writes passionately about it such as in her first letter to Agnes of Prague:

> O blessed poverty who bestows eternal riches on those who love and embrace her! O holy poverty, to those who possess and desire you God promises the kingdom of heaven (Matthew 5:3) and beyond any doubt,

reveals eternal glory and blessed life to those who have and desire her.
(Armstrong, 2006, p.45)

What is unique and even more challenging is that Clare lived in poverty
within an enclosed community. This way of living was the outward expression
of Clare's belief in the Providence of God. In practical reality this meant
depending upon the generosity and goodness of other people.

In 1216 Clare became the Abbess of San Damiano in Assisi, though for
a brief time, the order was directed by St Francis. Clare became the first
woman to write a rule for religious life for women, despite opposition from
members of the hierarchy of the Church who wanted her community to live
under the Rule of St Benedict. Clare's rule had at its heart the desire 'to live
according to the perfection of the Gospel.'

It is interesting to note that it was only in the last part of the twentieth
century that greater attention was given to Clare in her own right, rather
than as someone in the shadow of Francis of Assisi. Owing to this relatively
recent scholarship, Clare is now understood as a strong, determined woman
of her time. Her vision and passion have throughout the centuries inspired
countless women to follow in her footsteps, including the nuns who lived in
Belfast. It is clear from Clare's writings, suggests Jon Sweeney (2007), that
she was a woman of deep faith with a personal commitment to, and love of,
the person of Jesus Christ: 'Like St Francis before her, St Clare was always
looking at Jesus' earthly life for what to do and who to become. She read and
quoted from the Gospels more than any other Scripture.'

In 1253 Clare's rule was approved by the Pope as the governing rule for her
Order of Poor Ladies. Clare died on 11 August in 1253 at the age of 59. Two
years later Pope Alexander IV canonised her as St Clare of Assisi. Ten years
after her death, the order became known as the Order of St Clare or the Poor
Clares.

In addition to the influence of St Clare on the Belfast nuns, there is also the
part played by St Colette. The monastery in Belfast was officially known as
the Poor Clare Colettine Monastery and the nuns who set up there were
known as the Poor Clare Colettine Order.

The word 'Colettine' comes from the name of St Colette, who was born in France in 1381. As a young woman she joined a number of religious orders before going off to live a solitary life. In 1406, she ended her solitary way of living, having had a dream to reform the Order of the Poor Clares. She set about this and founded several convents which followed her approach. These convents began to spread beyond her native France including to Ireland.

Fr Aidan McGrath OFM (2012, p.19), Franciscan priest and former religious assistant to the Belfast community, charts the connection between St Colette and the eventual Poor Clare presence in the city:

> In her own lifetime she [St Colette] founded the monastery of Ghent; this, in turn, founded the monastery of Bruges; from this monastery came the monastery of Levenshulme in England; and from there came the monastery of Graiguecullen, in Carlow, in 1893; Carlow founded St Damian's in Dublin, and Dublin founded the monastery in Belfast.

## Request to set up a foundation in Belfast

With St Clare and St Colette as the guidance and inspiration for the Order, the initiative to set up in Belfast began formally when, following Church protocol, the superior of the monastery in Dublin wrote to the bishop of the diocese in Down and Connor in 1923 requesting permission to establish a convent in Belfast. The details of this are contained in the community journal:

> *On St Patrick's Day, 1923, Mother Genevieve, Abbess of the Poor Clare Colettine Convent, Donnybrook, Dublin wrote to the Most Rev. Dr MacRory asking his permission to found a convent of the Order in his diocese of Down and Connor. Mrs Hill, a personal friend of His Lordship approached him on the same subject; he promised to consider it but didn't seem too keen. However, as he himself admitted later, the Lord evidently wanted the foundation, for just then he was sending the usual reports to Rome and it struck him very forcibly that he had not a single contemplative Order in his diocese. He wrote to Mother Genevieve giving the necessary permission.*

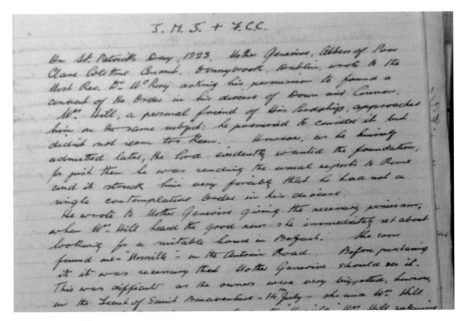

First page *Journal One*

From a human point of view, the actual timing of the request in March 1923 to set up in Belfast, in post-partition Belfast, is hard to understand. In the city, between July 1920 and June 1922, almost 500 people had been killed, many more were injured and countless others were made homeless or jobless in a series of incidents and widespread unrest. Yet less than a year after the mayhem began to subside, on 17 March 1923, Mother Genevieve was formally requesting permission from the local bishop to set up in Belfast.

When violence in Belfast is considered, most attention focusses on the 'Troubles' that began in the late 1960s and yet the city had endured a much earlier violent and destructive conflict in the early 1920s. On 21 July 1920 rioting broke out, beginning in the shipyard in the east of the city. This violence was to spread to all parts of Belfast, and the significant death toll it unfortunately produced is documented by Niall Cunningham (2013, p.56) in 'The doctrine of vicarious punishment': space, religion and the Belfast Troubles of 1920–22':

> In total, 491 deaths have been attributed to the conflict in Belfast over the two-year period from 21 July 1920, when the first fatality was recorded, through to 29 June 1922 with the last entry.

Cunningham (2013, p.53) also makes the point that within the first six months of 1922, 285 people were killed in Belfast, whereas in 1972, the worst year of the later 'Troubles,' 298 were killed during the whole year.

Jonathan Bardon (1982, p.202) writes that from July 1920 to July 1922:

> Catholic relief organisations estimated that between 8,700 and 11,000 Catholics had lost their jobs, that 23,000 Catholics had been forced out of their homes, and about 500 Catholic-owned businesses had been destroyed.

In February 1922, Bishop Joseph MacRory, wrote a Lenten Pastoral Letter (a public letter to the Catholics of his diocese) in which he described his understanding of how it all started:

> The trouble began with the expulsions of Catholic shipyard workers on the 21st of July, 1920, nine days after Sir Edward Carson had addressed a large Orange meeting in a suburb of Belfast on the Twelfth. Whatever may have been the motives for the onslaught, whether it was planned with a view to drive a wedge into the ranks of Labour, as it has unhappily succeeded in doing, or to terrorise Catholics into meek submission to the new 'Ulster' Government, or to provide work for Orange workers in the places of those expelled, or with all three objects in view, at any rate it was not a fact, and it was not even alleged at the time, that the great body of local Catholics had given any excuse for the fury let loose against them. (MacRory, 1922 p.6)

Various factors were perceived to have contributed to the rioting in the early 1920s. Belfast had experienced an economic downturn at that time, competition over jobs was intense and unemployment was very high. In addition, an RIC (Royal Irish Constabulary) officer from Banbridge was killed in Cork by the IRA. The rioting began when more than 7,000 Catholics and left-wing Protestants were forced out of the shipyards and pelted with rivets as they fled for their lives. Further expulsions took place from the Sirocco Works, Musgraves, Mackies and Combe Barbours. None of these expelled workers ever got their job back again.

Bishop MacRory, who was living in Belfast, regularly spoke out during the riots. In 1920, for instance, he had telegrammed the Chief Secretary of Ireland: 'the condition of Belfast is appalling. Our Catholic people are being brutally driven from their homes. Unless the men expelled from Queen's Island be reinstated and adequately protected, there is no hope of peace.' (*Irish Catholic Directory*, 1921, p.526)

In June 1921, in a cablegram to the Honourable Morgan J. O'Brien, chairman of the executive committee of the American Relief Committee, the bishop had declared:

> The position of Catholics in the city is simply intolerable. Thousands of men were expelled from their work nearly a year ago, their houses burned and their furniture burned or looted and they and their families – in all nearly 30,000 souls – have been forced to subsist during the past ten months on the generosity of the civilised world. They have also been so far as possible, disarmed and now they are largely at the mercy of the Special Constables who differ acutely from them in religion and politics. (*Irish Catholic Directory*, 1922, p.553)

Meanwhile, in his speech in June 1921 marking the opening of the Northern Ireland Parliament in Belfast, King George V, referred to the violence gripping the island of Ireland and made an impassioned plea to the Irish people:

> I am emboldened by that thought to look beyond the sorrow and the anxiety which have clouded of late My vision of Irish affairs. I speak from a full heart when I pray that My coming to Ireland to-day may prove to be the first step towards an end of strife amongst her people, whatever their race or creed. In that hope, I appeal to all Irishmen to pause, to stretch out the hand of forbearance and conciliation, to forgive and to forget, and to join in making for the land which they love a new era of peace, contentment, and goodwill. (*The News Letter*, 1921)

Sadly, his words were not acted on and the 'new era' did not materialise. In the month King George made his appeal, 14 people were killed in Belfast during riots.

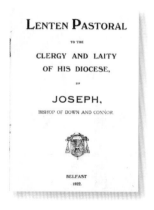

Bishop Joseph MacRory (later Cardinal MacRory) by
Seán O'Sullivan RHA, 1935. Image courtesy of the
Cardinal Tomás Ó Fiaich Memorial Library & Archive,
Armagh

Front cover of Bishop MacRory's
1922 pastoral letter

A year later, in his pastoral letter of 1922 (p.5), Bishop MacRory added:

> When I addressed you at the beginning of last Lent (1921), dearly
> beloved we all hoped that long before another Lent the cruel plight
> of Catholics in Belfast would have come to an end. … Thousands had
> already been expelled from work, and for many months denied their
> natural right to earn a living for themselves and their families; a large
> number had already been done to death; a very much larger number had
> been wounded; and several hundreds had had their homes or business
> premises looted or burned.

Whilst the community of the Poor Clares in Dublin may not have known
all the details of what was happening in Belfast, it is likely they would have
been aware of some of what their fellow Catholics were suffering. In deciding
to come to the North, the Poor Clare nuns would have known they were
moving to a city where some people were living in misery, where no Catholic
or Catholic property seemed to be safe and where the bishop had been living
under a death threat. (Phoenix, 2014)

G. B. Kenna, which was the pen name of a young Catholic priest called Fr
John Hassan, who was a curate in St Mary's Parish, Chapel Lane, describes
attacks on parochial houses, churches, convents and even nuns, including one
that took place on 23 July 1920, the third day of the Belfast riots:

At about ten o'clock at night a desperate attack was made on the convent of the Nuns of the Cross and Passion, beside St Matthew's Church in Ballymacarrett. The sisters who devote their lives to teaching the children in the adjacent schools, were about to retire to rest when the convent was attacked by a furious Orange mob, supplied with petrol and weapons for breaking in the doors. Military were telephoned for,

Cover page of J.B. Kenna's *Facts and Figures of the Belfast Pogroms 1920–1922*

but before their arrival the furniture of two rooms had already been sprinkled with petrol and set on fire. (Kenna, 1922 p.18)

Kenna also refers to a murderous attack on 'a number of Catholics engaged in relaying the tram-track on the Antrim Road, a supposed respectable Protestant residential quarter. These Catholic workmen were also ex-soldiers of the British Army who had seen service on many fronts during the European War' (p.74). In the same publication he describes an attack which took place just off the Antrim Road and a very short distance from 'Mossville,' the house in North Belfast where the first nuns would soon set up their small community:

On the 20th [May] the murder gangs operated over several areas of the city and thirteen person were slain, twelve Catholics and one Protestant and nearly a score were wounded. A Catholic lady and her daughter, Mrs and Miss Shiels were shot, though not fatally, by a gang who invaded their house in Alexandra Park Avenue. (p.91)

Close to the location on the Antrim Road where the nuns would come to live was Kinnaird Terrace, the scene of the brutal murders on 24 March 1922 of six Catholic civilians ranging in age from 15 to 50 years old. Two others were also shot and wounded. State forces, either the RIC or the USC (Ulster Special Constabulary), were believed to have perpetrated these murders.

Also nearby was Carrick Hill, a small neighbourhood of 13 streets; over 30 people were murdered there during these riots. Author and historian Jimmy McDermott in his book *Northern Divisions: The Old IRA and the Belfast Pogroms 1920–1922* (2012, pp.218–219) described the butchery meted out in the 'Arnon Street massacre' which was attributed to members of the police force of the time as a reprisal for the murder of a policeman. Five people including two children were murdered. 'Some were shot, others had their brains dashed out with a sledgehammer; one man who was in bed with a baby, one year old was battered to death and the baby was shot dead beside him.

Police on patrol in the York Street area of Belfast following a night of rioting in 1922 (image courtesy of Police Museum)

Parts of North Belfast in the 1920–22 riots experienced some horrific murders; poignantly this part of the city would again in the later Troubles suffer some of the worst violence, including human butchery and murder.

Page from St Damian's Journal detailing Mother Genevieve's desire to set up in Belfast

# Why Belfast?

Clearly then, in March 1923, when the nuns requested permission to set up in Belfast, the city was in great need of healing. The question is: why would Poor Clare nuns who were living in a monastery in Ballsbridge in Dublin want to set up a new foundation in trouble-torn Belfast? Thanks to the journal of events from St Damian's Monastery in Dublin, it is possible to answer that question:

> *For a long time Mother Genevieve* [Mother Abbess in St Damian's] *had cherished the desire to make a foundation in Belfast the capital of Ulster and the headquarters of Freemasonry and Orangeism. She saw what a benefit it would be to the City and to the whole of the 'Black North' if there was a 'powerhouse' of nocturnal prayer established there. It was not however until 1923, that she could take any steps towards putting her desire into execution. From 1921-1922 the religious 'war' raged in the city and to even dream of making a foundation at that time seemed nothing short of madness. Yet Mother Genevieve not only dreamed of it but asked a kind benefactor a native of Belfast to approach the Bishop of Down and Connor, Most Rev. Dr. MacRory, afterwards Cardinal Archbishop of Armagh, whose recent death the Christian world is now lamenting. This lady having broached the subject he asked, half seriously, half laughingly, 'Why do they want to be martyrs?' Mrs H. assured him that we did not fear the danger in the least for we knew that if God wanted us there He would protect us. He then told her to tell us to send a formal application. Mother Genevieve lost no time in doing this, and shortly afterwards in May 1923, he called to St Damian's to tell Mother Abbess he would accept us in his Diocese.*

Some other notes, which seem to date to the early 1930s, around the time of the building of the monastery chapel, explain that Mother Genevieve wanted to found a Poor Clare Monastery as a 'house of Prayer and Penance' in Belfast.

The decision of a Poor Clare community in Dublin to establish a foundation in a deeply divided and wounded Belfast makes no sense from the ordinary person's point of view. The nuns of this particular order were not going to be on the scarred streets of the city; they would be enclosed in their monastery, spending hours every day and in the night in contemplative prayer, petitioning God for the people of the city and beyond.

Perhaps their choice can only be understood in the light of faith. Yet the question remains as to what difference a contemplative order of nuns could make to a city in pain. This very issue was addressed in an article entitled 'Colettines In Belfast' in the *Irish Catholic* newspaper (1924) shortly after the nuns arrived:

> To many it may seem that this Order fulfils no worldly need, as their mission is not teaching, nursing, nor charitable works but their hidden lives of perpetual fast and abstinence and their untiring supplications for all states of life to which the rational creatures of Almighty God are called, rendered them, as it were, the elite of the Church, and worthy daughters of St Clare and St Colette, their saintly founders.

> ...The Poor Clare Colettines are, by reason of their secluded lives, little known to the outside world. ...Their hours are spent in contemplation of the Divine Perfections, on meditation on the Mysteries of the Faith, in the choral recitation of the Divine Office, in such manual labour as will remind them of their createdness, and in penitential fasting, Adoration, Expiation - the great needs of the present age. Their entire lives are passed in fulfilling them and who can tell what blessings will follow such sanctification?

> In the midnight hours they arise from their pallets of straw to chant the praises of God in their little oratory, and during the daylight hours they again at stated intervals return to the choral, recitation of their Office. Their frugal fare, into which fleshmeat never enters, consists of one meal and a collation, yet all is willingly, nay cheerfully borne, for is not the spirit of the Order one of simplicity, cheerfulness and joy?

Ilia Delio (2007, p.60), author of *Clare of Assisi: A Heart Full of Love*, says that 'though the traditional monastic path of contemplation leads to rest in God, Clare maintained that contemplation leads to action. Transformation and union with God does not mean retirement from ministry but rather new ways of being in the world.'

There is little doubt that the nuns believed they would be bringing to the city of Belfast 'new ways of being in the world.' As a contemplative order they clearly trusted that their way of being and life of prayer had some contribution to make to people in Belfast. In deciding to come northwards they would have known at least some of the details about the divided nature of the city at that time. They would have been aware not only of the religious differences over doctrinal issues of those times but also of the thorny issue of political identity, British versus Irish because Ireland was at war with itself and its neighbour. Above all they would have been aware of the most significant political change that the country ever faced, namely the partition of Ireland and the establishment of the Northern Ireland state.

Whilst it is not possible to know their individual or indeed collective thoughts and feelings, one might surmise that along with most Nationalists, Republicans and Catholics the partition of the country would have grieved the Poor Clare nuns deeply, as would the divisions and fighting throughout the island. It is very clear from the journals and correspondence of the Poor Clares whilst as an order they acknowledged the existence of the Northern Ireland state and refer to it as 'Northern Ireland' they in fact understood Ireland as one country with two separate jurisdictions. The Poor Clares, like the Catholic Church and indeed other denominations, operated throughout Ireland as one entity.

One might also surmise that all these different factors, the riots in Belfast, the suffering of its citizens (especially Catholics) and the partitioning of the country all played some part in the decision of this enclosed order of nuns living in Dublin to request permission to set up in Belfast.

In the history section of the website of St Damian's monastery in Dublin which established the Belfast foundation, is an additional clue as to the motivation for the Poor Clares coming to Belfast:

*In 1924 Mother Genevieve again led a group of sisters to Belfast wishing to plant another little shoot where **the need was great for prayer and reparation.** (Poor Clare Nuns, Dublin 2018)*

# Prayer and reparation

The words prayer and reparation offer a great insight into how the community at that time would have understood their desire to set up in the North. When Mother Genevieve first requested permission to come to Belfast, she would have believed the city needed prayer and reparation, and that prayer and reparation could make a difference.

In the rule which St Clare left to her community, prayer has a central role; in fact, it sets the pace of everyday monastic life. The rhythm of prayer in any monastic community finds its roots in the words from one of the Old Testament psalms: 'seven times a day I praise you for your just decrees' (Ps 118 [119]: 164). The Belfast community in coming together throughout the day before God in prayer followed a structure which provided stability and grounding not only for themselves but for those who joined them.

An important part of their rhythm of prayer was intercession for those in need. The nuns derived this form of prayer from the spirituality of their founder St Clare, who was renowned for her intercessory prayer. As a woman deeply committed to prayer she instilled this practice in her first community and it is still observed by the Order to this day. Clare also encouraged her community to rely on God's Providence. In early thirteenth-century Assisi she would have known well the words of St Paul: 'There is no need to worry; but if there is anything you need, pray for it, asking God for it with prayer and thanksgiving' (Philippians 4:6.).

The nuns living in their community in Dublin would have prayed for the people of Belfast during the riots in the 1920s and for all the people of the country during the War of Independence. During their years in Belfast, countless people acknowledged the importance of intercessory prayer which they experienced from the Poor Clare community. Many who called into one of the monastery parlours asked the nuns to pray for them. Former Irish boxer Barry McGuigan often made contact with the nuns before important fights to ask the nuns to pray for him. A woman who regularly visited the monastery over the years told me how the nuns 'held people in prayer' especially during the Troubles. Throughout their journals and correspondence there are numerous references in which the nuns acknowledge that God had answered their prayer. This prayer ministry continues to play an important part in the life of all Poor Clare monasteries throughout the world.

In *Clare of Assisi: A Heart Full of Love,* Delio (p.60) draws out the importance of contemplation for St Clare and in turn for those who will follow her in the Order of the Poor Clares. She explains that contemplation is a journey of transformation for the person who prays, which is to become ever more like the ultimate model, the person of Jesus Christ. Contemplation was not static but leading to growth in the individual:

> Both Clare and Francis (St Francis of Assisi) show us that the one who seeks to contemplate God must learn to gaze upon the beloved crucified Spouse which means coming to dwell in the mystery of suffering and love. The one who seeks union with God is to become a servant of love.

In other words, the nuns believed that contemplative prayer changed and transformed human beings, and, in this way, human life.

Mother Genevieve was well aware, too, of the need for reparation. The *Oxford Dictionary* defines the word as '1. the making of amends for a wrong one has done, by paying money to or otherwise helping those who have been wronged…2. archaic the action of repairing something….'

It is beyond argument that Belfast in 1923 and 1924 was in need of reparation. Over the years, Belfast had known many different riots, acts of violence including murder owing to sectarianism. In his book, *Holy War in Belfast,* Andrew Boyd (1987, p.9) details some of the more significant ones and argues that 'Sectarian riots in the town have …been traced back to as early as 1835.' At the start of the 1920s, the people of Belfast had endured two years of murder, mayhem and trauma. Boyd (p.199) acknowledges that both Catholic and Protestant suffered at the hands of one another, and it would be a mistake to assume that the Catholics of Belfast were all docile victims of loyalist aggression:

Thousands of families were terrorised by violent mobs. More than 200 Catholics were murdered. Ten thousand were driven out of the jobs in which they earned their living. The Catholic community suffered terribly. But those Catholics who had weapons shot and killed policemen, soldiers and politicians. They bombed the tramcars in which loyalist shipyard workers travelled along places such as York Street and Corporation Street. As Michael Collins admitted, the IRA in Belfast bombed and set fire to Unionist owned property.

Healing and repair were therefore essential. North Belfast, the area in which the nuns would settle, especially had suffered greatly after the years of rioting.

The decision of the Poor Clare community in Dublin to set up at such a time in Belfast might seem incomprehensible or even foolish if viewed from a purely human perspective. When it is viewed however with the eyes of faith, and understood in light of the radical determined decisions of St Clare of Assisi, it begins to make sense.

First page *Journal One*

# Chapter Two

## Moving to the Antrim Road
### Mossville

Mossville, 349 Antrim Road, the first Poor Clare 'monastery' in Belfast

—— 66 ——

*Restless would have been the sleep of the owners*
*that night had they known that plans had been*
*made to turn their house into a convent*

—— 99 ——

On Thursday 31 May 1923, the *Northern Whig and Belfast Post* carried an advert for the sale of 'Mossville,' a 'Detached residence, containing 3 Reception, 5 Bedrooms. Modern Conveniences. Garage. Grounds, 1 acre. Free of head rent.' The house was number 349 Antrim Road on the corner of the Antrim Road and Alexandra Park Avenue in an area of the Antrim Road known for large houses.

Sale of Mossville advert, *Northern Whig and Belfast Post*, 31 May 1923

In the 1924 *Belfast Street Directory*, Mossville was listed as belonging to a woman called Ella (or Elinor as she was also known) Deacon. In earlier editions of the street directory, it had been listed in her father's name, Rev Isaac Henry Deacon, who had been the Church of Ireland Rector of Holy Trinity Parish; Holy Trinity Church was in the Carrick Hill area of Belfast close to Clifton Street.

The advertisement was not lost on Mrs Hill, the aforementioned friend of Bishop MacRory.

> ...when Mrs Hill heard the good news she immediately set about looking for a suitable house in Belfast. She soon found one – 'Mossville' – on the Antrim Road. Before purchasing it, it was necessary that Mother Genevieve should see it. This was difficult as the owners were very bigoted.

After the nuns in Dublin had received the bishop's permission ('good news') to set up in Belfast, they had to find a suitable house, then check it would be appropriate and thereafter find a way to buy it. Even in the best of times that would be a challenge but even more so in the 1920s. In those day the matter of buying and selling land and property had the added complication of a sectarian twist. With an attitude of 'what we have we hold' there were unwritten rules about selling either land or property only within one's own religious tradition. Despite these 'rules,' the sale of large properties which had been lived in by Protestant families to Catholic religious organisations did take place.

This must have caused some consternation at that time, even giving rise to some conspiracy theories that such purchases were part of a plot by the Vatican for a Catholic take over in Northern Ireland!

The theories persisted even to the point that on St Patrick's Day 1973, fifty years to the day after Mother Genevieve had written to Bishop MacRory requesting permission to set up a foundation in Belfast, 'M.R.' wrote to *The Protestant Telegraph*:

> The desecration of Cliftonville Cricket Ground is really detestable and worthy of the greatest condemnation. Not content with the destroying of the pavilion and the theft of furnishings and fittings, the rebels from the adjoining erst-while exclusively Protestant areas which have been taken over, are now playing their primitive game of Gaelic football on the ground where once I played cricket. Of course, the old tactics are again being invoked, and once a foothold has been gained, the inevitable follows, and soon the entire district becomes rebel country. The cricket ground will make an ideal site for further papist buildings, and the 'poor clare' convent will becomes units in a large popish complex – again in a once predominantly Protestant district. The vatican stream roller is hard to stop, but stopped it must be, or our city will be taken over entirely!

In preparation for the setting up of the foundation, the nuns carried out at least one 'reconnaissance' trip from Dublin, which is recorded in the online history of St Damian's Monastery:

> *She (Mother Genevieve) herself travelled to Belfast to 'spy out the land.' However, the House in mind was in the hands of Protestants and she decided it would be best to view it discreetly from the top of a double Decker bus – in full Poor Clare attire!* (Poor Clare Nuns, Dublin 2018)

The notes from the St Damian's journal offer more information on this:

> *All necessary permissions* [from the bishop] *having been obtained, she* [Mother Genevieve] *lost no time in looking for a suitable house, and accompanied by the lady mentioned above (Mrs Hill) paid a visit to Belfast on the 14th July 1923* [the Feast of St Bonaventure, an important feast day for the nuns].

St Damian's Poor Clare Colettine monastery in Dublin

Dunmore House, 351 Antrim Road, former headquarters of the North Belfast Regiment UVF
(image courtesy of David Nixon, O.D. Cars Ltd)

"Why do they want to be martyrs." Mrs H. assured him
that we did not fear the danger in the least for we knew
that if God wanted us there He would protect us. He then
told her to tell us to send a formal application. Mother
Genevieve lost no time in doing this, and shortly after-
-wards in May 1923, he called to St Damian's to tell
Mother Abbess he would accept us in his Diocese all
necessary permissions having been obtained, she lost
no time in looking for a suitable house, and accompan
-ied by the lady mentioned above paid a visit to Belfast
on the 14th July 1923 We may regard this visit as a
very daring act for only two days before was the 12th
Orangemen's Day, when all the anti Catholic celebration
take place which end too often in riots between both
parties and when the echo of the Drums had hardly
died away, that this poor Clare Abbess in her full Religious
Habit should cooly go up North and calmly pass
through the City as though she were in Catholic Dublin
The house they had in view had been a Protestant
Rectory and as the lady who owned it, the former
Rector's daughter, was still in residence, they could
not approach her for had she known they wanted
the house for a Convent, she would never have consent
-ed

'Do they want to be martyrs?'
St Damian's Journal

*We may regard this visit as a very daring act for only two days before was the 12th, Orangeman's Day, when all the anti Catholic celebrations take place which end too often in riots between both parties, and when the echo of the Drums had hardly died away that this Poor Clare Abbess in her full Religious habit should cooly go up North and calmly pass through the City as though she were in Catholic Dublin. The house they had in view had been a Protestant Rectory and as the lady who owned it, the former Rector's daughter, was still in residence, they could not approach her for had she known they wanted the house for a Convent, she would never have consented to sell it for that purpose. The only way therefore to get a view of the property was to go on the top of the tramcar along the Antrim Rd., which they did and which may be regarded as the very limit of daring.*

This expedition led to the next step of viewing the property which at the time was not without its challenges. *Journal One* details Mother Genevieve's visit:

*… 14th July 1923 – Mother Genevieve and Mrs Hill travelled to Belfast and called at 'Mossville,' Mrs Hill explaining that she was thinking of taking the house for a friend of hers – Miss Janie Stead (Mother Genevieve's name in the world). They were shown all over the place and by the time they left Mother Genevieve had laid her plans as to which room should serve as choir, which as refectory etc etc and Mrs Hill declared herself satisfied with the house.*

Notes kept by the nuns at St Damian's add: *This former Rectory being considered suitable, it was purchased….*

Considering the size of Mossville, it is easy to understand how, when she came to inspect it, Mother Genevieve would have been drawn to it as very suitable to accommodate the needs of the community of the five nuns who would come to live in Belfast. The notes in the journal also record the fact that two of the nuns travelled on several occasions to Belfast to arrange for the house to be set up as a convent.

Owing to the high levels of enmity between Protestant and Catholic at that time it was no surprise that the nuns wanted the reason for purchasing

Mossville to be kept from the owners of the property before the purchase:

> *Restless would have been the sleep of the owners that night had they known that plans had been made to turn their house into a convent. Indeed, they themselves declared later that had their dead the power they would have risen from their graves in protest.*

The nuns were moving to a largely 'Protestant' area of the city. The 1924 *Belfast Street Directory*, lists Rev T. M. Johnstone, the minister of Newington Presbyterian Church, as living at 347 Antrim Road, known as 'Antrim Lodge' as their next-door neighbour. This was the church manse. In the first journal which the Poor Clare community kept, unsurprisingly there are no references to any contact or conversation with the minister and his family.

In his book written to mark the Golden Jubilee of Newington Presbyterian Church, Rev Johnstone (1926, p.25) makes a reference to Mossville as it was in 1876 and surrounding area:

> Cliftonville, where to-day there is quite a colony of Newington people, was then a quiet country lane named 'Solitude'. Antrim Road, another of our present day fruitful sources of membership, had no avenues leading off it, and practically no residences beyond the present Manse, Antrim Road, and its neighbour Mossville. Between these and the Waterworks (these reservoirs were constructed in 1840) lay another tract of unoccupied territory.

Rev T M Johnstone

He makes no references to his new neighbours.

On the other side of Mossville was 351 Antrim Road, known as 'Dunmore House;' in the 1924 edition of the street directory, this house was registered to several directors of a company called O.D. Cars Ltd (still in existence in the Dargan Industrial Estate today). The 1918 *Belfast Street Directory*, however, lists the occupants of Dunmore House as the 'headquarters of the North Belfast Regiment UVF' and a man called Alex Kennedy. One can only speculate about what the reaction would have been had the nuns arrived a few years earlier!

# Ascension Thursday, 29 May 1924

It was then time to move to Belfast. The St Damian's journal describes it in this way:

> *On the 29th May 1924, Mother Genevieve went up with her brave little band of five sisters who were to form the nucleus of the future community. The history of this foundation has been written elsewhere in detail taken for the greater part from Mother Genevieve's own notes so I shall not dwell upon it here except to say that like the great St Teresa, who never left her daughters in a newly made foundation, until 'she saw them in a house of their own', so the Foundress of Belfast did not abandon her children.*

The 'brave little band of five sisters' were Mother Colette Egan, Abbess and referred to in *Journal One* as the 'foundress', Mother Patricia Ward, Sister Paul Hobbins, Sister Mary O'Connor and Sister Paschal Hughes, who all bade farewell to their community in the Monastery of St Damian in Ballsbridge in Dublin to travel to Belfast. Mother Genevieve accompanied them to help them settle in. As they arrived at lunch time, it is likely the nuns would have taken the 9.20am train from Amiens Street station in Dublin for Great Victoria Street station in Belfast.

The decision of the nuns to leave Dublin was radical because in addition to leaving behind their community they were also saying farewell to their families. In those days nuns did not return home again even at the time of a funeral of a close relative. In addition, because these nuns had taken a vow of 'enclosure' they would be staying within the confines of their new Belfast home except in very rare occasions such as medical appointments or voting days.

The actual day on which the five nuns arrived in Belfast gives some clue as to the rationale of the new foundation. The 29 May 1924 in the Christian liturgical calendar was known as 'Ascension Thursday'. It is likely this date was specially chosen. For the nuns and for other Christians, this was a very important feast day commemorating the end of the ministry of Jesus on earth and his return or ascension to his Father in Heaven. The Feast of the

Ascension also recalled the command of Jesus to preach the Good News to the ends of the earth. For the Poor Clare nuns following Jesus Christ would have been the ultimate motivation in their lives and therefore it is likely they have would have viewed coming to Belfast in the light of the mission given by Jesus to his followers.

By choosing such a feast, the nuns were being 'missional' about their decision. Throughout their 88 years in Belfast feast days played an important part in the lives of the Poor Clare community. Significant events were arranged for important feasts such as the dedication of their new chapel which took place on 4 October 1992, the Feast of St Francis of Assisi. The importance of such days and the liturgical year can be traced back to St Clare herself who was acutely aware of times of the day, days of the year and their significance in the life of Christ, Mary, or the saints.

In interviews conducted with the nuns who lived in community with St Clare herself Armstong (1988, p.15) notes that they used feast days as points of reference:

> Thus many of the sisters respond to questions concerning the dates of the miraculous deeds of Clare by simply stating they can only remember the occurrence on or about some liturgical feast.

In choosing to come to Belfast on Ascension Thursday, 1924 the Poor Clare nuns were therefore following a liturgical time frame that underscored the contemplative tendency to interpret reality in the light of the mysteries of prayer, incorporate daily events into a different time frame, and consider time as yet another gift with which to praise God.

It is hard to imagine how the first nuns felt as they stepped off the train in Belfast on Ascension Thursday 1924. Although they were women of faith, inevitably they must have had human feelings including fear. They were facing into the unknown. Questions must have been on their minds regarding their safety, the success of their venture and the extent to which women from Belfast would join their community. They had no way of knowing the answers to such questions. The whole venture was one taken in faith and trust.

Whatever understandable feelings of fear and uncertainty they had, these would have been alleviated somewhat by the welcome they received. Indeed, right from the first moment the nuns of the Order of the Poor Clares came to live in Belfast they were warmly welcomed and this remained the case during their 88 years in the city:

> *They were met at Belfast by Mrs Hill; and when they got off the train, the first to welcome them was a number of poor factory girls. His Lordship (the bishop) had very kindly sent his own car and a taxi to take them to his house for lunch. He, himself was performing a ceremony at the Mercy Convent and Mrs Hill showed us all over his beautiful house and grounds and then we set out for 'Mossville.'*

Even in the early months of their time in the first 'monastery' in Mossville on the Antrim Road, the nuns were already giving thanks for various benefactors including people from other Christian denominations. That said, the nuns in the early days did however experience some of the divisions of their new 'home' city:

> *One day about 12th July Mr Hill was scuffling the sand outside the hall-door; he came across an extra big stone or something equally harmless, and he got quite excited and ordered us all to keep at a safe distance – it was probably a bomb!! It was evident "The Silent Five" were not regarded too favourably by the protestant [sic] element who so named us, but they didn't go so far as bombing us, though they did try to stone us and call out uncomplimentary remarks now and again. The Street Preachers too did their bit to win us round to their own way of thinking and arrived up under our windows regularly (until they found it was no use) to give us the benefit of their eloquence.*

With all the necessary legal, ecclesiastical and domestic arrangements completed the community of five accompanied by Mother Genevieve moved into Mossville at 349 Antrim Road to establish Belfast's first and only Poor Clare community. In those days it was referred to as a convent; it later became known as a monastery. It was dedicated to Our Lady and St Michael. Mossville had five bedrooms which meant that each nun had her own room or 'cell' as the rooms in a monastery are known. The house which had served as a rectory in its earlier days was now a Poor Clare monastery and the community was in place to be a contemplative presence and a sanctuary in a strife-torn city in need of prayer and reparation. In *Thom's Commercial Directory* (1925, p.836), officially the enterprise was known as the:

> POOR CLARE COLETTINE CONVENT, Our Lady and St Michael's, Mossville, Antrim Road, Belfast. Founded from St Damian's, Donnybrook, Dublin, May 29, 1924. Rev. Mother Abbess, Sister Mary Colette Egan. Community, 7. Chaplain, Rev. A. Greanen, B.A.

The reference to the chaplain as Rev. A. Greanen is a misprint. The priest's name was Rev Alfred Greaven, a curate in St Paul's Parish on the Falls Road. Before his appointment as the nuns' chaplain he had been a curate in Sacred Heart Parish. He died in 1927.

Once officially established, it only took a few months before the community began to grow. The nuns welcomed their first postulant on 8 September 1924, a local woman called Mary Grogan from Orient Gardens also in North Belfast and very close to where the nuns would eventually move to on the Cliftonville Road. The growth was described in this way in an article entitled 'The Franciscan Family: Poor Clares in Belfast' in *The Brief* magazine (1992, pp.6–8):

> Scarcely three months after their arrival their first postulant, a Belfast girl, came to join them. She had heard about them from a bread server who as our Annals report, 'did all he could to advertise the new nuns.' Soon other girls came to join them and before long 'Mossville' was proving to be too small.

In keeping with the practice of Catholic religious life at that time and the practice which still remains for many enclosed communities, Mary was given a new name, 'Joseph' in honour of St Joseph, the foster father of Jesus. This practice of religious orders such as the Poor Clares of giving members of the order a new name has a Biblical origin; a number of people including Abraham, Jacob, Simon in the Old and New Testaments received new names representing a new vocation from God in their lives.

By July of 1925 the community had received another member from St Damian's Monastery in Dublin, a young nun by the name of Sister Mary Oliver Feeney. She had made her final profession in St Damian's on 21 June 1925 and had accompanied Mother Genevieve to Belfast. As Sr Mary O'Connor, one of the original five, had become seriously ill, Mother Genevieve thought it would be better for another nun to join the community in Belfast for additional support.

Within two years of their arrival in Belfast, the Poor Clare community, now numbering seven, faced a problem. The new foundation was making an impact in the city. The community was attracting vocations and had outgrown Mossville. It was time to move to a bigger house.

> 'Mossville' was too small for a Convent, and there was not enough ground for building purposes; so after much consideration, Mother Genevieve who visited us occasionally, decided with our own Mother [Mother Colette Egan] to buy some land on the Glen Road, and build a new Convent, but when plans were drawn up the price exceeded all speculation and the thought of building had to be abandoned. Many prayers were said that we might get a suitable house.

The St Damian's journal provides further information:

> The house on the Antrim Rd. having proved to be unsuitable Mother Genevieve never rested until she saw them [the Belfast community] well established in another – a large well built house that could be easily adapted to Conventual usages and to which in a comparatively short time they were able to add a new Church and choir. In 1930 she paid her last visit to her children in the North but she kept up a constant correspondence with them and they always turned to her for advice especially in doubtful matters and abided by her decision.

The nuns moved to new accommodation in 1926 and Mossville was sold. The house was later demolished to make way for the Capitol Cinema, which opened in 1935. The cinema was in turn demolished and the site became a supermarket, which it remains at the time of writing.

# Chapter Three

## Growing and Building

> [Photo, Dorothy Horton.]
> new Chapel attached to the Poor Clares' Convent, Cliftonville Road, Belfast, which was dedicated last week

| HER AND SON OR TRIAL. | POOR CLARE COLETTINES. | DRAMA OF SWE TICKET. |
|---|---|---|
| RATION OF INSURED ERSON'S DEATH. | BISHOP DEDICATES NEW CHAPEL. | Clerk and Two Bar Share Over £100,00 |
| REPRESENTATION ALLEGED. | SUBLIME CEREMONY IN BELFAST. | OTHER PRIZE WINNE |

Front page news – the new chapel on the Cliftonville Road monastery

*" Our Lord evidently wanted us to stay this side of the city "*

Once the first community of Poor Clare nuns in Belfast recognised they needed to move, they looked to the west of the city to build their new monastery. When the costs of the purchase of land and the building involved were considered they soon recognised this was not a realistic option for them. Inevitably, this would have been a disappointment. As a contemplative community, they would have prayed and sought guidance from God. *Journal One* records what happened next:

> *Mrs Barclay visited one day, and the Portress told her of our dilemma, 'O, I know a place that would suit you,' she said. The Mothers were called and they decided to go and see 'Dunowen.' They went, and there was no little rejoicing at finding an ideal house and large garden attached. As many said, Our Lord evidently wanted us to stay this side of the city, and in the Parish of his own Sacred Heart too.*

It is not clear how Mrs Barclay who was a friend of the community had found out about 'Dunowen' on the Cliftonville Road, which had been put for sale. The house had been advertised on the front page of the *Northern Whig and Belfast Post* on Monday 4 August 1924 as 'The Residence of the late ADAM DUFFIN Esq., J.P., containing 3 Reception and 8 Bedrooms, Dining-Rooms, Cloakroom with Lavatory.

Advert for 'Dunowen,' *Northern Whig and Belfast Post*, 4 August 1924

Large Garden, Tennis Lawn, Garage, and every accommodation.'

The timing of the sale of Dunowen and its location in the Parish of the Sacred Heart suited the nuns very well. In fact, they were likely to have viewed it as an act of Providence which was a key element in the spirituality of St Clare who encouraged her community to trust in God's provision.

> *So, Dunowen on the Cliftonville Road was purchased, and was soon to become the Poor Clare Colettine Monastery of Our Lady and St Michael.*

When the community moved into their new home on the Cliftonville Road, they placed the monastery under the protection of Our Lady and St Michael.

*Journal One* records it in this way:

> By the end of May [1926] 'Dunowen' was ready to receive us, so Mother Genevieve came again to be with us for the great event. The last Mass in Mossville – the day of our departure was the Feast of Corpus Christi, 3rd June 1926 and the first Mass in Our Lady and St Michael's was on the First Friday. We were indeed grateful to God for bringing us into such a beautiful house in such lovely surroundings.

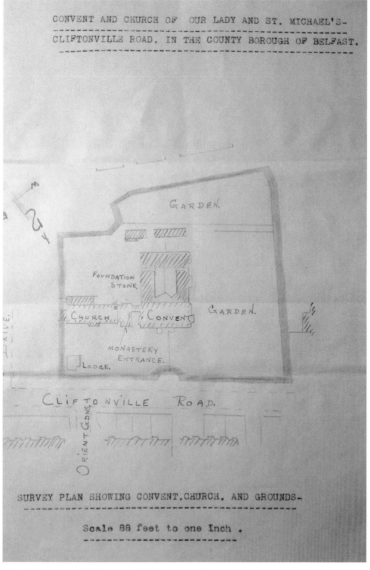

A hand-drawn map of the grounds of the convent

# Solitude – A good place for contemplation

The house was located in an area of North Belfast known locally as 'Solitude.' It is evident from several sources that this name had been in existence well before the arrival of the Poor Clare nuns in 1926, though it is hard to imagine a more apt name for a contemplative community!

The area clearly took the name from the house and lands of a property that seems to have stood on the upper pond of the Waterworks. Indeed, Paul Treanor from Cliftonville Football Club, which then backed on to the Waterworks and still does now, refers to a newspaper report in 1889 of a match that mentions the club ground as Solitude.

Cliftonville FC team in the 1940s
(courtesy of Cliftonville FC)

In addition to the historic Cliftonville Football Club, the nuns had another well-known neighbour when they moved to Dunowen – Cliftonville Cricket and Lawn Tennis Club. The club started in 1870 as Enfield Cricket Club but took on the name of Cliftonville Cricket Club in 1880 and moved to a site on the Cliftonville Road also referred to as Solitude by the cricketers.

Cliftonville Cricket Club 1st XI, 1954, overlooking back yard of John Morgan & Sons (furniture removers) and beyond that the rear of the Poor Clare Monastery. Image courtesy of Crawford McCully, Cliftonville Cricket Club

Although the club continues and is now located within the grounds of Ulster University at Jordanstown, sadly, its last years on the Cliftonville Road were marked with difficulty as will be seen later in the book.

After the effort and excitement of familiarising themselves with their surroundings and moving into their new monastery the community experienced a death of one of its members for the first time in Belfast. Sr Mary O'Connor had only been 10 days in her new home. Sr Mary, who had been ill for some time, died on 14 June 1926.

Sr Mary's grave, St Damian's Monastery, Dublin

Later in the summer of 1926, as a way of settling in and strengthening their spiritual lives, the community had their first retreat (a series of talks, times for reflections usually following a specific theme). It was given by Fr Collier CSsR, a Redemptorist priest who according to *Journal One* took a special interest in the community and hoped that:

> *Our presence as contemplatives in protestant Belfast would bring about many conversions.*

Within three years of arriving in Belfast, the small community had developed their way of life:

> *By degrees everything began to shape itself, and we were soon living the regular Poor Clare Colettine Life as far as circumstances allowed.*

Yet, it is clear from one journal entry that the nuns perceived they had moved into a divided and an anti-Catholic state:

> *In 1927, Cardinal O'Donnell and Bishop MacRory came to visit the community in their new monastery. 'They went through most of the Convent blessing it, and us, praying that our Monastery would be a Power House of prayer in the Black North.*

One of the first matters the early community wanted to sort out was the establishment of a cemetery within the enclosure. The legalities were completed by 1926, though the journal records that the cemetery 'could not be put in order until the chapel was built in 1930.' The monastery site was beginning to take on its own character with the building of a gate lodge, additional sheds for storage as well as trees and laurels planted in various parts of the garden.

The community continued to grow in number with two novices being received in 1928, one of whom, Sr Catherine, was described as 'a most generous all round sister.' The early community also received:

> Sr Thérèse a fully trained nurse from the 'Mater' [hospital] – a great God send to any Community – she has faithfully looked after the sick all these years and is now so devoted to our Mother Foundress octogenarian – little Mother Colette – likewise our good Sr Francis was received at this Enclosure Gate also soon after Sr Thérèse which shows what a flourishing Noviciate there was.

According to *Thom's Commercial Directory* (1928 p.693) the number in the community was '12', whilst the chaplain was still Fr A. Greaven.

As the community settled into their new home, the nuns decided to develop their monastic life by building 'extern' and 'choir' chapels. The extern chapel was for external visitors, a place where people from outside the monastic community could worship, whereas only the nuns would worship in the choir chapel. The nuns were completely separated from the public and could not be seen by them in those days.

The architect, Frank McArdle sent out tenders but received only one back. The community journal records with some surprise that the successful candidate to build the chapels was a Mr Carson and Son; the name Carson was particularly resonant at that time given that it was Edward Carson who was the first signatory of the Ulster Covenant of 1912 opposing Home Rule:

> When the big board went up in front of the Convent we had mixed feelings and guessed there were many comments from various denominations as to the reason for our choice. It could have been for Policy or Protection or Proficiency – and it was really none of these. It was necessity – someone must be got to do it and no one else offered. The name 'Carson' would surely remind everyone who saw it of the one-time 'Idol' of the Ulster people but when he proved himself anything but their friend and Protector but simply used them for his own… they could have murdered him.

Whilst the Poor Clares were an enclosed community, it was clear they had some knowledge of the politics of the era. The nun writing the journal for that time period describes the very positive way the community saw the builders with 'not the least hint of bigotry, in fact they became quite friendly.'

The laying of the foundation stone for the new chapels took place on 7 June 1928, on the Feast of Corpus Christi – another example of an important Poor Clare event taking place on a major liturgical feast day, this time celebrating the Catholic belief that Jesus Christ was fully real and present in the bread and wine consecrated at Mass:

> *The ceremony of the laying of the Foundation Stone of the New Church in which this document is enclosed in a copper sealed tube will be performed by Mr Frank Egan, brother of Sister Colette, the first Abbess in Belfast on the feast of the Sacred Heart the seventh day of June in the year of Our Lord One thousand nine hundred and twenty nine.*

A copy of the document placed in the copper tube contains the following touching detail:

> *The work at the new church which adjoins the Convent of Our Lady and St Michael was commenced on the Feast of the Assumption One thousand nine hundred and twenty eight when the ceremony of cutting the first sod was performed by Miss Maura McArdle, age 6 years, daughter of the Architect.*

The document goes on to state that the Colettine Church and Convent was one of four convents belonging to the Order, the other three convents being in Dublin, Carlow and Cork.

This early history contains the names of those present in the community at the time:

> *Sister M. Colette Egan, Abbess, Sister M. Patricia Ward, Sister M. Paul Hobbins, Sister M. Clare Gaynor, Sister M. Paschal Hughes, Sister M. Oliver Feeney, Sister M. Joseph Grogan, Sister M. Thérèse Hoey, Sister M. Francis Bryce, Sister M. Catherine Megan (Novice), Sister M. Emmanuel Donegan (Novice).* [The M is short for Mary, the Mother of Jesus]

The document was signed by the architect Frank McArdle. Later in that summer of 1929, the final profession of the new monastery's first postulant took place on 12 August. Mary Grogan was from Orient Gardens, which was on the other side of the road from the monastery. The first profession of Sr Catherine also took place on the same day.

Later in the month, 25 August 1929, Fr Daniel Mageean was consecrated the Bishop of Down and Connor following the appointment of Bishop MacRory as Archbishop of Armagh. *Journal One* speaks of the very close and supportive presence of Bishop Mageean to the community during his time as bishop:

Bishop Daniel Mageean

> *…Among the many blessings which the Belfast Foundation received from the very beginning, one of the greatest is – that in their Bishop they found both a Father and a friend. Dr MacRory always showed himself kindly disposed towards the Community, and his successor Dr Mageean was equally kind.*

On the Feast of St Clare, 12 August 1930, a bell which the community named 'Clare' was erected in the bell-tower of the chapel. This bell was rung at different times throughout the day as a call to prayer, primarily for the community but for others as well. Over the years, a couple of stories developed around this bell. One concerned some people in North Belfast believing that if the community ran out of food, the nuns rang the bell outside the usual times for Mass and the hours of the Divine Office to indicate their need. The rumour seems to have started from a time when the rope which was used to pull the bell became frayed and had to be replaced. The workmen who came to replace the rope checked everything was in order by ringing the bell several times outside the normal timetable. It would seem this additional ringing started the rumour about running out of food. Similar stories also spread about the nuns ringing the bell if they needed salt. It appears, however, that both rumours were urban myths.

The chapel was finally opened on 19 November 1930 and was dedicated to the Most Holy Trinity. This event was considered sufficiently important to make the front page of the *Irish News* on the following day under the title 'Poor Clare Colettines'.

The article described the 'sublime ceremony in Belfast' and gave a very detailed account of the chapel:

> The new chapel which is situated at the south-east side of the convent, has a frontage to the Cliftonville Road of 120 feet, an overall width of 26 feet and a height of 36 with a bell tower of 60 feet.
>
> A diaphragm wall divides the main portion of the building into two sections, the choir and the priest's chapel. The choir section, which has direct communication with the convent, consists of the choir chapel, ante-choir and the monastery enclosure, whilst the other section consists of the private chapel, sacristies, etc.
>
> The altars in the chapels are situated back to back on each side of the diaphragm wall.
>
> The chapel is of Gothic design, and the whole of the buildings are constructed of cast stone faced with granite. To ensure uniformity of colour throughout the whole of the exterior, the mouldings, corbels, etc., have been so designed as to be cast direct from the moulds.

The newspaper article also described the arrangements the nuns had made for a type of prayer known as 'exposition of the Blessed Sacrament.'

> The monstrance with the Blessed Sacrament was then placed in the top tabernacle where it always remains. Poor Clare abbesses having the great privilege (since the time of their holy mother, St Clare) of being able to open their tabernacle on the side of their own choir whenever they wish. They have exposition of the Blessed Sacrament all the time that they are in choir, and sometimes even during the night office. (*Irish News*, 1930)

As well as the dedication of the chapel, Bishop Daniel Mageean performed what is called the 'Ceremony of Enclosure':

*We all gathered at the Enclosure Gate and His Lordship presented the Keys of the Monastery to Mother Colette and we all returned to the Choir to chant the 'Te Deum.' The Portress locked and barred the big doors. How can we thank God enough for our Lovely Enclosure?*

The nuns were clearly at home within the enclosure; meanwhile, outside, the local community had grown in appreciation of the Poor Clare presence:

> *It speaks well of the generosity of the people of Belfast that in less than seven years the Community were able to build the new church and choir and make all necessary alterations to the Convent, without any delay in the work through lack of funds.*

The journal gives details of the help the nuns received from female factory and mill workers who gave generously of their time as well as gifts to the community. Several people had organised activities such as bazaars, raffles and whist-drives to raise money to pay for the building work.

Later, at the time of the Belfast Blitz in 1941, the nuns came to appreciate even more the work the Carsons had done to build the chapels:

> *We realised how well it had been built when it withstood the Blitz of 1941. Nothing but the Glass windows were broken and the big Enclosure door hinges while the old house was wrecked so much as to be unfit for us to stay in.*

The same however could not be said for the company who installed the central heating:

> *The firm who did the work were not Catholics as would be expected but they had very little respect if any for people like us – they were noisy and dirty-talked, smoked and whistled through the House – this was a real trial to us – we were glad when they were finished.*

During the early 1930s, further building work took place within the monastery grounds, including raising the height of the enclosure wall. This was not without its objectors and it is clear from the journal that some of the neighbours who were described in the notes as 'well-wishers' did not appreciate the high wall. Part of the problem may have been due to a lack of understanding from their neighbours of the enclosed contemplative life of the community. Although at the same there was an understanding of the enclosed life from some of the doctors, solicitors and even a dentist who came to the nuns instead of expecting the nuns to go to them.

Despite the objections and even a petition from some neighbours, all the work was completed. The high wall still stands to this day.

As the building work was going on the community continued to grow in number as more women were attracted to the Poor Clare life: 'These 1930s brought us several very good vocations.' The 1930 edition of *Thom's Commercial Directory* (p.693) records the Poor Clare Community with 12 members. Others joined during the 1930s and in December 1939, the community received two new members from Scotland: *'Mother Maria (Henry) and Sister M. Francis Assisi (O'Neill) came to us from Liberton as their Convent there had been closed.'* From the original five who came to Belfast in 1924, the number had reached 17 members by 1940.

During the 1930s the community celebrated two Silver Jubilees (25 years of service) – Mother Colette's in 1935 and Sister Patricia's in 1937. The journal descriptions of these occasions present the celebrations not only as faith events but also as full of fun. As well as the joyful celebrations, there were times of sadness to contend with, such as the death of the community's foundress:

> *1939 has special memories for us all here and Donnybrook because dear Mother Genevieve the real Mother Foundress as has been recorded, died, February 21st. Needless to say there were sorrow stricken hearts everywhere – but especially among her own children and grandchildren as she called those who had entered this convent while she was alive.*

In fact, as Britain and France declared war on Germany in September that year, 1939 was to be memorable not only for the Poor Clares in Belfast but for the whole world. The monastic peace and quiet on the Cliftonville Road was about to be shaken.

+ 6/

The foregoing pages were written by Sister M. Paschal (Hughes) — one of the Sisters who had come from Donnybrook in 1924. They were written a few months before her death. She had been in poor health for many years. She was always an exemplary Religious, and had a wonderful devotion to the Blessed Sacrament and the Holy Sacrifice of the Mass, and an ardent love for the Divine Office. She was Mistress of Novices for several years until her health failed. Her death came as a great shock to us on Christmas Eve 1949 R.I.P. She was the first to be buried in our Cemetery. (See also notice of her death in second Manuscript by Mother Colette.)

The following passages are taken from Sister M. Paschal's notes — (written in pencil.)

Some of our very first friends at Ursuline were the Tinsleys — May Bresing, John Savage who collected for the beautiful Statue of Our Holy Mother Saint Clare (which now stands on first landing of the Professed House cloister.) — Kay R.I.P. and Gertie Hughes who supplied us with vegetables and fruit regularly. — Mr Hamill R.I.P. who frequently sent us beautiful flowers — Cassie Hughes R.I.P. who never failed to bring her weekly collection, and poor Maggie O'Hanlon R.I.P. who said she recovered her sight on the way up to the Poor Clare Monastery She came every week with the neighbours petitions and generous offerings — Tom McReevey whose proudest title was "The Poor Clares' Messenger" would need a book to do him justice. He was dock-yard worker and one of the first problems he came to have solved was "Sister, when I bes carrying them heavy planks down at the docks, I bes thinking of Our Lord carrying His Cross — is it any harm?" Poor Tom!

# Chapter Four

## 'How we prayed that night!'
### The Belfast Blitz

High Street after the Blitz (PRONI CAB 3/A/68)

—— 66 ——

*The general idea is that the Germans think this
is a barracks and that we are the target for their
bombs falling around us*

—— 99 ——

As a contemplative community, the nuns would most certainly have been praying for peace as World War II was raging. They possibly believed as did many others in Belfast that they were sufficiently far away from the German bombers and therefore had no reason to be concerned for their personal safety. Yet, like so many other people in Belfast, they would eventually be affected by the bombing. The monastery on the Cliftonville Road in North Belfast was in an area which sustained heavy bombardment, with a significant number of fatalities, people wounded and property destroyed or damaged.

Although the declaration of war was made on 3 September 1939, the community journal makes no mention of this or the war until 16 April 1941 and the bombing of Belfast. As it happened, Belfast was bombed on four occasions in 1941: 7/8 April, 15/16 April, 4/5 May and 5/6 May. The journal does not refer to the first April bombing, possibly because it did not affect the area where the monastery was located. The most significant attack on Belfast took place on 15/16 April 1941.

The envelope which contained Mother Colette Egan's letter,
postmark: 'Belfast, 9.15am, 21 April 1941'

On Sunday 20 April 1941, Mother Colette Egan wrote to the community in St Damian's in Dublin. She gave a first-hand account of how the Belfast Poor Clares had experienced the blitz:

*Sunday*
*Praised be Jesus Christ*

*My dear Mother Abbess your letter came yesterday. Although I am very busy as you can imagine I must write to you. Poor Frank wired again yesterday to know if we're here. I have just sent a line.*

*Well on that memorable night the 'siren' went at about quarter to 10 so we got up and went down to Choir. I opened the Tabernacle and we chanted the Office. As things seemed to be getting worse we recited the Office to get finished and put out the electric lights.*

*The choir doors began to rattle. We continued praying with just the candle light until suddenly there was a tremendous crash and all the windows came in on one side of the choir. The sisters made towards the door as I called out to go to the sacristy and confessional. I went up and shut the Tabernacle and we put out all lights. Mother Vicaress remained on the altar steps the remainder of the time and I gave out prayers and aspirations without ceasing and 'oh dear me' what weight went into every word. I often had recourse to O.H.M. St Clare's prayer when she raised the Blessed Sacrament over Assisi – 'Ne tradas bestiis animas confitentes tibi etc.'* ['Do not give over to the wild beasts the souls of those who trust in you' – from the Vulgate translation of the Bible of Psalm 73, verse 19]

*As for those whistling bombs, they seem to be right over you and you just wonder where they are going to land. Well, when that crash went, it was not only the Choir windows went but every window in the Convent, doors and shutters and all the houses around. – It was the blast of a bomb that fell about 200 yards from the Choir, surely St Michael kept them off us. – One of the enclosure gates was blown wide open and one half wrenched off its hinges – St Michael remained in his niche over the gate without a scratch and the Infant of Prague was smiling at us from behind the gate with his night light lighting as if nothing had happened.*

*We were certain the out-houses were on fire as the flames seemed to be rising up just outside the choir windows but Sister M.* [possibly Sr Magdalen] *looked out of the sacristy door and saw we were safe. It was the row of houses where the bomb had fallen and the men had no water to attack the flames, the mains was cut off.*

*We started a 'Te Deum' for own safety and we called on all the angels to put out the fires and save lives. The siren began soon after. When the 'all clear' went we said another 'Te Deum' and remained in Choir until daylight. The raid lasted 5 hours and how we kept up the aspirations etc all the time I wonder now. Certainly God was liberal with his Grace. The sisters were grand D.G. and have been so generous in cleaning up the house.*

*When we went up through the convent what a sight met our eyes – mortar and glass everywhere, shutters and doors on the ground. In the refectory our table was standing on its head in the middle of the room and the big shutter and windows broken. In the parlour it was really wonderful – the big windows and shutter had burst in and the altar was just in front of it – the altar was there and Our Lady of Lourdes standing but she had turned round towards the window. St Bernadette had fallen on her side.*

*We went on to the top of the house to see if there were incendiary bombs lighting but D.G. there were none. The scene was the same everywhere – mortar and glass and window frames lying about – it would make you sad but I thought it's God's Will and he has some good purpose in it all. We are certainly having a fresh air cure at present!!! but we are in great spirits D. G.*

*The house is not habitable for many so I am sending 9 away, Sister Paschal as Abbess!!! I will let you know later their destiny.*

*God help the poor people outside. Mrs Barclay's house was ruined, they have gone to the country. Our bread came next day and some milk, how God watches over us. David and Nellie spent their night in the sacristy. It has a flat roof. There are many sad tales about the people outside but I have no more time now.*

*Much love to all and keep us in your prayers.*
*Your loving sister in Jesus.*
*Sr M Colette.*

Mother Colette wrote again after the air raid that took place on Sunday 4 and Monday 5 May 1941:

*Praised be Jesus Christ*
*My dear Mother Abbess*

*Dear me the worst has come at last and yet it must be the best – God's Holy Will. We had a terrible night last Sunday worse than the first, a mine was dropped in the same place again but did not make such a flash as the houses were all down already and it fell on soft ground. Still our garden is full of debris and one of the homes just outside our wall suffered badly … our out-house roof also and the green house. The general idea is that the Germans think this is a barracks and that we are the target for their bombs falling around us. God watched over us wonderfully and we are leaving the convent and chapel in charge of Our Lady and St Michael and the Infant of Prague. They will be the wardens. Human aid is no use these times. Sunday night was chiefly on the centre of the city. Big buildings with watchers and fire brigade and everything and they could not save them.*

*The PP [Parish Priest] was very sad taking the Blessed Sacrament out of the Tabernacle yesterday. We brought the Monstrance and chalice to the Glen Road Convent, the ciborium to the Sacred Heart Presbytery. 4 of us slept the last 2 nights at the Glen Road. They gave us a great welcome although they have 18 or 19 in community and about 200 refugees are there every night from the city in the cloisters – classrooms etc.*

*The first night Sr Magdalen and myself got up at the siren and went down to the parlour with the community – they were hammering away at their aspirations to the Sacred Heart – I felt I would not keep up with them so when they stopped after a while I began in an under breath on our prayers slowly so Mother Anne asked me to give out the prayers. She said afterwards they were lovely. It was well it was dark – I just felt I was at home saying them as we did when the 'siren' went – but the noise up at the Glen Road was just child's play to here - Of course the raid was not much on Monday - Sunday was the worst of all. ...Mother V. Sr Malachy and Sr Magdalen are with me now. We leave at 1.15 for Newry. (The others went 2 days ago) Today is the apparition of St Michael isn't it strange and we never thought of it until yesterday – it gives me great confidence – We were at Mass at St Teresa's Church Glen Road the two mornings. I could not get Mother Genevieve R.I.P. out of my head. I lit a candle for her and also 1 for all of you and many for ourselves that we will be back again soon. D.V.*

*We had a letter from Newry this morning, they seem very happy already D.G. –
There are 6 professed Carmelites, 1 Novice and 9 lay sisters – complete solitude
– they arrived just after Benediction. Father Nash S.J. is coming for the retreat on
the 24th so we are just in time. I had asked the Poor Clares at Newry to take us
the same time as Drumshanbo (in case the latter failed) and they said certainly. I
had a letter from Mother Abbess the other day they were getting anxious about us
to be sure and come but I believe their convent is right in the middle of the town
and it is a garrison town so it might not be very safe there. I will call perhaps this
evening on our way to thank them.*

*The Carmelites said 'come immediately.' How wonderfully God has settled
everything but oh dear me I hope we will be home again soon. I have just sprinkled
the whole house and garden with Lourdes water. Newry is only 1⅓ hours away so
it will be easy to get up here if we want to –*

*David will be here all day and will sleep away somewhere. Thousands go to the
hills every night – Nellie has gone to Draperstown.*

*I was out on business the other day with Mother V. in a taxi. If you saw the state
of the place around, you would weep. Mrs Barclay's house was wrecked. They have
gone to the country and anything like everyone's anxiety about us - we might be
their own family.*

*Mr Cairns was over –*

*I forgot to tell you an incendiary bomb fell in our cemetery just outside the sacristy
window and set the tree in flames we had against the covered walk.
There were two big warders here that night who put it out. Plenty of large holes,
clay etc all over the garden. A policeman was in all through the place last evening
with David and when he saw the place he said 'How did they stay there?'*

*I want to get Vespers said now before we go. Please thank Mother V[icaress] for
her last letter. You are dears to take such an interest in us. If we want anything for
Drumshanbo we will call on you. Please send Sr Paschal some stamps for her Feast
[day]... – I only sent a wire with our new address – Sister M. will write on the
train, she won't have any Office to say.*

*Mother good bye and I know you will all pray for us for the safety of the Convent
and Chapel – God has given us all great grace D.G. as we are in good spirits
despite all.*

*Your loving sister in Jesus
Sr M. Colette
Much love to you all.*

The peace of the enclosure had been shattered, and the nuns like so many
others in that part of Belfast must have wondered if they would see daylight.
Despite a traumatic number of hours of bombardment the community had
survived, yet such was the seriousness of the barrage Mother Colette as
the abbess contacted Bishop Daniel Mageean, the bishop of the diocese, to
ask his permission to disperse. This cannot have been an easy decision but
the nuns, like many others, realised that Belfast was now a target and the
community was no longer safe. In due course, the community was evacuated
with some nuns going to a convent in Co. Leitrim, others to a convent in
Newry. Sr Colette recorded events for the community journal, though in the
upheaval of the circumstances she repeats the name of Sr Malachy, which
should probably have read Magdalene:

> *I got leave from the Bishop and sent 9 sisters off to the Franciscan Convent,
> Drumshanbo, Co. Leitrim. Sisters Joseph, Paschal, Anthony, Anne, Francis,
> Thérèse, Oliver, Assisi and Mother Maria (RIP) who died there later. After
> the second raid 9 of us went to the Carmelites at Newry – Mother Paul,
> Clare, Malachy, Michael, Malachy, Emmanuel, Catherine, Patricia and
> myself.*

Cleaning up Oldpark Presbyterian Church
(courtesy of *Belfast Telegraph*)

Mother Colette's letter, 20 April 1941 (courtesy of Northern Ireland War Memorial)

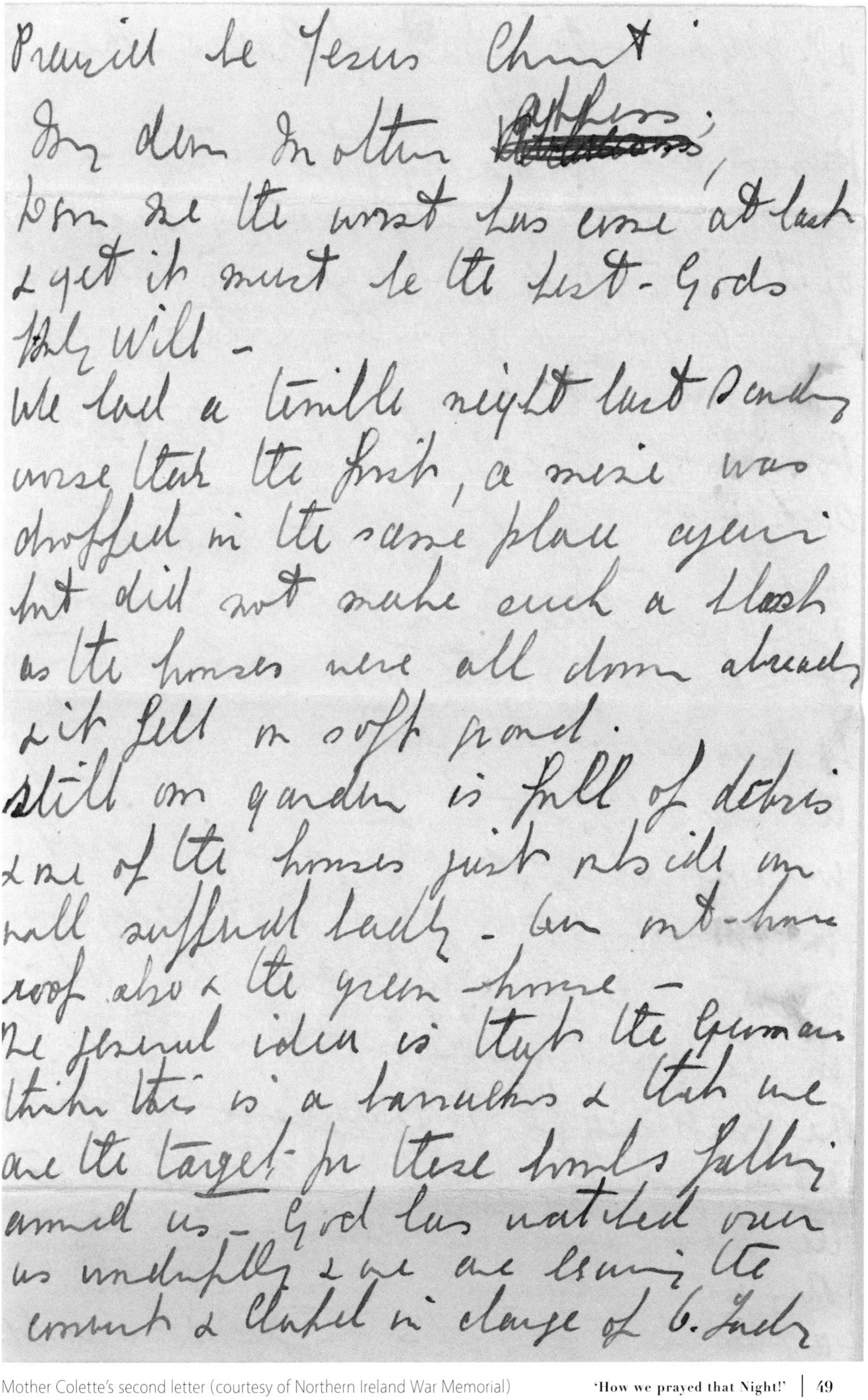

Praised be Jesus Christ

My dear Mother ~~[illegible]~~ Abbess;

Here we see the worst has come at last
& yet it must be the best - Gods
Holy Will -

We had a terrible night last Sunday
worse than the first, a mine was
dropped in the same place again
but did not make such a crash
as the houses were all down already
& it fell on soft ground.

Still our garden is full of debris
& one of the houses just outside our
wall suffered badly - our out-house
roof also & the green-house -

The general idea is that the Germans
think this is a barracks & that we
are the <u>target</u> - for these bombs falling
around us - God has watched over
us wonderfully & we are leaving the
convent & Chapel in charge of O. Lady

Mother Colette's second letter (courtesy of Northern Ireland War Memorial)

(1)

J. M. J. + 7. 6. 6.

Monastery
Glenvale,
Newry.

Praised be Jesus Christ.

My dear Mother Abbess and dear Mother Vicaress.

St. Bernardine's Feast day gives me an opportunity of writing to you. and to say a big God reward you for all the prayers which you and all our dear Sisters offered up on our behalf during our big trial. It was indeed a big thing to close our dear Convent. one of the big graces which do not often come in the Religious life. so please God we hope to profit by it. Mother would have stayed as long as the Choir stood, what ever about the house, but being a mother with a large religious family to provide for. She first thought of the safety of the community. Looking back on those terrible eventful nights I thank God, we were there to share in the terrible strain and suspense which so many thousands had to endure. without our wonderful consolation of knowing full well, that nothing could or would happen to us, but what God willed and how our faith and confidence increased as the hours of terrific noise

Mother Paul's letter, 20 May 1941 (courtesy of Northern Ireland War Memorial)

a big loss of his very best friends - one of them mended the shoes I am wearing R.I.P. There were five in the house & for Easter a married sister and her little girl of 5 came from Dublin. On Mon eve, I think they were at the lodge for tea - The little girls was blown right away from the house and found dead in a protestant church - the other six were buried under their house - we heard when we came here the loss of life was, I think 500. Oh but there was cutting down things!! before we left Belfast the loss was estimated to be 4, 500 and it was by no means the full amount - during the week, there was a constant stream of funerals to the cemetry and a great number of little blue coffins - I wonder did Mother tell you how the night light to the Divine Child of Prague burned right through the raid although the enclosure ? in which it stood was broken in, the big iron bolts snapped like matches, - & there was a high wind - In the parlor in front of a big window was a statue of our Lady of Lourdes - the shutters were closed & barred - the bar, not a very strong one was blown right off the shutters and the window itself strewed the floor - the statue of our Lady was turned right round facing the chair & remained standing - it was really very

Mother Paul, who was evacuated to Newry, wrote to the community in St Damian's:

*J.M.J. F.C.C.*
*Carmelite Monastery,*
*Glenvale,*
*Newry*

[Tuesday 20 May 1941]

*Praised be Jesus Christ.*
*My dear Mother Abbess and dear Mother Vicaress*

*St Bernardine's Feast Day gives me an opportunity of writing to you and to say a big God reward you for all the prayers which you and all our dear Sisters offered up on our behalf during our big trial. It was indeed a big thing to close our dear Convent, one of the big graces which do not often come in the Religious life, so please God we hope to profit by it. Mother would have stayed as long as the Choir stood, whatever about the house, but being a Mother with a large religious family to provide for, she first thought of the safety of the community.*

*Looking back on those terrible eventful nights I thank God, we were there to share in the terrible strain and suspense which so many thousands had to endure, without our wonderful consolation of knowing full well, that nothing could or would happen to us, but what God willed and how our Faith and confidence increased as the hours of terrific noise dragged on. You should hear the screams of the ton weight bombs, as they whistled close to the convent and dropped a few hundred yards away. We believed our convent was finished when the 6000 incendiary bombs were sent shooting through the air, the sound was as if houses were crashing down.*

*Mother was prostate up the front altar steps and I was as the side. I said in a whisper to Mother, 'the Convent is down.' Mother said: 'I think so.' Then as our blinds on the Choir window were blown in and the bright red light from the flaming houses lit up the choir we thought: if not the Convent, at least the outhouses of coal and coke were in flames, but thank God no: Mother's prayers removed the mountains that night. Certainly the barrage of prayers that went up that night, filled us with extraordinary courage and calm and you should have heard our clear steady voices chanting the 'Te Deum' twice during the night and our prayers were not book prayers either. Mother would say 'All ye holy Angels,*

*(Response) Put out the fires and save Belfast, etc. Our Lady and St Michael Drive them away and save Belfast. Dear Sacred Heart we are so tired, please let the 'All clear" sound.'*

*We were in pitch darkness and I went down the choir, with my two hands out in front of me, to get a look out, and what was my surprise to see the enclosure door burst open and to see the face of the Child Jesus of Prague lighted up and smiling, the glow of the little night light shining on Him, and though the iron bars and bolts were broken in two and heavy doors through the house were torn from the hinges, and smashed on the floor, the dear little Holy Child stood firm on His pedestal the little flashes of light during all the terrible blasts at the open door. I was so glad to have lighted the night light as we ran to choir. You should hear us on the 2nd bad night running to our Choir, 'Here we are Lord, for they're coming' and we know for certain He was there to save us, even one's blood would run cold.*

*We were a full week clearing the glass, and even then you would think the mats were sprinkled with 'sequences' there was so much glass dust buried through them. The Portress' room is a large room it is cloistered as well as we pass through it to choir there are two long narrow windows in it at either side of the glass door leading to the choir one window only was broken which I boarded up the first morning. Six sisters slept there on the floor and three of us remained all night in Choir, but the first three nights after the 1st big raid we all remained in choir.*

*I think it must have been the way the Apostles slept round Jesus, when after the heat of the day. He invited them to 'come apart and rest.' We too sat around Jesus and rested, then one Sister complained of a swollen ankle, then another and another. So Mother said, it must be from sitting up, and then added I cannot afford to get swollen ankles, pulling her habit aside and sure enough, without knowing it, she had a pair of them.*

*It was then we lodged up in the P. room, and we had camp chairs. When the nine went to Drumshanbo, the men had the windows in the 6 cells felted, so we were in great form, as all were on the 1st landing. Sr Malachy, and myself were still in the P. room and Mother had a companion in her cell. We intended to remain so for the duration of the war, when two other cells downstairs would be ready for myself and Sr Malachy. Well our security was of short duration as we had only two nights in bed, when the 2nd raid occurred.*

*We were in no draughts as the wind blew, in four directions, in that way we did not catch cold, as the outer doors were taken away hinges and bolts etc and many of the inner doors were down or smashed and all windows gone. We were like the shop in B.??? with the notice up 'Open and never more opened.'*

*Then the delayed bombs, kept us to the back of the house, as the only glass left was in the front, and the blast from the bombs was expected to break all that, so we had to take up our beds and walk, sleeping (3 of us) at night in the kitchen; and the 1st night a little mouse kept us company, giving me more annoyance than the delayed bombs. The military were able to remove bombs and mines in our district and only one exploded killing eight soldiers.*

*The last raid the time bombs were exploding all the next day and night with terrific noise. Mother had a letter from the Bishop today and he said the bombs were still exploding and one did much harm the day before which must have been on Monday. So many lives could not have been lost at the last raid, as every night thousands leave the city for neighbouring towns, and the poor to the hills. It was a very sad sight when we were on our way to the Holy Cross Sisters at night to see the procession of mothers with babies and tots following, little boys and little girls carrying bundles (a blanket or a top coat a pillow an old chair etc) the men staying behind to put out the fires, sometimes you would see a few of them carrying a bed. They were on the way to the hills for the night, and this procession goes on every night and going to Mass in the morning, we walked to St Theresa's Church, we met some of them wearily returning.*

*It will take much to convert Belfast. Yes, many of the protestants, had their eyes opened, and many more their eyes closed. For instance, the famous Shankill Road, believed it was the Free State planes that did the first day's destruction and when they knew it was not so, then they said the planes were Italian ones and the Pope was in the leading one; at the next raid poor Shankill Rd and its inhabitants were nearly wiped out.*

*The incendiary bomb which fell in our garden was just outside the Sacristy window where the Sisters were. It burnt away to dust, burning also a rustic trellis work nearby.*

*Poor David's nerves nearly gave way. We (the nuns) were a great responsibility, he could have stayed another night, but comes early each morning and stays until dark.*

*When we went to the Glen Rd, he stayed with a relative in the District, but as the Sirens went both nights he and the family, a young married couple and their baby went to Cave Hill with hundreds of others. The enemies were over on those nights also, and the anti-aircraft guns sent up volley after volley. At the H.C. Convent we heard them, but of course we felt and knew we were out of the way.*

*We heard most tragic tales of the dying and dead R.I.P. and of those buried alive etc. etc. Mrs Barclay's and the Hughes houses, our best friends, were shattered from the blast and it was the risk of their lives they tried to get some necessaries out. We saw Mossville, the smoke still coming from the remains as we passed on our way to the Bishop's.*

*The sounds we now hear are so different from the sirens, cocks and cows and sheep and lambs and crows and birds. The place is full of rabbits or hares. I don't know which, they run up and down the hill towards evening, there are plenty of wild violets and primroses.*

*Mother says the Convent reminds her so much of the old house at St Damian's, as it was when she entered.*

*I hope you will be able to read this letter. Mother wishes us to write in pencil for the present, and it is so much quicker also.*

*With my best, love to you and all*
*Affectionately*
*Your little Sister in Jesus*
*Sr M Paul of Jesus.*

North Belfast had been badly affected by the German bombing, with several public buildings destroyed or badly damaged including the LMS railway station, the adjacent Midland Hotel on York Road, and Salisbury Avenue tram depot.

Crater on the Cliftonville Road at Wyndham Drive (courtesy of *Belfast Telegraph*)

One bomb destroyed houses on the Cliftonville Road close to Wyndham Drive and left a crater on the road less than half a mile from the monastery. The community would most likely have heard the noise from this bomb when it exploded though it is hard to know whether this was the bomb which Mother Abbess described hearing. Given its proximity, it would seem to explain the damage to the monastery and the enclosure gate. There is no detailed description of how the nuns must have felt during the nights when Belfast was bombed, but it is reasonable to deduce that it must have been terrifying. The phrase 'How we prayed that night!' used by Mother Colette in her account in the community journal of that night indicates this.

Ballycarry and Ballynure Streets off the Oldpark Road (courtesy of *Belfast Telegraph*)

She writes powerfully:

> *1941. April 16: the memorable day or rather night of the Blitz during World War II. We were all in choir after Matins, the Blessed Sacrament exposed when an aeroplane came over the choir and a minute later there was a terrific noise and all the windows on the enclosure side of the choir crashed in…I sent the community at once to the Sacristy, closed the Tabernacle and M. Vicaress (Paul) and myself remained on the altar steps - the bombs and anti-aircraft guns continued until early morning. …How we prayed that night!*

Mother Colette's letters tie in with Brian Barton's (2015, p.157) account of the bombing of 15/16 April.

> 180 (enemy aircraft) were active over Belfast, some of them for two hours or more. …Luftwaffe records also indicate that, over the four hours of the raid on Belfast, their aircraft dropped 750 bombs, an average rate of over three per minute, and that these contained 203 tons of high explosives.

Mother Colette's letters refer to the anti-aircraft guns; Belfast had only 16 heavy calibre anti-aircraft guns in total, which made little difference in the defence of the city. The Luftwaffe first targeted the city's Waterworks which was very close to the monastery. There is some dispute about whether the bombers mistook the Waterworks for the docks or if indeed the Waterworks was the intended target to disrupt water supplies. Certainly, there were reports of fire crews finding water pressure very low thus making it difficult for them to put out fires.

The Poor Clare monastery, while certainly damaged, was not destroyed though it had at least one unexploded bomb in the grounds. Barton (2015, p.394) refers to several unexploded bombs in North Belfast including 'fourteen at Belfast Royal Academy, the Poor Clare Convent on the Cliftonville Road, etc) six of which were subsequently exploded.' Some local churches in North Belfast were less fortunate. According to *Bombs on Belfast* (2011, p.52-60) in which Dr Ian Adamson wrote the foreword, the churches in this part of the city that were either destroyed or very badly damaged were Macrory Memorial Presbyterian on Duncairn Gardens;

Duncairn Methodist, Castleton Presbyterian on York Road; St Silas's on the Oldpark Road; St James's on the Antrim Road; Newington Presbyterian on Limestone Road; Crumlin Road Presbyterian; Holy Trinity on Clifton Street and Clifton Street Presbyterian; York Street Presbyterian and York Street Non-Subscribing Presbyterian.

In addition to the damage to the Cliftonville Road, bombs either wrecked or caused considerable destruction to other roads and streets within North Belfast, including Percy Street; York Park; York Crescent; Eglinton Street; Carlisle Street; Ballycastle, Ballycarry and Ballynure Streets off the Oldpark Road; Southport Street; Walton Street; Antrim Road; Annadale Street; Hillman Street; Atlantic Avenue; Hallidays Road; Hughenden Avenue; Sunningdale Park; Shandarragh Park and Whitewell Road. Burke Street, which ran between Annadale and Dawson streets in the New Lodge area, was completely wiped off the map with all its 20 houses flattened and all the occupants killed.

Emma Duffin, a previous resident of Dunowen (which the nuns had bought in 1926), wrote a diary of her experiences as a nurse at the time of the Blitz. She describes walking from the south of the city to the north and close to where the monastery was.

Trevor Parkhill (2016), who transcribed and published Emma's diary, describes her journey in the aftermath of the Blitz on Easter Tuesday, 15 April 1941 in this way:

> She [Emma] travels on foot or in a car, through quarters of the city centre and via Carlisle Circus up the Antrim and Oldpark roads. There is almost an eerie sense of calm after the storm as the transport system, or what was left of it, struggled to maintain a service. Even the evacuation of families stricken or left homeless seemed to be undertaken in a calm, if shocked, orderliness. (p.68)

Emma Duffin, who lived in Dunowen with her family from 1890s until 1924 (PRONI D2109/18/4)

Emma described some of the devastation to North Belfast very close to the monastery:

> We passed the Mater hospital where many victims had been taken. The nurses' home had been hit. As we got higher up the road we began to realise the extent of the damage. Little side street in ruins, houses reduced to dust. We were diverted into another road, not much better. We saw a street shelter which had received a direct hit, killing most of the occupants. (p.75)

As a nurse who had served during the World War I and had tended wounded soldiers, and who was based in Stranmillis College which had been taken over as a hospital, Emma volunteered to help at St George's Market where the dead bodies of those killed in the Blitz were taken for identification. It was clearly traumatic, as she records in her diary:

> …it was a job for an older woman and my former experience in hospital should have prepared me to a certain extent for the sight of death. I say should have, but I had seen death in many forms, young boys dying of ghastly wounds, men in the prime of life dying by inches of dysentery or septicaemia, but nothing I had ever seen was as terrible as this. …The place was full of coffins, some varnished but the majority plain deal. … A man watered the ground with disinfectant from a watering pot, a wise precaution as the place smelt. (p.79)

Letters written by Poor Clare nuns shortly after some of the air raids on display in the Northern Ireland War Memorial (images courtesy of Northern Ireland War Memorial)

Sr Paschal Hughes, who had gone to Drumshanbo, wrote to the Poor Clare community at St Damian's in Dublin thanking the Mother Abbess for all the community had sent to them whilst they were there:

*Drumshanbo*
*Friday 30th [May] 1941*

*Praised be Jesus Christ!*

*My dear Mother Abbess,*

*God bless and reward you for your prompt and generous reply to our demands– we are most, most grateful…*

*Two Belfast ladies …called to see us this eve - one of them had her house ruined – she said it is quite extraordinary that the Catholic part of Belfast & the Catholic churches have come off with little or no damage - of course how our convent escaped in the first raid was a mystery to everyone & still more so in the second raid. Of course there is hardly a door or window left are boards on doors & windows felt but otherwise it seems to have [had] a wonderful escape - we could write pages on the raid but as we all said the morning after we could not possibly convey to anyone outside the experience– I think a good many of the sisters would agree with me that we would not have missed those 9 or 10 hours of our lives for anything– we got a few ordinary lives into them D.V.*

*Poor David had a big loss of his very best friends - one of them mended the shoes I am wearing R.I.P. There were five in the house & for Easter a married sister and her little girl of 5 came from Dublin. On Mon Eve, I think they were at the lodge for tea- the little girl was blown right away from the house and found dead in a protestant church - the other six were buried under their house - we heard when we came here the loss of life was, I think, 500. Oh but that was cutting down things!! Before we left Belfast the loss was estimated to be 4,500 and it was by no means the full amount - during the week, there was a constant stream of funerals to the cemetery and a great number of little blue coffins…*

*It was the 16th of April & we renewed our holy vows …in the pitch dark, with the guns shrieking & the fires crackling round us and worst of all to hear the houses toppling down, wondering if part of our own was one of them & wondering, please God, ready – if it were His Holy Will that we should be buried, … [writing illegible]. Oh, He did test our trust and we will trust Him now to make good our want in it – God help the poor sisters who had to face two more such raids – God grant us peace soon – How we are longing to open again that little tabernacle!…*

*Sister Thérèse' sister sent word that a priest in America after the first Belfast raid made an appeal to all priests to say Holy Mass for the preservation of Eire … you can hardly imagine the different atmosphere between Eire & the North; we felt it even in the train – The first bell we heard when we crossed the border was the Angelus so we all stood up & said it aloud in the carriage – we were alone – we hadn't heard a church bell for about a year…*

*I better close this letter, as it is to go in this post.*

*With all my love and again God reward you always.*

*Your grateful little sister in Jesus,*
*S. M. Paschal of the Blessed Sacrament PCS*

In the aftermath of the bombing, the decision for the nuns to return to Belfast fell to Mother Colette, who had to consider the risk to the lives of the community members balanced against staying on in the separate monasteries, which was fragmenting the community. Being in community is central to the Poor Clare way of life and this would have featured prominently in her prayer:

> *Shortly after I made a Novena asking for a decision about returning myself – the 4th day a letter came from David (who remained in the lodge) to say that the police had been making enquiries if we were returning as if not they would take over the place. I wired the Bishop and returned 2 days after with Srs Malachy and Magdalen – Srs Francis, Anne & Anthony came from Drumshanbo and we kept the House until the following Easter when all returned except Mother Maria and Sr Assisi.*

Community life could then get back to normal – or as normal as it could be during World War II. Nothing is recorded about the return of the full community in April 1942. By 1943 when the next entry in the journal is made, it would seem that the community was back to their daily timetable. Bishop Mageean visited on 17 October 1943 to bless the Lourdes grotto. Later that year, news came through of a second community death, this time Mother Maria who had come from Liberton in Edinburgh. She died on 24 November 1943. The last entry in the notebook for the 1940s describes the death of Sr Paschal Hughes. She was the first member of the community to be buried in the new cemetery, created in 1930; 20 more nuns would in the years to come also be buried there.

The Belfast Blitz was a dramatic episode in the story of the Poor Clares in Belfast, and indeed a tragic one for the whole of the city. Interestingly, there is a plaque in the Shankill Graveyard acknowledging those killed on 15/16 April 1941, however, there is no public memorial to the 1,000 or so people who were killed during the whole Blitz. Historian Brian Barton has been among those calling for one.

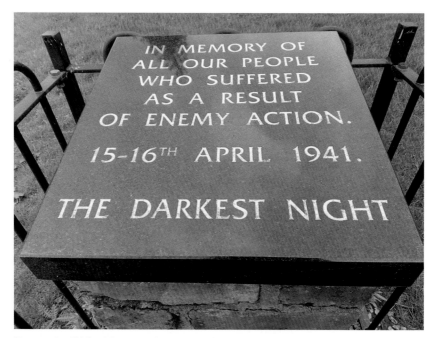

Plaque in the Old Shankill Graveyard in memory of all the people killed in Belfast in the 15/16 April 1941 air raid

# Chapter Five

## From Autonomy to Federation

Forty Hours' Devotion

> **" **
> *Now I am coming to a very*
> *unforeseen event in our life*
> **" **

By the time the 1950s came around and the thoughts of war were passing, celebration was playing an important part in the life of Belfast's Poor Clares. In 1951 the community journal records, albeit briefly, Silver Jubilee celebrations for Sr Joseph and Sr Thérèse. These were the first two women who joined the community when the nuns were still living in Mossville on the Antrim Road. In later entries, there were more details given to the various jubilee celebrations that were part of community life. There were also final profession ceremonies marking the decision of a nun to take life-long vows as a Poor Clare. Befitting the Poor Clare mindset of following a liturgical timetable, the Birthday of Our Lady on 8 September 1951 was chosen for Sister Helena and Sister Petronilla to take on these vows.

Alongside these important community developments, there was a significant physical development. The community had decided to build an enclosure wall. The practice and indeed vow of enclosure plays a very significant role in the Poor Clare way of life. The issue of monastic enclosure is one that raises considerable discussion within religious life. St Clare of Assisi is considered to have played a key role in the development of the practice of enclosure. Armstrong (1988, p.63) explains that in her rule Clare states that her sisters may leave the enclosure 'for a useful, reasonable, evident and approved purpose.' Poor Clare nun and author Patricia Rumsey (2011, p.249) also shows how St Clare saw enclosure:

> …according to her [Clare] understanding, enclosure is a filter to remove pointless distractions rather than an impenetrable barrier within which the nuns are contained for life in order to 'condemn the vanity of the world,' as it was becoming for other Orders within the Church.

*Journal One* notes the efforts of the community to secure planning permission from the local authorities to build an enclosure wall, which was eventually given on 6 March 1953. The wall was completed three months later. The nuns had a plaque attached to it with the Latin words Ego vos semper custodiam meaning 'I will always look after you'. The community marked 1953 with various celebrations as it was the seventh centenary of the death of Saint Clare on 11 August 1253.

Following on from the centenary year of the death of St Clare, in 1954 the nuns along with Catholics throughout the world took part in what was called a 'Marian Year' declared by Pope Pius XII which was dedicated to Mary the Mother of Jesus. The year began on 8 December 1953 and continued until 8 December 1954. There were special prayers and ceremonies to mark this year. As the community grew in number and became more settled in Belfast, they developed their religious practices. The purpose of all these practices, talks, retreats and conferences was to help the nuns grow in faith and nourish their contemplative life. These have their roots in the thinking of St Clare herself. In her third letter to Agnes of Prague, Clare writes:

> And through contemplation, transform your entire being into the image of the Godhead Itself. (Armstrong, 2006, p. 51)

The Poor Clares observed another Catholic practice known as the 'Forty Hours' Devotion' which began on 11 June 1954. This is the practice of putting a large Eucharistic host in a receptacle known as a monstrance which was placed in a central point on the altar. Catholics believe that Jesus Christ is present in the host and are invited to pray during the 40 hours of continuous prayer in the presence of Jesus. This practice of prayer in the presence of the Eucharistic host known as the Blessed Sacrament goes back to the words of Jesus to his disciples in the Garden of Gethsemane on the eve of his Passion and death. 'He came back to the disciples and found them sleeping, and he said to Peter: "So you had not the strength to keep awake with me one hour? You should be awake, and praying not to be put to the test"'
(Matthew 26:40-41).

The community records various changes which were happening within the Catholic Church at large and how these were received in the Belfast community: *we had the new Easter ceremonies like all the churches – evening Mass etc.'*

The journals also record some of the work that needed to be done inside and outside the monastery including the painting of the 'Professed House Cloister' and an additional room added on to the lodge and the kitchen was enlarged. Mother Colette seems to have been surprised by the bill when it came in from the builders: *'We got a shock when the account came from Mr Kerr, over £800, the men's wages were half the amount.'*

# Religious Processions

## in the monastery grounds

May procession around the garden reciting the rosary

Procession to Our Lady of Lourdes grotto

Community procession around the cemetery

Sr Patricia Ward in Poor Clare habit pre-Vatican II

Mother Paul and Mother Michael

# The Federation of the Poor Clares of Ireland

Until October 1959, when Mother Colette went to a meeting of the nine abbesses of the Poor Clare Colettine Order in the order's monastery in Galway, the Belfast nuns had lived in relative independence. In Galway, the journal records that a series of meetings took place: 'in connection with the Federation of the Poor Clares of Ireland which Pope Pius XII had ordered.'

The meetings were to establish a federation for the Poor Clares in Ireland, which would foster a greater sense of cohesion and facilitate the sharing of members and resources. The abbesses met each day to draw up statutes for the federation which would then be sent off to Rome for approval. The journal records that the abbesses made use of the statutes which had already been approved by Rome for the French Poor Clares and made some additions to these.

Once the Irish federation was established, it became very important for the Poor Clares in Belfast, with many references to it throughout their various correspondences. It was especially significant in the last years of life of the Poor Clares in Belfast.

One of the purposes of the federation was to create an overall sense of community for the Poor Clare monasteries throughout Ireland. This meant moving beyond a situation of autonomy where a monastic community was completely independent and had little or no dealings with other communities.

Within a few years of the meeting of abbesses to agree the statues, there was a request for assistance from a monastery within the federation. These sorts of requests would become common whenever the federation was finally established. The request took the superior of the time, Mother Colette, by surprise:

> *Now I am coming to a very unforeseen event in our life. At the beginning of March 1960 I had a letter from Father Rogan O.F.M., he said it was on the part of the Bishop of Killaloe. The Poor Clare Colettines in Ennis (founded*

*about 2 years ago) were very badly off for sisters as Mother Agnes (Abbess)*
*was dying of cancer and they found it hard to keep things going so he asked*
*if we could give 1 or 2 sisters and that the request was urgent. I immediately*
*put on my thinking cap & prayed & settled on Sr Anne (Cummings). She*
*consented to go although a little fearful – I had arranged for our usual*
*'Triduum' to begin the 21st March so I thought it would be a good idea for her*
*to go on the 28th March. Donnybrook had been asked for sisters also, they gave*
*Sr Magdalen – the whole affair was settled up speedily – Sr Anne's people*
*brought them both down after staying at Donnybrook … they got a great*
*welcome in Ennis & settled down wonderfully well D.G.*

It is clear from Mother Colette's description that the request to transfer
nuns from one monastery to another was not commonplace. The expectation
would have been that a nun once she was finally professed would remain
in that monastery for the rest of her life. In the last years of the Belfast
community, there were several requests made to the Irish federation for
nuns from another Irish monastery to come to Belfast to supplement the
community to 'keep things going'. But it is clear that at the start of the
1960s, the Belfast community had sufficient members to be able to send a
nun to the Poor Clare monastery in Ennis.

The Poor Clare monastery in Ennis

In 1962, Mother Colette, who was keeping the community journal at that time, wrote of the priest tasked with setting up the Irish federation:

> *The beginning of May Father Rogan OFM died rather suddenly RIP. …He was the Father of the Federation of the Poor Clares in Ireland ordered by Pius XII. I have been told it is doubtful if the Federation will continue. The other Fathers are not much interested in it and the Sisters are not anxious for it. It is not actually needed in Ireland – the people are very good to us wherever we make a foundation and God will arrange Himself as regards postulants D.V.*

The Irish federation did survive, and at the time of writing continues.

In the 1960s there were further community celebrations to mark three jubilees of profession:

> *Sister Malachy McHenry and Mother Michael Sheridan – who were due the end 1960 but owing to other celebrations, they decided to wait until 1961.*

The third jubilee celebration was for Sr Anthony. The journal records that family and friends were an important part of these celebrations and they were also occasions of fun as can be seen for the entry for 3 September 1963:

> *We had Mother's Golden Jubilee - Everything went grand D.G. Sister Magdalen kept her Silver Jubilee the same day – the Sisters got up several amusements.*

The joy of the celebrations was soon tinged by the death of their chaplain, Fr O'Neill, in September 1963:

> *On Sunday 29th Father O'Neill our Chaplain had left his mother's home to come here to say Mass – it was a Sunday. He was very late so Nora at the Lodge looked out of our gate to see if he was coming & got a shock when she saw Father lying on the foot path – a Protestant lady …saw him also & telephoned immediately for an ambulance – Father was taken to the Royal & died almost immediately. R.I.P. He was anointed by Father Murphy as soon as he got to the hospital. He was buried in Cork at the African Missionary College.*

# Vatican II

One of the surprising points about the community journal is how little reference it contains to Vatican II, which had started in Rome in 1962 and continued until 1965. This council, which had been initiated by Pope John Paul XXIII, introduced major reform within the Catholic Church. These reforms meant the re-organisation and re-ordering of the altars in churches and chapels and affected Catholics throughout the world including the Poor Clare community on the Cliftonville Road. There is a reference to the nuns asking permission of the local bishop, Dr William Philbin, for some changes to the structural layout of the community chapel:

> *He gave leave for Mother to go ahead about getting the altar in the choir to be changed according to the new liturgical regulations.*

Although the notebook gives very little detail of what was happening when Vatican II was taking place it does have passing references to some of the changes which the community made, such as the movement of the altar to allow the priest to face the congregation. These regulations which had emanated from Vatican II meant that the altar needed to be moved forward to allow for the priest celebrating Mass to go behind the altar and face the people.

> *In Sept. and Oct. alterations were done in the Choir. We had Holy Mass in the Refectory & the Blessed Sacrament reserved there. The Choir Altar was arranged so that we could see the Priest. It is very satisfactory & all are very pleased with it.*

Vatican II as a time of reform had far ranging implications for Catholics throughout the world. Some changes led to how the nuns dressed, as recorded by Journal One in August 1966:

> *On the Feast of St Clare we changed to the new white veils. The first appearance caused much merriment as we did not recognise each other. We also discarded the long Enclosure veils.*

Later, in December 1966, a very good friend of the community who is often mentioned in the notebook, Fr Theodore Crowley, a Franciscan priest and philosopher, began to teach the nuns theology *'which he hopes to give weekly for a period of 4 yrs. Let us hope we shall be good Theologians by that time.'*

Another of the changes coming from Vatican II was 'concelebrated Mass', which meant that more than one priest could celebrate the same Mass together; prior to Vatican II the norm was for only one priest to officiate at Mass. On 24 September 1968, the nuns were present at their first concelebrated Mass.

As a community in 1968, the Poor Clares were still attracting new people to their way of life: *'We had one Simple and two Final Professions & the Entrance of 2 Postulants.'* However, the last reference in Journal One in August 1969 starkly read: *'Serious riots in Belfast. Continued more or less until 1970.'*

The nuns would hear at first hand of the suffering of people deeply traumatised by what became known as 'The Troubles'.

# Chapter Six

## Solace and Survival in the Seventies

'Anguish'. Image courtesy of Brendan Murphy

> *Few people realise what mothers in Belfast*
> *are enduring these times*

Towards the end of the 1960s, Belfast was once again to experience a sustained period of violence that would last until 1998. In the course of almost 30 years, there are many reflections and references in the Poor Clares' community journals and newsletters about the ongoing violence on the streets of the city and further afield.

Some commentators look to a Civil Rights march in Derry on 5 October 1968 as the beginning of this period of the Troubles, with the ending considered to be the signing of the Good Friday Agreement on 10 April 1998. In the early months of 1969, loyalist paramilitaries planted bombs in various places in Northern Ireland, including in Castlereagh in East Belfast where an electricity substation was destroyed. Serious rioting broke out in Belfast on 12 July 1969, then eased but broke out again on Thursday 14 August and continued into the following day. British soldiers were deployed on the streets of Belfast on Friday 15 August 1969. Seven people were killed in the city from Thursday 14 to Saturday 16 August in these early days of the Troubles.

As already mentioned, *Journal One* contains a simple reference to the start of the Troubles. The next reference, which immediately followed, contained some more details, though it read like a telegram with the briefest of information:

> *July 1970. Serious riots and burning continued – Military control enlarged this month. 'Twelfth' quietest for many years – it was a Sunday & all Churches in the North had Exposition of the Blessed Sacrament & prayers for peace. Orange Parade on 13th passed over quietly.*

In fact, there was serious rioting in Belfast on Saturday 27 June 1970, which resulted in the deaths of five people. On the following day, there was more rioting as well as the expulsion of Catholic workers from the Harland and Wolff shipyard. Homes and businesses were also burnt out as noted in a publication by the Ulster Unionist Party:

> Saturday, June 27 1970. Many buildings are burned and looted as troops and police fight off attacks from rioters. (UUP, 1970)

With regard to the journal's comment about 'military control enlarged this month,' this may be a reference to what was known as the 'Falls Road Curfew' where the British Army conducted extensive house to house searches and raids in the Falls Road in West Belfast. A military curfew was put in place from 10pm on Friday 3 July until approximately 9am on Sunday 5 July.

Along with many other people of faith, the nuns prayed fervently and frequently for peace. But there were no more references to any violence or what was happening in Belfast for the rest of 1970.

The next entry in the community journal to the Troubles again reads like a telegram: *May 1972. Serious rioting and bombing continues all over North.* It also gives details of a visit by two Franciscan priests to show solidarity with the nuns and contains these words: *They were very concerned about us during these Troubles.*

This is very understandable in the light of the murders of two men, Hugh Clawson and David Fisher on 2nd July 1972 whose bodies were found by children playing in the grounds of Cliftonville cricket club next door to the monastery. In the history of the cricket club, the horrors of those years are acknowledged:

> The outbreak of civil disorder in August 1969 and the geographical positioning of the ground had made it increasingly difficult to travel to and from practice/games etc. with bomb scares and street protests a regular occurring event. …By 1972 a campaign of intimidation had begun against the Club, its members and what it represented in the area. Members were verbally and physically attacked, two young Protestant men were abducted, executed and their bodies dumped within the grounds of Cliftonville Cricket club. Whilst the British Army stood idly by and watched, the club was looted and set on fire by a hostile crowd. With no assurances coming from local or national government regards guaranteeing members' safety, the Club had no alternative but to make the heartbreaking decision to abandon the ground.
> (Cliftonville Cricket Club)

McKIBBINS WHITE RUM (THE LADY IN WHITE)

# The Irish News
AND BELFAST MORNING NEWS

113th YEAR · No. 31,435 · BELFAST, MONDAY, AUGUST 27, 1973 · ESTD. 1855 · 2p

HIGH & DRY Really Dry Gin

**Three seriously injured in 700lb. Ballycastle blast**

# MASSGOERS MIRACLE ESCAPE

A 700lb. car bomb exploded outside a Ballycastle, Co. Antrim, Catholic Church yesterday as 800 men, women and children attended Mass inside, injuring more than 200, three of them seriously.

And an RUC officer at the scene said: "I dread to think what would have happened if this bomb had gone of five minutes later when the bulk of the congregation were leaving the church. It is a possibility too terrible to contemplate."

The car was left outside the Church just as 11 o'clock Mass was being brought to a close. The three seriously injured — one had an arm blown off — had left at the Last Gospel and were on their way to their parked cars when the car bomb exploded, blasting in the stained glass windows of the church, badly damaging two nearby schools, and tearing a crater eight foot wide and four-and-a-half feet deep in the roadway.

A section of the large crowd which attended the anti-internment meeting at Dunville Park, Belfast, yesterday, listening to the speakers.

**Provos shot 'undercover'**

**LONDON BOMBS—HEATH NOT DEFINITE ON IRA'S PART**

**A 'milk shortage'**

# Victims of blast also shot

THREE Catholics who were killed in a Cliftonville Road, Belfast, car repair workshop at the weekend, were the victims of a Protestant extremist murder gang. It was established last night that they had been shot before the workshop was torn apart in a massive explosion that cut one of the bodies in-two and sent the torso and head rocketing through the roof onto a cricket ground some distance away.

A police spokesman said the bodies of brothers Sean McDonald (50), Harvey Park, Upper Cavehill Road, and Ronnie McDonald (25), La Salle Park, and 14-year-old Bernard Rice, Plumtree Lodge, were taken. Personal effects and announcements were quietly on the scene.

*Shots, then explosion*

A woman who lives near the scene said last night that the brothers and the youth started work until about 11 o'clock—and before three men arrived. Neighbours heard shots and saw a car moving at speed from near the workshop. Then the explosion tore the inside of the workshop and the bodies were blasted over the wall and into the next night. The remains of all three murder victims were...

'Victims of blast also shot.' *Irish News* coverage of Cliftonville Road murders, August 1973

The notes kept during the 1970s are interspersed with what was going on in the community (such as the various liturgical celebrations and the priests who officiated at them) and references to the ongoing violence such as this one in March 1973: *Serious trouble continues in the City.*

These few words give a brief idea of what was going on in Belfast at that time, and it was very unpleasant. On Thursday 8 March 1973, father of six David Glennon, aged 45, from Divismore Drive in Ballymurphy, had been abducted and shot dead by the UDA/UFF. In *Lost Lives*, the main authority of the killings during the Troubles, describes his death this way:

> He was found hooded with his feet bound, shot in the head in a stolen car in Summer Street just off the lower Oldpark Road. (McKittrick, Kelters, Feeney and Thornton, 1999, p.339)

The Oldpark Road runs at stages parallel to the Poor Clare Monastery. On that same day British soldier, Private John Green, was shot dead by the IRA outside St Joseph's Primary School, Slate Street, off the Grosvenor Road in West Belfast which was used as a polling station. In addition, bombs went off in the city.

On 23 March three soldiers, Sergeant Richard Michael Muldoon, Staff Sergeant Barrington Foster and Sergeant Thomas Penrose – all Catholic – were killed by the IRA after being lured to a flat on the Antrim Road by two women. A fourth soldier was seriously wounded. The following day, 28-year-old factory worker John Huddleston was shot by the UDA, according to reliable loyalist sources as mentioned in *Lost Lives* (p.345).

As part of a DVD called *Voices from the North: The Poor Clares* made at the time of the closure of the monastery in 2012 Sr Paschal McMeel was interviewed about her memories of the Troubles from 1969 to 1998. She talked about some of the inspirational people she had met who had called into the monastery to find solace. Sr Paschal recalled some of the events such as the blowing up of a filling station further up the Cliftonville Road from the monastery and how that explosion broke several of the monastery windows. She also recalled 'the constant presence of helicopters; with helicopters flying so near to us, rising and landing and their searchlights.' In her interview on camera she spoke of her lasting memories of the people she met:

> …wonderful people. People came here from all parts and especially those who had suffered tragedy in normal families – shootings, deaths. There was a lady in particular, her husband had been working in the Shipyard. Like many others, he was shot, coming out of his work. Two of her sons were coming home from the club one evening, not very late, and yards from their own entrance gate, a motorbike with a driver and a pillion rider, came flashing past and shot the two of them, probably just on their doorstep. That lady has been coming to us all the time now and we can see it, she should be canonised, a wonderful, wonderful lady and that's only one experience of an awful tragedy. Of course there are many others who have lost members of their family, young, nearly all, many young people. (Multimedia Heritage, 2014)

# Ministry of listening

During the early Troubles, there were very few opportunities for counselling. As people of faith, the nuns would have assured their visitors they would be praying for them. Whilst the Poor Clares did not providing counselling – none of them were trained counsellors – they did provide a safe place for people to share their stories and a space where people could be guaranteed a listening ear in confidential surroundings. In the *Voices from the North* DVD, Sr Paschal explained:

> It is a matter of being there for someone, to listen to them, this is what people need desperately at this present time.

In reality, the nuns exercised a 'ministry of listening,' which Sr Paschal described in this way:

> …They come to us not to get anything but just to unburden themselves … and even yet, people will come and sit down and just burst out crying… and we'll say to them 'take your time, take your time' and after they settle down a little bit, they say, 'this is something I couldn't do in front of my own family.' …I said, 'time, it's yours, just be here.' (Multimedia Heritage, 2014)

Donegal Road beside Celtic Park, 1974. Image courtesy of Brendan Murphy

As the Troubles continued on a daily basis, North Belfast bore much of the worst of the violence. Whilst many people were resilient, they found in the monastery a place where they allowed themselves to be vulnerable in the presence of a listening and caring Poor Clare nun. There was a tendency amongst women whose husbands had been murdered or who were imprisoned, and who were bringing up children, to believe they needed to be strong for their offspring. They did not want their children to witness their pain. When they were in a parlour with a Poor Clare nun, many of these women allowed their mask of being strong and coping well to come down as they experienced their pain and brokenness. In the entry for 24 December 1977, it was clear there was an increasing need for space to listen to people:

> … *lives are in danger every day and night; so people felt the need of spiritual help as much as they can get. It was thought necessary to have another Parlour for Visitors – this was arranged by making the big Extern Parlour into one where Sisters could meet their people. Our good man at the Lodge – Jack with the help of his brothers did the work and had it complete before the Parlour opened again after the Advent Silence. It is a lovely place and bigger than the other which is kept now for a few visitors and a long passage beside it leads up to the Turn where the ordinary everyday people can come and talk with the Portress, quite separate from the other two places – leaving them shut off from the Public and private. Two different sets of visitors can be received at the same time and enjoy Privacy.*

In addition to the community journal, which at this time was kept sporadically, in 1975 the nuns began to produce an annual newsletter called *Tel-A-Vision*. It continued until the monastery closed in 2012. This newsletter was compiled in each of the monasteries within the Irish federation and then sent to the others. It was a record of key events which occurred during the previous year. The 1977 edition contains this description of their ministry:

> *Through the letters sent to us and conversations in the parlour we get many an insight into the anguished hearts of countless people; things that elude the notice of newspaper and other reporters.*

Another edition gives some idea of the painful stories that people shared with the nuns when they sought a place of sanctuary.

*There is the wife who sits by the window night after night awaiting her husband's return from work, in a Protestant centre, fretting lest he is murdered, and in the end her nerves give way.*

*A most kind hearted couple who had only two children, two boys; they adopted seven other children over a period of twenty years, and then one of their own two was shamelessly tortured and murdered. The mother said that at first she just sat on a couch all day and wept.*

*There is the mother of six, a nervous wreck in hospital week after week, as a result of the assassination of her husband.*

*Workmen on a building site at Ardoyne, and many others like them, never sure of their safety, send an urgent petition for our prayers.*

*Countless parents ask prayers for sons and daughters having to appear in court, that the judge may be lenient to them. They will say: 'He is a good boy or girl but…' and the 'but' ending is the parents' torture. The list is endless.*

At different times in their writings, the nuns acknowledge the pain of the people of Belfast.

*…It is good to know that you unite with us in praying for these sorely tried people.*

*On the rare occasions when we go out – to the dentist, optician etc. – we notice that there is scarcely anyone among the people who speak to us, who hasn't had someone belonging to her killed, maimed or imprisoned. The same is true of those who come to visit us here. There is so much silent suffering around that it must be effective in hastening the day of peace.*

For some people, relying on their faith was very important:

> *If any of you watched 'Walls of Tears,' produced by RTE in late February, you may be interested to know that the Mass, of which you saw a few flashes was our Sunday Mass on 13th January. This was a programme on North Belfast, and in it people who had lost dear ones by violent deaths, or who had themselves been attacked, were interviewed. One of these Mrs. McGuinness, whose husband, Dermot, had been shot in Rosapenna Street, just outside our wall last October, God rest him. Being a spiritually minded person she wanted her contribution to have a religious slant, so, at her wish, she and her family were televised attending our Mass.*

Whilst it is true that the nuns were living an enclosed contemplative life, the large wall which surrounded the monastery did not shield them from the horror and scale of the Troubles. There were times when a relation or relations of a community member were affected by the violence as the 1976 annual newsletter testifies:

> *Around 6.30 p.m. on 17th January Mother heard that her sister's shop in Belfast had just been bombed! [It was Sheridan's bar and not a shop.] In horror she tried over the phone to get news. No answer anywhere! She came down to the refectory to us and very bravely gave us the news and asked us to pray. After some time her niece, Colette Martin, phoned to say that her Mother had been rushed to hospital where it was found that, beyond shock and some bruises she was unhurt. It was truly miraculous! To Mrs Martin's great grief, two people, to one of whom she had just been speaking when the bomb exploded were killed and several people injured. The building was of course, completely destroyed.*

Children playing 'war games' in Balaclava Street, Belfast, 1975 (courtesy of Brendan Murphy)

The editors of *Lost Lives* (p.616) record it in this way:

January 17, 1976. Sarah O'Dwyer, North Belfast. Civilian, Catholic, 47, married, 5 children. James Reid, North Belfast, Civilian, Catholic, 47, married, 10 children.

Sarah O'Dwyer and James Reid were killed by a UVF no-warning bomb thrown into the Sheridan bar on the New Lodge Road. In all 26 people were injured in the explosion. Sarah died instantly and James Reid died a short time later...

# Death toll 4 in bomb and bullet attacks

THREE men and a woman died violent deaths from bombs and bullets in Northern Ireland at the week-end but there were no casualties when an explosion badly damaged the UDA centre at Navarra Place, between Serpentine Road and Ballyroney Hill, Newtownabbey, last night.

The murder of a man and a woman in a Catholic-owned and frequented public house at New Lodge Road in a "no warning" explosion, the assassination at Hannahstown, near Belfast, of a 25-year-old Catholic by the Provisional IRA who claimed that he had been working for the Security Forces and had passed on information about both wings of the Republican movement, and the death of a British soldier shot at point-blank range by a teenaged gunman in Derry, brought the death toll from violence for the first three weeks of this month to 28.

The victims of the pub bombing were Mrs. Sadie O'Dwyer Street and Mr. Jimmy Reid (44), a married man of Upper Meadow Street, The Hannahs. A town victim was Mr. Seamus Brendan O'Brien from Andersonstown, found shot through the head on a lonely road. The soldier was 19-year-old Mark Ashford from North London, shot dead at an Army check-point in the centre of Derry on Saturday morning. He was a Catholic and unmarried.

Eighteen other customers many of them elderly were injured in the bomb attack on Sheridan's Bar on Saturday evening. Four of the injured were still "very seriously ill" in hospital early today.

A teenage youth was seen planting the brown parcel bomb inside the doorway of the pub. "It exploded within seconds, giving the customers inside no chance of escape," an RUC spokesman said.

A statement signed by the heads of the four main Churches in Derry said: "We recall that at Christmas upwards of 20,000 Derry people of all sections signed the Declaration for Peace, in which they declared that they were opposed to assassinations 'for any sectarian or other purpose'. We believe that they expressed the view of all but a very few in this community who respect neither the law of God nor the will of the people.

"These few are therefore without justification in conscience and without any proper mandate. They must therefore ask themselves what authority they have for their actions, and we appeal to their supporters to deny them any further help."

The statement was signed by Most Rev. Dr. Edward Daly, Bishop of Derry; Rt. Rev. Robert Eames, Bishop of Derry and Raphoe; the Rev. James Williamson, Superintendent of Derry City Methodist Mission; and the Rev. Philip Breakey, Moderator of Derry Presbytery.

The Provisional I.R.A. statement said the only reason the British Army patrolled the streets of Derry was purely for the harassment and oppression of the people of Republican areas and this was blatantly obvious to the majority of people in the city.

"Those who are so quick to speak about the defensive measures of the Republican movement become dumb or semi-dumb when it comes to commenting on the misdemeanours of the British

Army," the Provisionals said. "We want to make it clear that if there is to be peace in Derry then the oppressive methods of the British Army must be spoken out against by everyone. Their very presence on our streets armed with rifles and other war materials is in itself provocative and aggressive.

"They are slowly reverting back to indiscriminate raids and arrests and we will not stand by much longer.

## Retaliation

The Provisionals said that Saturday's actions were in retaliation for all these oppressive measures and they wished to give civilian searchers, male or female, a special word of warning that if they continued to inconvenience the people of Derry they would not hesitate to pursue them relentlessly. "Let to-day's experience be a warning to them," the statement said.

A statement by the British army in Derry said that after the deliberate murder of one soldier and the wounding of two others in the midst of Saturday shopping crowds the Provisionals IRA had again shown that it totally disregarded the purpose of 20,000 Derry people who only recently declared their wish for a lasting peace.

"Nothing could have been done in a more cold-blooded and callous way," the Army statement said, "and it has dealt the image of peace and

(Continued on Page Six)

*Irish News* coverage of Sheridan's bar murders January 1976

# The Troubles close by

It is very clear when studying the nuns' community journals and annual newsletters that they were impacted by the stories they were hearing. Towards the end of her interview in *Voices from the North: The Poor Clares*, Sr Paschal recalls an event that made a huge impression on her. This was a gruesome murder of three men on the Cliftonville Road in a garage next to the monastery. In the interview recorded in 2012 she speaks with a freshness about the event that took place on 25 August 1973, describing it in this way:

> One Saturday afternoon, we had come from prayer to the Refectory and we had just said 'Grace' and were sitting down to start our meal, when we heard a mighty explosion and then we saw black smoke flaring up all over the place.

> At that time, we had Caretakers at the Gate lodge, and the gentleman came over and said 'please don't allow anyone to go near the windows' and he told us then what it was. Just over on the other side of our enclosure wall, behind the little shrine of Our Lady of Lourdes, there was a garage and being Saturday afternoon, …a gentleman and his friend and his little son…were about to close their garage for the weekend and … there was a group of men came up and shot the three of them and set fire to the garage.

It was recorded in *Lost Lives* (p.388) in this way:

> August 25th 1973 Sean McDonald, North Belfast Catholic, civilian, married, 8 children, garage owner.

> He was killed with his brother Ronald and their apprentice, Tony McGrady, in a UVF gun and bomb attack at their car repair shop near a cricket ground on the Cliftonville Road. The police said all three bodies had what appeared to be bullet wounds. At first people in the area thought the explosion could have been accidental because gas cylinders were used in the workshop. It later emerged that some people living nearby had heard gunshots and saw a car driving away at speed just before the explosion.

One man told reporters, 'My son said he heard shooting. Then there was a terrific explosion. I ran to the yard and the garage was blazing.' Two bodies were found beside a car in the workshop and the third was lying outside. Firemen braved flames and exploding paint cans to carry the bodies from the premises. According to one report, security forces in the area said there had been reports of a suspicious car on the Cliftonville Road a short time before the blast.

Sean McDonald came from Slievetoye Park, Belfast. He and his brother started their workshop on the Cliftonville Road after they were forced to leave their former premises in Perth street by loyalists in 1969. According to reliable loyalist sources the UVF was behind the attack.

There were separate entries in *Lost Lives* for Ronald McDonald and Tony McGrady. Yet again Belfast was going through another time of sectarian murder and strife. According to Johnston (1998), the largest number of people to be killed per year in the Troubles in Belfast and elsewhere occurred during the years of 1972 and 1976.

While the Troubles were going on, most people, including the Poor Clares, tried to get on with life as best they could. The nuns continued their daily rhythm of prayer from the Divine Office, also known as the 'Liturgy of the Hours,' which marks the different times of the day when psalms and scriptures are read and prayers said. They also had their individual times of contemplative prayer, community retreats led by a visiting preacher as well as celebrating important community events.

On Tuesday 29 May 1974 the community celebrated the Golden Jubilee of the order's foundation in Belfast in 1924. Fifty years in Belfast was an important milestone for the Order, however, the journals show that celebrations were in the context of a very unsettled city:

> *Father David OFM and Fr Cassian OFM were unable to come from Dublin owing to train stoppage threat, and the very 'tense' condition of the City during the Big Strike set going by the Ulster Workers Council. However, their absence was 'made up' for, by the presence of 3 Anglican Franciscan Brs wearing their holy Habits and one had a beard!*

While the journal records that *'every part of the Monastery was painted'* and that there had been *'additional tiling work,'* it also continues: *'there were serious troubles in the City at the time but thank God all those involved in the painting etc arrived safely every day.'*

There was indeed serious trouble, which included the murders of 12 people in Belfast around this time. The nuns would have been aware of these deaths even with their limited access to the media. Within their community and personal prayer they would have prayed for the dead, their families and for those injured. Through word of mouth, it became known that the Poor Clares offered a safe place where people could go to share their story and where they would receive a listening ear and an assurance of prayer and support. Clearly this meant a great deal to those who called with them. Over the years, the nuns met many people whose loved ones were killed or injured during the Troubles. There was a mutual appreciation in these relationships as indicated from this reference:

> *...the people of Belfast keep us well supplied with food and we daren't refuse them. They say: 'we need your prayers, the only thing we can rely on.'*

The nuns praying for people and for peace was a very important part of what they saw as their role in Belfast. They believed in the power of prayer:

> *As on last year, with the approach of the marching season – July and August especially – tensions were high and there were bleak forebodings of the awful things that might happen, but, thanks be to God, and to the power of the many prayers offered, most of the imagined evils were averted, and people can relax a bit. Now we have the new situation of loyalist paramilitaries fighting among themselves and taking lives. It is drug related, we are told, and not political, a bit better than usual, but still not acceptable.*

Some of the people who regularly worshipped with the Poor Clares often said that the nuns were very well informed about what was going on in Belfast. Their knowledge can be explained quite simply – they garnered a great deal of news and information from the many people who called with them.

Falls Road, Belfast after the Queen's Silver Jubilee visit (courtesy of Brendan Murphy)

Springfield Road Barracks under attack (courtesy of Brendan Murphy)

# Continuing unrest

As the 1970s continued so did the unrest, and even though the nuns were living an enclosed life, it was impossible for them to escape the Troubles affecting Belfast and beyond. This included soldiers coming in to search their grounds for caches of weapons. The nuns accepted these 'visits' graciously.

> *The 'Army' and Police regularly inspect our spacious garden and Mother Abbess has to meet them at the enclosure gate to shake hands with the Colonel and others! They are usually 6-footers but our little Mother rises to the occasion.*

As has been mentioned previously, one of St Clare's principles of life was a reliance on Providence, the belief that emphasised trusting in God to supply all one's needs. This central tenet in Franciscan spirituality encouraged Clare to advocate for a radical poverty relying on total trust in Divine Providence. It was from this belief that Clare and the nuns in her community chose not to own any personal material property. The Poor Clare nuns in Belfast also lived by this belief in Providence and in the midst of the Troubles they regularly expressed gratitude to both God and the people of the city for looking after them during the distressing times:

> *Despite the sad situation here, we are full of gratitude to God. During this long period of almost daily bombings, shooting etc., He has given us graces and blessings without number, such as monthly lectures by the Redemptorists,… the extraordinary generosity of our benefactors, especially during Advent and Lent when the parlour is closed, and during the bread and milk strikes.*

But the tension in the city was never far away, even at Christmas. Around this time in the mid-70s many parishes in Belfast changed the Christmas 'Midnight Mass' to an earlier time because of the fear of people being out late and therefore being a target. The community records give a flavour of the anxious situation in Belfast at Christmas 1975:

> *Christmas passed over peacefully and we had Midnight Mass, thank God, but few people could attend in case of trouble on the streets.*

For those living at some distance from Belfast, including the nuns from other Poor Clare monasteries, there was always a concern for the safety of the members of the Belfast community. That concern even expressed itself in the offer of accommodation from other Poor Clare communities from within the Irish Federation had the situation deteriorated any further and had the nuns believed they were at risk. It is clear, however, that the nuns had no desire to leave the city and its people during these difficult times:

*Belfast for the world at large means a city of violence, murder, bomb and bullet. … When we receive letters from all the Monasteries expressing their admiration at our courage for living in the midst of such tragedies, we thank God for His sustaining grace. We would like to take this opportunity to thank all the Monasteries who have repeatedly assured us that their doors and their hearts are open to us at any time should the need arise. Naturally none of us would wish to leave our dear cloister 'Home' and indeed should this happen the poor people would be on the verge of despair, so great is their faith in the power of prayer. They come to us or write about their heart-breaking troubles.*

Yet there must have been moments when the nuns wondered about their own safety. There were occasions when some damage was caused to the monastery such as an explosion in 1976:

*Sunday 24th April: At about 9.30pm there was a huge explosion just a short distance away, with the result that several of our windows were broken, but thank God, no one was injured by flying glass. Sunday morning saw all available hands brushing up broken glass for a considerable length of time, and we had a surplus of fresh air for some days! However, Sister Rain and Brother Wind obligingly did not intrude.*

Clearly the area was unsettled and one of the consequences was that their Unionist neighbours could no longer put up with the various attacks on their property.

*June 10th 1976 The big house next door to us – we used to call it 'Erskines' from the name of the people who lived in it when we came here originally, was demolished to-day.*

*It had changed hands several times since the Erskine family lived in it, but the last residents were people called Morgan and he was a big light in the Unionist party, with the result the house has been constantly attacked. The Morgans finally decided to quit. Since then the place has fallen into complete ruin and we often see small boys crawling on the roof pulling off lead which could be used for many warlike purposes. To-day, however, a bulldozer sent every speck of the building crashing to the ground, and now we have a splendid view of Cavehill. It is an enormous relief to get the unsightly building removed as we never know what arms dump might be in it or what devilry went on in it during the night.*

Community celebrations in 1976 such as the Golden Jubilee in September of that year of the two women who entered the Belfast foundation some 52 years previously were kept low key due to the ongoing unrest:

*Owing to the dangerous and difficult times it was all kept very quiet – neither sisters letting the few relations they have even know of it.*

Meanwhile, the perception that Belfast was a dangerous place to visit persisted:

*November 8th Our annual Retreat began and continued for 6 full days given by Fr. Sebastian Lee O.F.M. It was a most wonderful Retreat – so Franciscan and was a real treat for us up here in the 'North' who have very few chances to her our own Fathers since Fr. Theodore has left* [Fr Theodore Crowley, OFM]. *He had the courage to face the North which many or few would not, owing to the dangerous times of Violence of all kinds…*

As well as meeting family members of people killed or wounded in the Troubles, some of the nuns would have known personally some of those affected by the violence such as the case of one man who had a narrow escape but was left with life changing injuries:

*November: One of our benefactors was almost fatally injured (he lost one leg) in a booby trap in his car as he was returning from visiting his wife in hospital. He attributed his escape from death to our prayers and in gratitude he gave us a very beautiful and costly carpet for the sanctuary in our extern chapel.*

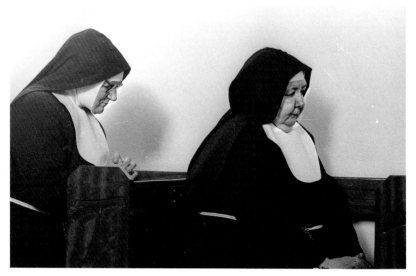

Sr Petronilla and Sr Helena at prayer (courtesy of Brendan Murphy)

Riots at the time of the Queen's visit (courtesy of Brendan Murphy)

Local girls clash with the British army after soldiers smashed in the gates of Milltown Cemetery on Easter Sunday 1976 (courtesy of Brendan Murphy)

'Arrested!' Image courtesy of Brendan Murphy

There is another account in the 1977 annual newsletter of how the nuns responded when they were confronted with a nearby bomb, a common feature of Belfast in the 1970s. They clearly went on with their lives as best they could unsure as to whether the bomb would explode and if they would be among its casualties.

As people of faith, they sought refuge in their belief in God and found comfort in the Scriptures that were part of their communal prayer every time they met. The account even has a certain black humour to it, something that was common amongst people during the Troubles as a way of coping with the dreadful things happening in Belfast:

> On the feast of St Agnes, January 21st we had a bomb scare. There was a ring from the lodge at about 11.20 a.m. to say there was a suspect bomb in a vacant house across the road, and we should go to the back of the house. ... When everyone was alerted it was time for Midday Prayer, so we went to the Chapter room. False notes or slips of the tongue would not have surprised anyone as we awaited our doom, but if there were any they went unnoticed, we were so intent on our prayer. ... With what sincerity we called out: 'You Lord who dwell in the heavens, have mercy on us.' Our confidence and abandonment increased as we prayed: 'Our help is in the name of the Lord.' The Lord surrounds his people both now and forever.' As we chanted: 'Those who put their trust in the Lord are like Mount Sion that cannot be shaken, that stands forever,' we could visualise our sturdy 16" thick stone and mortar standing up to any blast. ... Our suspect bomb featured on the midday news... After about an hour's suspense the bomb went off. It was audible only to those of us with keenest hearing. ...It was another half-hour before the all-clear signal was given, and then we sincerely thanked God that we were still alive.

The nuns were clearly struck by the contrast between the peace of their enclosure and the chaos in the city:

> The atmosphere in the Community was so peaceful & happy & cheerful – so different alas to that outside where people are under awful strain Violence continues Bombs, Robberies Burnings etc. etc (Provisional I.R.A.)

Even though several organisations were involved in the Northern Ireland's Troubles, it is interesting to note the only grouping singled out in this reference was the 'Provisional I.R.A.'

Apart from exceptional reasons the Poor Clare nuns never left the grounds of their monastery at 120 Cliftonville Road. They lived in the peace of the monastery and yet were acutely aware of the violence and mayhem going on around them. They were sensitive to life in Belfast and throughout the North/Northern Ireland at that time and understood the general anxiety about living and working in Belfast at a time when people were aware of where they should or shouldn't go in the city: *'People are always in danger of death especially here in the North of Ireland.'*

The nuns also understood that one of the great qualities the people of Belfast showed during throughout the Troubles was resilience, as indicated by some of the references in the monastery journal:

> *24th December. We had Midnight Mass this year 1977 which we did not have for several years on account of the danger of Bombs etc. etc. …Churches are filled even for Daily Mass. Six new Churches have been opened since the troubles began. God can bring good out of anything, lives are in danger every day and night, so people feel the need of spiritual help as much as they can get.*

Bottle attack on a Saracen tank on Andersonstown Road Belfast, 1976 (courtesy of Brendan Murphy)

The nuns' records during the 1970s clearly indicate that the Troubles had an impact on them. As well as dealing with the deaths, casualties and insecurities of the times, they also had to come to terms with the reality of bereavement within their own community. Sadly, during the 1970s eight Poor Clare nuns died, three of them in 1977.

What is most apparent about the Poor Clares in the 1970s period, however, is that they were always able to endure. Despite their calamitous surroundings, living the Poor Clare way brought the nuns peace, calm and the ability of absorb and salve the suffering of the people of North Belfast with love and compassion. In the midst of the trouble they were even able to display another example of black humour:

> Though the problems of Northern Ireland have by no means been solved, we enjoyed a measure of peace, or at least freedom from continual bombing and shooting, during the year. However, a few incidents which occurred in this locality stand out in our memories. On the night of 17th August, shortly before Matins, there was some shooting just outside our gate. A sister with deep concern, peered out and saw a military truck draw up at our gate. A soldier put a ladder to the gate, climbed up, crossed the gate, opened it on the inside, another soldier drove the truck in, and then they did whatever they wanted to do. They went all round the house flashing powerful searchlights on our windows – they must have penetrated to the marrow of our bones! We were up by this time as the Matins call had gone. (There's nothing to beat a bit of shooting as a Matins call! It gets everyone down in record time. Even those who usually travel on the 'last train' are in time for everything.) Fortunately the soldiers did not ask to be let inside, but they searched the Lodge…

As if to contrast the peace of the Poor Clare enclosure, as the decade was drawing to a close, the nuns were disturbed once again by tragic events happening a short distance from them:

> One evening late in October [25 October 1977] we were just cosily tucked in bed when we heard three shots outside. Then followed the usual procedure: traffic hold up, loud talk, ambulance, helicopter with its sweeping searchlights, and we wondered, prayed, thought of people agonising, of broken hearts and broken homes, and at last slept, hoping that the morrow's news would not be bad. It was too bad.

*An eighteen year old had been shot… The lad died R.I.P., after two hours in hospital. He was from the famed Unity Flats, and his father had died suddenly a few months previously. You can imagine his mother's anguish. Few people realise what mothers in Belfast are enduring these times.*

The event referred to was the shooting of teenager Denis Michael Neill and was described in *Lost Lives* (p.738) in this way:

*Denis Michael Neill, North Belfast, Civilian, Catholic, 16. The teenager from Stanhope Drive in the Unity Flats area of west Belfast, was shot by the army in disputed circumstances at the junction of Cliftonville Road and Oldpark Avenue.*

The nuns' newsletter also paints a picture of the area in 1978 where the monastery was located:

*Cliftonville Road still retains its notorious name, so much so that people, such as some taxi drivers, will not travel that way.*

The reference was to the fact that the Poor Clare community at 120 Cliftonville Road was smack in the middle of what by then had become known as 'Murder Mile'.

Bomb attack on Smithfield, Belfast (courtesy of Brendan Murphy)

Community at prayer

# Chapter Seven

## Living with Uncertainty

Left to right: Sr Petronilla, Sr Francis (from Ennis) and Sr John at prayer (image courtesy of Brendan Murphy)

— 66 —

*We pray and hope for justice*
*and a genuine peace*

— 99 —

Like so many people in 1980s Belfast, the nuns continued to live with uncertainty, unsure of what was going to happen next – as indicated by this reference in the 1981 newsletter:

> *The hunger strike here is world news, but we scarcely realise now, that it began several weeks before Christmas. As the holy season drew near, it seemed that Midnight Mass was out of the question for us, because, due to the tension and trouble outside, our chaplain said there could be no late travelling for him. We prayed and we hoped. 'The Lord looks on those who revere Him on those who hope in His Love,' and he rescued us from our dilemma. The strike – at least that phase of it – came to an end about a week before Christmas, and we had our Midnight Mass with greater appreciation than ever.*

This was known as the '1980 Hunger Strike' which began on 27 October 1980 when seven Republican prisoners went on hunger strike. It was called off on 18 December 1980.

Often in their annual newsletter they would describe aspects of the atmosphere and surroundings in North Belfast to give the other nuns in the different Irish monasteries in their federation a glimpse of life in the 'North'. The writer of this 1984 extract was aware of the irony:

> *Just now 'the Twelfth holidays,' as they are called, (12th July), are in full swing. The 12th itself was a particularly quiet day at 120. No bands passed up or down the road; we just heard a few in the early morning going to 'the field' and returning late in the evening. Not one person called to the parlour. That did not surprise us, as a great number of Catholics leave the city altogether at this time and go elsewhere on holidays. Most of those who remain prefer to stay indoors that day. Every place is closed – no post, no milk, no work at all that can be avoided. We got a double supply of milk on the previous day. The only other unusual thing that caught our attention was a small plane hovering around, with a scroll attached, which in bold lettering invited: 'Have your holiday in Ulster.'*

The relative peace of July 1984 was different from that of July 1986:

*There seems to be widespread relief here that the 12th celebrations passed off without any great calamities. ... There had been such a build-up of tension and violence beforehand that people dreaded the worst. Some streets near us witnessed a few bad nights. There were clashes between the police and civilians in Rosapenna Drive, which runs along our wall, when a black taxi had been fired on. There were some violent outbursts also in Manor Street, which is just below that. A lady who has recently come to live in Rosapenna told Sr John she didn't get to bed till 4 a.m. and she gave Sister her phone number, so that we could call on her if we were molested in any way! How thoughtful of others these good people are in their hardships!*

An *Irish News* report of that time contained the following details:

Dozens of police in full riot gear were drafted into the area and Land Rovers took up position to keep the rival factions apart. Stones and petrol bombs were hurled at police from the loyalist end of Manor Street and a police Land Rover was later set on fire. At the height of the trouble police fired plastic bullets to drive back the mob who tried to force their way into Catholic homes. Earlier in the day police discovered five petrol bombs, a number of acid bombs and iron bars in the mainly Catholic Rosevale Street, only yards away from the houses which were attacked in Roe Street. (Moloney, 1986)

## Peace prayers

The original reason the Poor Clare nuns came to Belfast in 1924 was their desire to make a difference through prayer and indeed to contribute to peace making. Throughout their journals and newsletters this desire is often reflected:

*Oct 27th 1986: We joined the Holy Father and the world church leaders gathered in Assisi to pray for peace. N. Ireland was the only country not to have a day of peace.*

# THE IRISH CATHOLIC

Volume 98    Number 27

THURSDAY, OCTOBER 30, 1986

Price 25p

- 3 NOV 1986

**YOUNG IRELAND PRESENT**

Pictured at right are part of a group of young people from all over Ireland who travelled overland to Assisi to join the Pope on Monday in his appeal for world peace.

**IRISH BISHOP AT ASSISI**

Bishop Anthony Farquhar, Auxiliary in Down and Connor at right as Chairman of the Bishops' Commission for Ecumenism represented the Irish Bishops' Conference at Assisi last Monday.

## RELIGIOUS LEADERS UNITE IN PRAYER

# GO IN PEACE
# WORLD URGED

El Salvadorean guerillas laid down their arms, and saffron-robed Buddhists intoned mantras in a Christian church as part of the Pope's Day of Prayer for Peace in Assisi.

Across the globe regional conflicts were briefly interrupted in response to the call for a 24 hour ceasefire. The truce was widely observed in South America, and three African guerilla movements pledged to heed the Pope's call.

More than 150 representatives from the twelve major religions joined the Pope in his capacity as host, rather than president, of a multi-religious day of prayer in Assisi. After a symbolic pilgrimage across Assisi, the leaders assembled in the Shadow of the Basilica of St. Francesco to pray. Seated on a platform

lined with white lilies, the leaders ended the event by an exchange of olive branches as a flock of white doves was released into the evening sky over Assisi.

In his final speech the Pope dwelled on the need for action towards peace to complement prayer. Christians, he said, should go away with a ". . . deeper resolution to commit ourselves to continuing the search for full unity and to overcoming the serious divisions which remain".

Among the 60 government leaders who sent messages of support were President Reagan and General Duarte of El Salvador. PLO leader Yassar Arafat also expressed support, saying that "the appeal by the Pope had a large echo among my people".

### NORTH MARKED EVENT

Last weekend Ireland heeded Pope John Paul's Peace Appeal with special ceremonies, prayer and fasting in most dioceses. Cardinal O Fiaich preached at Mass and a special prayer vigil in St. Patrick's Cathedral, pictured at left, on Saturday. The Cardinal also presided at a special ecumenical service in the cathedral on Monday evening at which Bro. Tadhg and Bro. Jean from the ecumenical community of Taize attended. Homilies and bidding prayers at all Masses in the Armagh diocese on Saturday evening and Sunday were on the theme of peace in the world and especially peace in Ireland. In Derry there was an all-night vigil in all churches ending at 6 a.m. on Sunday with Monday being observed as a day of fast and abstinence.

### IN DUBLIN

A Holy Hour was held in Dublin in the parishes of the diocese on Saturday at the request of the Archbishop Dr. Kevin McNamara and prayers for peace were offered at all the Masses on Sunday.

### PIPE OF PEACE

Without doubt the most colourful pilgrim to Assisi was Chief John Pretty On Top, a member of the Crow Tribe from Montana. As the Pope and the Archbishop of Canterbury bowed their heads respectfully, the Chief, who wore a bonnet of eagle feathers, buckskins and moccasins, passed the pipe of peace to his nephew and a group of friends from another church. Buckskins were perhaps more appropriate than the colourful robes worn by many of the representatives of 1,000 million people worldwide as a chill wind lashed Assisi during the day-long ceremony.

### Focus Point Needs Help

The founder of Focus Point, Sister Stanislaus, has made a plea for more money to fund her projects. Focus Point helps to house the homeless victims of family violence and other difficulties which have forced them onto the street. She needs £100,000 to support her projects.

The Archbishop of Canterbury, Most Rev. Dr. Robert Runcie, embracing the Pope when they met in Assisi to celebrate Prayer for Peace Day, last Monday.

## PRIEST URGES SHARING OF JOBS AS SOLUTION

A warning was given out to a group of Cork people about the risk that they might become passive regarding the present situation in the employment industry. "We cannot, as a people, allow ourselves to become passive regarding the present situation in the employment industry. "We cannot, as a people, allow ourselves to become passive, helpless victims of unemployment — we cannot allow the life blood of our young people to drain into the ground" Fr. Gus Murray told the congregation at St. Mary's Church, Popes Quay, Cork.

Fr. Murray, outgoing Diocesan Youth Director gave his homily at a Mass for Industrial Peace last week. According to Fr. Murray the main source of our problem is our unusual population structure. For some years now our birth rate has been over double our death rate and the number of people coming on to the job market is also over double the numbers that are retiring. He advised us all to examine our conscience and ask ourselves if there is not someone else who is more in need of our job than ourselves.

Many people just keep their job in order to be occupied and not for the sake of money. "Surely creative and imaginative alternatives could be discovered to provide for these

people and somebody who needs a paying job could take their place," he said. He felt that a realistic concept of this would be the idea of job sharing — where two people can share the same job.

Fr. Murray urged us to make the most of the jobs that we have, and pointed out the continuing urgent need to create new jobs. He told them "I marvel at the courage of those individuals and groups who are starting or developing projects, in spite of the gloom which the recession brings.

IRISH CATHOLIC
55 Lower Gardiner St., Dublin 1. Phone: 747538

CHURCH FORCED TO DRAW THE LINE — PAGE 8

*Irish Catholic* coverage of Assisi, 1986

● March for peace: people on their way to the City Hall to mark World Day of Peace pass through the Docks area yesterday.
Picture by Brendan Murphy

Peace rally in Belfast

*The 27th October, the great Peace Day in Assisi was unforgettable. On the previous evening the Friars had an ecumenical service in St Joseph's, and on the actual day they, with some hundreds of people, all carrying white flowers as a sign that they pledged themselves to work for peace, marched to the City Hall. They left their flowers there, and prayed in silence for peace.*

This inter faith initiative which came from an invitation by Pope John Paul II was called World Day of Prayer for Peace. In 1987, there were further efforts to make peace:

*In October a Peace Group from Assisi visited Belfast – a Franciscan Sister and four other people. They were received at the City Hall by the Lord Mayor, to whom they presented an olive branch, symbol of peace. Fr. Diarmuid O.F.M. brought them to see us. Because the Sister could speak English, it was possible for us to have an interesting conversation.*

Throughout the Troubles the nuns met many people affected by the opposite of peace and the Poor Clares always offered those who were touched by the violence their support. The nuns were impressed by a woman called Christine McKay, who was in the Holy Land on the same day as the Assisi event in 1986:

*On that same day, a Belfast lady, Christine McKay, at Father Liam's request, placed a white flower on Mount Tabor, in the Holy Land.*

*Christine had been happily married about eleven years ago, but before her first baby was born, her young husband, Noel, was shot dead before her eyes, outside her home one evening, as both of them returned from church, where they had received the Sacrament of Reconciliation. Noel was completely innocent of all political involvement. It was a case of mistaken identity. After his tragic death, Christine went through a very trying time, … Then God's healing came to her and changed everything..*

The murder of Noel McKay is recorded in this way in *Lost Lives* (p.764):

July 26, 1978. Noel McKay, West Belfast

The post office engineer was shot, apparently by republicans, just after he had parked his van outside his house at Ardmore Drive, Finaghy Road North. Two gunmen, one armed with a shotgun and the other with a pistol, fired around ten shots at close range. …The victim's wife was pregnant at the time.

In the midst of all the painful stories the nuns were hearing throughout the 1980s, they were able to keep a sense of humour, as this 1987 entry describes:

*Occasionally a large bonfire is lit to consume what we don't want to keep – call it rubbish if you like. The smoke of the fires usually attracts the army helicopters, to the scene. We must present an amusing sight, stoking the fires and piling on the combustibles!*

# Man gunned down in mystery murder

A 29-YEAR-OLD Post Office engineer was gunned to death outside his home at Ardmore Drive, Finaghy, Belfast, last night. Mr. Noel McKay had parked his van and was on the way inside when two gunmen, one armed with a shotgun and the other with a pistol, fired ten shots at close range.

Police said afterwards that Mr. McKay had no connection with the Security Forces and was not connected with any paramilitary organisation.

Mr. McKay was married and his wife is expecting their first baby. The gunmen escaped in a car which they abandoned at Ladybrook Grove where they hijacked a blue mini-car. This was later found abandoned at Hillhead Crescent, off the Stewartstown Road.

"The motive for the murder is a complete mystery," an RUC spokesman said. "The van used by the gunmen had been hijacked at the railway bridge at Finaghy Road North. It was a well-planned murder in that a van and a car—both hijacked—were used in the killing."

Eye-witnesses said the murdered man's wife heard the shooting outside and threw herself across her husband's body. But he was already dead.

The RUC spokesman said: "It was a particularly brutal murder. The man was gunned down as he arrived home for his tea. His wife is eight months' pregnant and expecting their first child."

Mr. McKay had worked for the Post Office since he was a teenager.

**IRELAND TOP**

Murder of Noel McKay, article *Irish News* 27 July 1978

The uncertainties of the Troubles surrounded the monastery and no doubt had an impact on the community:

> *The Federal Assembly took place in Galway in August, and Mother Paschal and Sr Mary attended it. In their absence, a workman was shot dead in a house opposite our monastery shortly before noon one day – one of the many murders that have taken place on building sites. While all the murders and tragedies continue here, we praise and thank God for having protected us so lovingly all along.*

The 1989 *Tel-A-Vision* recorded the workman's murder in this way:

> *We cannot say we were surprised during our stay in Galway to learn that a man had been shot in a house opposite our monastery, because nothing, in the way of violence or barbarity coming from this part of the country, surprises people any more. However, this was the nearest of such tragedies to our house.*
>
> *The scene of this particular murder was a house undergoing renovations. There were three brothers employed there, one being a quantity surveyor, and he was the victim; God rest him. A man with a gun just walked into the house at about 11.30am and shot him point blank. Our sisters had assembled in choir for Sext etc. They heard the shots and wondered if there was trouble in the extern chapel. …it was only later they learned what had really happened. It gives a sickening sensation when you hear of someone having been murdered, to be able to recall that you heard the actual shots that struck him down. We have experienced it on a few occasions.*

*Lost Lives* (1999) indicates that more than 160 people connected to the building trade were killed during the Troubles. The vast majority of those, around 130, were civilians. While many of the deaths had nothing to do with their occupation – many of them random victims – a significant number were killed as they went about their work on sites.

# Concern for suffering

In the 1990s trouble was still never too far away from North Belfast and again tragedy struck three more families in the local area:

> *Three men from our parish were brutally killed in a bookie's shop in this locality early this year.*

The men were Francis Burns from Manor Street, Peter Orderly from Glenview Street and John Lovett from Rosapenna Street – all within Sacred Heart Parish. This happened on 14 November 1992 in James Murray's bookmakers on the Oldpark Road, which was less than half a mile from the monastery.

> *As a mark of solidarity with their families in their grief, we had a Mass offered for them in our chapel, the celebrant being Father Liam. All the families and some friends attended, and were greatly consoled by Father Liam's comforting and strengthening words to them. They were deeply touched by our concern for them.*

Finding hope in suffering, line drawing from *Tel-A-Vision*

## Lifestyle

### Who said Irish is dead?

An island somewhere off the Kerry coast hosts a celebration of the social, musical and linguistic aspects of culture. Gerry McLaughlin returns to tell all. P7

### On the line

Did Stormont blame Dublin for the talks deadlock or did it not? There is something fishy going on P6

### Headlines

- Anglo-Irish conference resumes P2
- WP criticises Dublin talks stance P3
- Lamont warns of more job losses P12
- Joyriders crash into home P12
- Important win for Tyrone P18

---

## In brief

### Bosnians escape in city ceasefire

ABOUT 1,500 people crammed into buses to escape the Bosnian capital of Sarajevo yesterday while a ceasefire continued to cool guns that have pounded the city for months.

Seth women and children fade a tearful farewell to husbands and fathers and were evacuated to the suburb of Lukavica.

Later 900 Croats, former residents of the battered western suburb Stup, climbed into the same buses and headed west toward Kiseljak, 15 miles away.

### Police seek man over assault claim

POLICE at Omagh are hunting a man believed to have indecently assaulted a 12-year-old girl at Royal Arms Mews at about 4.15pm yesterday.

He is 18 to 20, tall and thin with short light brown hair. He was wearing light blue jeans, carried a dark coloured haversack over one shoulder, and had a creamy brown scarf tied around his face.

Anyone with was in the area or who may have any information is asked to contact police at Omagh 246177.

### IRA admits gun attack killing

THE IRA in Fermanagh last night admitted responsibility for a gun attack at Belroo in which 25-years-old RUC man Alan Corbett from Banbridge was killed.

Meanwhile, the IRA in south Armagh admitted carrying out a gun attack on an army patrol near Forkhill. No one was injured.
● New weapon — Page 5

### Lennon killer 'disgusted'

THE man who killed John Lennon says he often finds autograph requests stuffed in his mailbag and is disgusted that some people even want to set up fan clubs to honour him.

Mark David Chapman describes himself as a "walking void" at the time of the killing and says he regards the present hero worship as pathetic.

### Tories attacked over Iraq arms

Labour's Robin Cook has said he will produce "damning evidence" today on the role of British ministers in the arms-for-Iraq affair.

Mr Cook has alleged John Major was "fully aware" during his period as foreign minister that Britain was supplying arms to Iraq.

---

### Lotto

There was no overall winner of the weekend Lotto jackpot of almost half a million pounds. Wednesday's jackpot is likely to be more than £750,000.

The numbers drawn were:
13 15 21 30 33 38
The bonus number was 10

---

### Weather

Rain will clear in the morning but showers, some heavy will persist throughout the day. Wintry showers on high ground. Winds increasing from the north west. Max 7C
Details P4

---

### Inside

Family notices............................2
News.......................3,4,5,12
Editorial..................................6
Letters.....................................6
Lifestyle............7,8,9,10
Crossword..............................5
Arts........................................11
Classified.............................13
Tat, radio...............................17
Crossword.............................17
Sport............14,15,16,18

---

## Victims' relatives tell of unbearable pain after murders

# Harvest of hate

❝ I was ashamed of my own humanity as I stood there among that carnage. I could feel the harvest of hate

*Fr Don O'Rawe*

❝ John pushed two young boys to one side. He then got down on top of two other men to protect them.

*Peggy Winter, victim's sister*

❝ Francis always warned our two sons about using that bookies. He said it was too wide open

*Mary Burns, victim's widow*

❝ No one ever thought that this could happen again. The people who did this must be devils

*Kathleen Kennedy, mother of Ormeau Road betting shop victim*

❝ I saw all the television pictures, the blood and anguish, but I hadn't heard any names.

*Robert Orderly, victim's brother*

**Full reports: P4-5; editorial: P6**

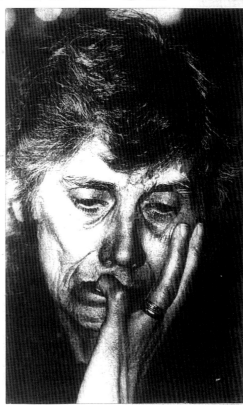

● Mary Burns... her husband died in the bookie shop gun and grenade attack          Picture: Brendan Murphy

**BELFAST VICTIMS**

● Frank Burns
Cancer victim

● Peter Orderly
lived nearby

● John Lovett
RAF veteran

**POLICE VICTIM**

● Alan Corbett
on patrol

---

## RUC declares drugs finds to mark Euro campaign

By Mary McCollum

A HUGE increase in the amount of LSD, Ecstasy and amphetamines seized by police is being highlighted today to mark the beginning of European Drug Prevention Week.

According to new figures, 9,018 doses of LSD have been recovered so far this year, against 800 last year. Police also have seized 4,668 grammes of amphetamines, compared with 625 grammes last year and 3,325 tablets of Ecstasy compared with 2,711 last year.

❝ It's only within the past year that we've become aware of the dangers

*Alan Green, RUC*

The amount of cannabis seized fell from 37.5 kilos to 14.75 kilos but 36 plants were found this year compared with 19 last year.

Only 71 grammes of cocaine were found and nine grammes of heroin. There were 477 drug-related arrests in the first 10 months of 1992.

The sharp rise in the amount of LSD, amphetamines and Ecstasy found by police proves that Northern Ireland has developed a drug culture in the last two years, according to community groups.

The Dunlewey Substance Advice Centre, which published figures earlier this year showing that more than 50 per cent of 14-17 year olds in north and west Belfast had used illicit drugs, called for a co-ordinated approach to the problem by all groups involved.

Welcoming the RUC's recognition of the problem director Jo Vernon said it was "quite remarkable" that they had traced such large quantities of these drugs which are very easily concealed since they are so small.

But she said the police must work closely with community groups to tackle the problem effectively.

Ms Vernon accused Sinn Fein and the SDLP of delaying action to stop the drug problem by trying to score political points over the issue.

"The political parties here used the drug scene to draw attention to themselves but that is negative and has hindered progress".

Detective Chief Inspector Alan Green, head of the RUC drugs squad said the increase in drugs found was due to the police being more effective in detecting these drugs than before and the upward trend reflected what was happening throughout the United Kingdom.

His primary objective was to reduce the supply and demand for drugs through investigation and education — targeting young people aged between eight and 21, their parents, teachers and youth leaders.

"There has been a significant increase in the amount of LSD, Ecstasy and amphetamines seized by the police in recent months. A major concern is it's only within the past year so that we've become aware of some of the dangers of these drugs

home-made in "unhygienic illicit laboratories" were potentially lethal. No one in Northern Ireland has died from taking Ecstasy, but 14 deaths have been recorded in the United Kingdom.

Detective Chief Inspector Green said wouldn't say there haven't been any Ecstasy-related deaths. We don't know how many have been killed in traffic accidents under its influence."

---

In the face of the yet more sickening violence of the period, there is a poignant account in the nuns' 1994 annual newsletter where it is clear they are keen to support a 'vote for peace' initiative:

*Violence has continued here with little remission. The names of Shankill, Greysteel and Loughinisland are etched on people's minds because of the atrocities they witnessed. It was the revolt of thousands to the massacre in the first two above named places, that sparked off the idea of taking a vote for peace by phone. The venture was very well organised. A day and half were allotted for the voting. All one had to do was dial a given number. A voice replied: 'Your vote has been registered. Thank you. Now hang up.' We were among the 150,000 odd who voted for peace. The people of violence might have been credited with enough sense to see that the general public in Northern Ireland were telling them loudly and clearly that they were not acting on their behalf, but they sadly, they failed to heed the message. Loughinisland and many homes are witness to that.*

As women of faith, the nuns responded to the ongoing violence with prayer, which, in 1993, they combined with an ecumenical side by uniting with their Anglican counterparts:

*The various Franciscan families and groups here, including the Anglican community, have thought up a lovely, peaceful way of combatting terrorism. On the first Saturday of every month, they meet at a particular venue, pray there together, and then go in pairs through the streets praying for peace, one on either side of the street. Only God knows what bullets, bombs and heart-break they stave off. The monthly hour of prayer for peace by Franciscans – Franciscans Together – is still well patronised. We are hosting the meeting on three occasions this year.*

Sr Paschal lighting the community paschal candle (courtesy of Brendan Murphy)

# Signs of hope

The nuns also were paying close attention to the positive political developments that were happening in the later 1990s within the North. It is possible to detect their hope in reading the 1996 annual newsletter to the nuns within the Irish federation:

> *These are historic days in Belfast – the days of the long-awaited Peace Talks. Now on the fourth day into the sessions, the participants are still squabbling over who should be chairman, not that this is surprising. With people walking out, and others being kept out, it will be a miracle if it ever gets off the ground, and a series of miracles if it progresses, and comes up with a solution to Northern Ireland's problems. A lot of people expect it to follow the pattern of all earlier attempts to form some sort of governing body here. Every time, at a certain stage, disagreement reached us a pitch, that the whole body had to be disbanded, and the situation was 'back to square one,' as we say.*

In this next entry, it is ironic that the nuns would talk about the world's media focussing on Stormont; when it came to elections, there were usually photographers jostling to get a photo of some of the Poor Clares on their way into a polling station. This would have been one of the few times they would have been spotted on the streets:

> *Of course, we are deeply interested in the talks, as their outcome will affect everyone here. Bright and early one the morning of the elections last month at 7.10, to be exact, we headed for the school, about a hundred yards up the road, to cast our votes. We pray and hope for justice and a genuine peace. The majority of people here yearn for them. The eyes of the world must be focussed on Stormont just now, judging by the number of media reporters and photographers, we are told have swooped down on it. What a picture it projects! God help us. Only He can.*

Their prayers for peace continued:

> On Friday evening, the 7th, the three branches of the Franciscan Family
> and others, had a vigil for peace in our chapel. It was very well organised by
> members of the S.F.O. All felt we needed a little extra united prayer in view
> of the Peace Talks, and for a settlement of the many differences of opinion that
> float about here.

In the 1997 edition of *Tel-A-Vision*, there is a mention to the 'monthly
Franciscan hour of prayer for peace and the healing of our nation.' The
newsletter then continues:

> Never was such prayer so urgently needed as now, when tensions and fear
> are mounting, with the marching season fast approaching. Following recent
> atrocities – callous murders, burning of churches, intimidation, the persistent
> haggling and persecution at Harryville Church, Ballymena (forty weeks of it
> to date), no one feels safe, except in trusting in God's protection. We do hope
> and pray that before the parades start, some sort of solution will be agreed
> upon, to prevent another 'Drumcree.'

Even though there were serious political efforts underway to end the
violence and to find a political solution to bring peace there were still
ongoing occurrences, such as in May 1997. It coincided with a visit from the
President of the Federation, Mother Francis:

> Something out of the ordinary would have to happen while she was here. On
> the morning of the day before she left, a call came from the local police station,
> saying there was a suspect device in one of the streets off the road, quite close
> to us, and asking could we take in some evacuees. …Remembering our big
> meeting room, (we said) 'Yes.' Sometime later the police brought a man over;
> some women had remained at 'Portiuncula.' The poor man was in his sixties,
> and he was suffering from angina. However, his biggest worry was that he
> had left a pot of potatoes on the gas ring, and couldn't remember whether or
> not he had turned off the gas! He had to endure the anxiety for a few hours
> until the all-clear was given, and he could go home, or at least go and see if
> his house was still there. … The suspect device turned out to be a hoax. All the
> precautions had to be taken anyway.

The annual newsletter also gives details of a visit by a priest called Father Schneider who called to see the nuns shortly after Christmas 1997:

*After lunch he took a walk through nearby streets, and on his return expressed shock at the signs of destruction left by the violence that he saw. He would have been trebly shocked had he seen some of the far more scarred places. It puzzled him how Christians could act so inhumanly towards one another.*

The year 1997 came to a bleak end on New Year's Eve with the murder of Edmund Treanor a short distance away from the monastery:

*Clifton Tavern is about ten doors down on the road from us. Opened a few years ago, it is, people say, the first of its kind on this road. The owners, the McGrath family ...do not live on the premises. On New Year's Eve, at bed time, our bed time, two masked Loyalists rushed in to the bar, and fired several shots indiscriminately wounding six men, one of whom died in hospital, within a few hours, R.I.P. The only member of the McGrath family there at the time, [was] Michelle, a teenager, who was serving tea in the café upstairs. We heard the shots but thought it was fireworks, as there had been some about an hour earlier. It was only next morning that we heard the harrowing story.*

It is described in *Lost Lives* (p.1420) in this way:

December 31, 1997. Edmund Treanor, North Belfast. Civilian, Catholic, 31. Single, civil servant. He was critically injured when two loyalist gunmen entered the Clifton Tavern on the Cliftonville Road and opened fire with what is believed to have been an Israeli-made Uzi submachine-gun. The shooting took place after 9pm and the victim died in the Royal Victoria Hospital minutes before the new year began. Five other people were injured in the attack on the new red-brick building close to one of the city's sectarian interfaces.

*Irish News* coverage of murder of Edmund Treanor

The 1998 annual newsletter captures the mood of optimism which the nuns clearly began to feel during that year. This newsletter charts how the nuns experienced the momentous events of that time:

> *…weather moods reflect to some extent the moods of life, political and social here in Northern Ireland, over the past several months. The peace process was much talked about and prayed for, and everyone was waiting for some positive results from the Stormont talks. After weeks and months of seemingly futile talks, a date was set for the signing of an Agreement. The date was the 9th April, Holy Thursday. The politicians then did get down to serious talking, especially during the time immediately preceding the decisive date; they worked hard and long, day and night. However, the Agreement wasn't signed till Good Friday morning, and it has since been known as the Good Friday Agreement, very appropriately, since all blessings come through the Cross. The majority of people were overjoyed, because it seemed at last that we had one foot on the road to peace.*

> *The next step was the Referendum. Hopes were high, but there were also fears, misgivings, anxieties, as the days passed. A great momentum of prayer rose up from all the Churches. As usual, Brother David Jardine, S.S.F. (Anglican Franciscan), was tireless in organising prayer sessions, with various denominations in St Anne's Church of Ireland Cathedral. As our contribution we had exposition of the Blessed Sacrament all day every day throughout May, and again in June in preparation for the Assembly elections. This gave people an opportunity of coming to the very source of life and peace in the Holy Eucharist.*

*On the polling day, we were out bright and early – perhaps a few minutes later than on other occasions – to cast our votes. As we left the polling station, one of the policemen on duty looked at his watch and said: 'You are late this morning ladies.' He must have been there last time, and seems to be blessed with a very keen memory.*

Brother David Jardine

The nun writing the annual newsletter is unable to contain her excitement at the developments:

> *The result of the Referendum is well known. It was almost unbelievable. People were dazed, hugging one another in sheer joy. There was the dissident minority of course, one of whom, referring to the Nationalists said: 'they will pay for it.'*

It was clear the nuns were in favour of a 'yes' to the signing of the Good Friday agreement:

> *As the election campaign for the Assembly got underway, hopes were kept high, and there was a great sense of peace and expectation around. People prayed especially that a very large majority of the seats would be obtained by the 'Yes' voters of the Referendum. They did get a good majority, but some disappointment was aroused by the number of 'Nos' who got in. Only time will tell how they will fare together.*

1998 was a year of highs and lows, difficult moments such Drumcree Sunday as it was known were also part of the year. In typical fashion, the nuns resort to prayer:

> *The first Assembly meeting was held on the 1st July, and then came Drumcree Sunday with its aftermath of the Orangemen's stand off, of protests, destruction and violence to equal some of the worst of the so-called 'Troubles.' The mood of the people is very low again, after the high of last month. Great tension and fear are very palpable, as we now find ourselves in a critical situation, but we know God is working in it and through it, and happy days will come again.*

Even with all the tension of that time, the nuns appreciated some lighter moments:

> *Everything connected with Portadown these times is not all evil. Today, the eve of the Twelfth, we enjoyed some delicious strawberries and cream, from the farm of a loyalist there. Of course he did not send them to us, but a good Catholic friend of ours brought them for us, an annual treat, and risked the danger of accosting loyalist road blocks, to bring them to us.*

The various editions of their annual newsletter in the 1990s describe the ebb and flow of the peace process. The 2001 edition of the inter-monastery edition, however, begins with these striking words:

> *Army helicopters coursing the sky, sometimes two or three at a time, the roaring of police cars, fire brigades, gun shots, disturbing pictures in the newspapers, and probably on TV also, of people being driven from their homes, the frightened faces of crying children as they cling to their mothers, fires and desecration of churches, and the all-too-familiar funeral corteges of innocent victims gunned down or bomb blasted, the very palpable tension and foreboding, have once again become the pattern of life, especially night life in many places in Northern Ireland, and in our city in particular. Having enjoyed a relative peace since the Assembly got under way, we wonder how people can so blindly barter its blessings for the selfish satisfaction of gaining supremacy for their own political party. They will learn some day.*

Whilst very seldom on the streets of the city of Belfast, the nuns were well aware that it would take very little to set off trouble, as acknowledged in this newsletter entry:

> *This happens to be the marching season in this part of our country, always a time of tension and anxiety. It is so easy to initiate violence; a few children can do it, and then it can escalate out of all proportion. We are hoping and praying that this year will not witness such a disaster.*

By the time the new millennium had come and gone, the community of nuns which had been in Belfast since 1924 and lived through some very difficult times, were able to take a more trusting perspective – as recorded in the 2001 edition of their newsletter:

> *Fortunately God is in control, and eventually all manner of things will be well. In the meantime we try to live our Poor Clare lives as best we can, hoping that in some way we are channels of comfort and love to the many frightened and distressed people, who come to share their burdens with us.*

# Chapter Eight

## The Dark Night

Line drawing by artist Liam Horner, brother of Sr Assumpta (courtesy of Liam Horner)

—— 66 ——

*Was God telling us that He didn't*
*want us any longer in Belfast?*

—— 99 ——

Following the nuns' move to Dunowen House on the Cliftonville Road in 1926, various repairs had been carried out to the house over the years. By the 1980s more serious issues had begun to emerge. In November 1982, for example, the community employed men to re-plaster and paint the sacristy as plaster was falling off due to dampness. Significant leakages along the roof had been discovered and at the same time some of the cork tiles in the choir floor were beginning to sink.

Investigations showed that there was dry rot underneath and that the floor would have to be taken up. The choir walls were also damp and would need stripped and cavity walls put up. What may have seemed like small enough jobs at the start were becoming more involved. The community began to realise the scale of the work that needed at the monastery:

> *Feb 7th 1983. Extensive renovations began in the choir, the walls and floor have been greatly damaged by damp due to too shallow foundations and salt in the old plaster. The repair is likely to take months. It has also been found necessary to take up the floor in the extern chapel and sacristy, due to rotted joist boards left when the little mosaic type of floor was laid about 3 years ago. 'Twas June 1980. Bishop Daly also engaged a Sculptor and Artist Mr Ray Carroll to design a new altar, so that there will no longer be the glass separation.*

It is clear at that point that the community had no idea of what was going to emerge. The work took much longer than was expected and was eventually completely in 1984, coinciding with the Diamond Jubilee of the foundation of the original community in Belfast on 29 May 1924. Following the usual format, the nuns chose an important feast day, the Immaculate Conception of the Blessed Virgin Mary (8 December) to celebrate the occasion:

> *Our new sanctuary was dedicated at last. It has been almost two years but we all say a sincere 'Thank God!' It is so beautiful, worth waiting for. Our stalls are also new.*

The bishop of the diocese, Bishop Cahal Daly (1984) preached at the celebration Mass, during which the altar was dedicated. He spoke about the vocation of the Poor Clares and the rationale behind their contemplative life:

The Poor Clares have withdrawn from the world, not to turn their backs on it, but to turn their face to the Lord of the world and therefore to influence the world more powerfully than anyone ever did by words or deeds.

He then went on to expound on what he saw as the contemplative nature of the Poor Clares:

Since the Eucharist is the beating heart of the Church, the very heart of Christ, which draws life from the eternal source of life in the Blessed Trinity to be the life of the world, the Poor Clare Sister, in her Eucharistic contemplation, is at the heart of the Church, the 'still point' where eternity meets time and history is lifted up to God. (p.273)

The joy of the celebration however did not last long because within a short time of the completion of the refurbishment work, problems began to occur again. There was a growing recognition that all was not well and this became a source of concern for the community. When they faced difficulties, as the journal entry indicates, the nuns always dealt with it by turning to prayer:

*April 18th 1986. First mention of building – much prayer needed.*

Then came a growing concern about the future of the community in the context of declining numbers in the community:

*July 26-29th 1986. Our new Religious Assistant Fr Seán Collins made his first visitation. Father was to have a meeting with Bishop Daly concerning the future of our community – we are only seven and Sr Veronica on loan from Bothwell.*

The community faced some difficult questions: the nuns lived by a vow of poverty; they had spent money on repairs and now they faced more expenditure. In addition, they were finding it difficult to attract new members to the Poor Clare life:

*We have all been through the 'Dark Night.' ... That was during the second half of last year and the early weeks of this year, and it all happened unexpectedly.*

*Experts left us in no doubt about the deteriorated state of our house and
different options were forced upon us. Should we have it repaired, at the
colossal cost that would entail, and knowing it would still be an unfinished
job? Should we demolish it and rebuild? The shortage of vocations seemed to
indicate otherwise. Was God telling us that He didn't want us any longer in
Belfast?*

The public area of the old chapel before demolition. The centre doors opened for public exposition of the Blessed
Sacrament. The small square on the left is the tabernacle. HOYFM.L3956.1 © National Museum NI Collection
Ulster Folk & Transport Museum

Church before demolition. HOYFM.L3956. © National Museums NI Collection Ulster Folk & Transport Museum

The nuns' choir chapel before demolition. The quotation Ego Vos Semper Custodiam from St. Clare means 'I will always defend you.' The circle at the centre is where the Blessed Sacrament was exposed. The small square, right, is the tabernacle. HOYFM.L3956.5 © National Museums NI Collection Ulster Folk & Transport Museum

## A decision to rebuild

This was a time of deep uncertainty and crisis for the Poor Clare community as the reality of the seriousness of the work needed on the monastery became clear and as the numbers of their members continued to fall. On the human level, there was clearly anxiety; yet as women of faith, they relied on God in all things:

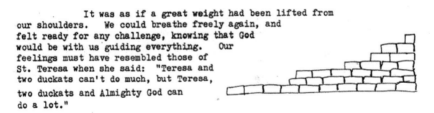

Excerpt and line drawing from *Tel-A-Vision* 1987

*These and similar questions with all their painful side-issues, confronting us at every turn, brought us to a deeper experience of our poverty than we had ever known before – our utter helplessness in a big crisis and our absolute dependence on God. We did all we could, we prayed, consulted those empowered to help us, and waited patiently, even when there seemed no reason for delays, though, of course, we know God had a reason. His light and help came to us eventually through Dr Daly, Fr. Seán Collins and Mother President of our Federation, Mother Marie-Céline. The long awaited meeting between our Bishop and Fr Seán, took place on the 31st January 1987, and that evening His Lordship came down to tell Mother the outcome. He and Fr. Seán were agreed that we should go ahead and build, if we had an assurance of help from the Federation. At Dr Daly's invitation Mother President procured that for us. God's will in our regard was manifest at last. It was as if a great weight had been lifted from our shoulders. We could breathe freely again, and felt ready for any challenge, knowing that God would be with us guiding everything. Our feelings must have resembled those of St Teresa when she said: 'Teresa and two ducats can't do much, but Teresa, two ducats and Almighty God can do a lot.' Only the first step had been taken, but it was, perhaps, the most decisive step.*

After all the prayer and consultation, the decision to rebuild had been made, and it seemed to empower the community. In the spirit of St Clare, their foundress, the nuns believed that God would assist them if they stepped out in faith and it was with confidence that they embarked on their ambitious journey:

*Things have advanced very favourably. A Committee of Friends of the Poor Clares, about thirty persons, has been set up to raise funds. They are working on several projects and meet here every few weeks. Just now we are in the process of selecting an architect, considering plans for the new building, and are even packing up … The building will not start until next spring at the earliest and we rejoice to think it will still be the Marian Year. In the meantime we have plenty to do.*

McCormick, Tracey and Mullarkey Architects based in Derry were eventually selected to do the work with Joe Tracey taking the lead on the project. But like every other human undertaking, the whole project had its hitches, as was explained in an annual newsletter:

*You must be wondering why our building project hasn't been making more progress. You would probably need to be in our place to understand the situation. Some months ago, the fund-raising committee had to be disbanded because of disagreements in the group, and because some members wanted to get much more deeply involved in the whole project, than had originally been conceived or desired. It was a matter of treading on thin ice sometimes, and one needed great tact in dealing with these people. …*

But the nuns' continual trust in Providence gave the them the belief that that things would work out:

*As things dragged on, some of our best friends were becoming disheartened, but, thank God, within the last few weeks, things have taken a dramatic change for the better. Almost 'out of the blue,' a new committee chairman turned up, and he has set the wheels in motion in the right direction. He is manager of the largest Woolworths store in the city, an exemplary Catholic, who wants prayer to have priority in all the committee meetings. Actually he doesn't favour the term 'committee' at all, he wants it to be called just 'Friends of the Poor Clares.' He has a very comprehensive plan of collections and functions for the coming months till Christmas. He is making quite challenging demands on the ever expanding group of helpers, but he himself is leading the way. His wife and family have also caught his enthusiasm, and are working tirelessly for us. This has all meant more work for us; writing letters, duplicating, typing etc., but it is our concern, so we must keep in step with those who are making such sacrifices for us.*

There were moments when the nuns must have wondered if progress was being made, and then it all seems to come together and begin to move:

> *The plans for the house are nearing completion, so if the fund-raising makes the progress now envisaged, the actual building will probably start early next year D.V. Please keep us in your good prayers.*

It is at around this point in the nuns' story in Belfast that their second journal starts to record the main events in the life of the community. It was kept by Sr Assumpta, who later began to record her own thoughts as well as the most important events related to the monastery. At the start of *Journal Two*, Sr Assumpta writes on 30 May 1989:

> *Almost 65 years later, 1989 would see the start of our New Beginning. We had known for sometime that 120 was to be rebuilt but the first signs of the activity began to show on March 2nd '89 when a group of men arrived with huge machinery to test the foundations. On March 6th the great dispersion began, Sr Assumpta (self) went to Nazareth House, Ormeau Rd. Apart from the difficulty of travelling I had also hoped, prayed and requested permission to stay in Belfast, near home.*

The 1989 edition of the *Tel-A-Vision* newsletter provides further details of the progress of the work:

> *As you can imagine, this past year has been a unique and historic one for us, a tiring and demanding one too, but full of the experience of God's love and the goodness of so many people. ... When the date for commencing the demolition of the monastery had finally been decided on for the 17th April, we had to get our spurs on. ... Everything had to be taken out of every room, and when what we didn't want to keep had been disposed of, the rest had to be stored in a limited space – in part of the choir that had been curtained off and in the passage between the enclosure gates.*

Inevitably the process of moving out of the monastery which had been home to some of the nuns for several decades must have been stressful. There was also the fact that as a community they had to separate, which would have brought its own pain:

*Our own little group had to split up, as the gate lodge can accommodate only three. Sr Assumpta was taken by ambulance to Nazareth House on the 6th March (1989). On the 12th, Sr Petronilla left for the Poor Clare monastery in Drumshanbo, and on the 20th, Sr Helena and Sr Patrice left for Dublin. There were just three of us left – Mother Paschal, Sr John and Sr Mary, and when we had waved the last goodbye and closed the door behind us, we felt a real pang of loneliness. It was as if something of our lives was being torn away from us, was dying, and we were unsure of what the future held for us. However, there was so much to be done those days, that there was no time for nursing our emotions.*

It was also a physically and emotionally draining time for those left behind in Belfast:

*We began sleeping in the lodge at night on Spy Wednesday, in order to accustom ourselves to the new way of things, but we spent the days in the monastery. Our last day there was the 16th April, and it really was a full day. It was almost 2 a.m. when we had the last of our luggage over to the lodge, and we just fell into bed exhausted.*

The early community had moved into 'Dunowen House' as it was known then, in June 1926; after all the years there, the time had come to knock it down. This began on 17 April 1989:

*Bright and early next morning the demolishers were on the scene, with a ten ton caterpillar. After that day's work they spent a fortnight taking off the slates, and salvaging all that was of value in the house. The greater part of the house came down on the 1st May. Almost the last part of the house to come down was the hall door. It was standing there by itself for some hours. In a sense it was sad seeing it all crumble down, but it just had to go. It was the Lord's will and His designs are always full of mystery and wonder.*

Sr Paschal lending a helping hand with the building work (photo courtesy of Brendan Murphy)

Sr Assumpta recorded it in this way:

> *200 lorry loads of 25 tons each. Our house reduced to rubble – 5000 tons. An 8ft barricade of wood and corrugated iron was erected around the bare site. Nothing remained but a thick layer of dust, it was silent as never before – 'twas lying as if in waiting, for the time of God's visitation. When the new building would begin was to be His secret, not as soon as we thought or hoped.*

Following their usual pattern, the nuns commended the whole project to God in prayer and by giving thanks for all the blessings the Poor Clare community had experienced since Thursday 29 May 1924 when the first nuns arrived in Belfast:

> *Days, weeks and months stole by. On July 30th Bishop Daly celebrated a Mass of Thanksgiving, …we had many reasons of our own to give thanks to God. There were the blessings on the community since we came to Belfast and there was the generosity He had inspired in our wonderful people.*
>
> *As a great act of thanksgiving to God for the singular way in which He is blessing our fundraising efforts, and also as a 'thank you' gift for our fundraisers and other helpers, Mass was celebrated by Dr Daly, with ten priest concelebrants, on the site of the old monastery, on the 30th July. It was a wonderful occasion, with about five hundred people taking part.*

Sr Paschal (left) and Sr Patricia (right) from St Damian's, Donnybrook with Barry McGuigan's boxing gloves and Sr Mary (centre) as referee. Image courtesy of Brendan Murphy

# Support from far and wide

It was only possible for the nuns to demolish and rebuild because of the support they received from people both near and far. The fundraising committee had begun the task of raising money to pay for the work. Several journal entries record the generosity of people up and down the country.

> *The first parish collection was taken up on the first Sunday of August and they are practically finished now. They were all very well organised. The committee members wore white sashes, on which was written 'Friends of the Poor Clares' and one of them usually spoke in the pulpit on our behalf at every Mass. They got a wonderful reception everywhere and the collections were always at least twice as big as the usual Sunday collections. They said they seemed to bring a new spirit to each parish, and they had many lovely and touching stories to tell us, such as that of the old lady who gave one of them a 1941 half crown, saying it was part of her wedding day silver; it was all she had and it was worth much more to her than a half crown.*

Sr Assumpta writes about the many blessings the community had received over the years since they came to Belfast, and then continues:

> *There was the generosity He had inspired in our wonderful people. They were ingenious at thinking of ways to raise funds.*

She describes in some detail the sponsored walk undertaken by 'our good friends' Michael Mullan and Leo McCarthy to raise money for the building project. The progress was noted with these details:

> *Our fundraising is progressing very favourably. Parish collections are now being taken up in the Northern part of Armagh Diocese, with the permission of our late Cardinal, Tomás O'Fiaich. Our committee members and others are organising various functions to raise funds – 'Night of the Races'* [the recording nun described it as a Night of the Races rather than a Night at the Races, indicating she probably had no idea what such an event entailed but was relying on what members of the committee had told her about it], *a treasure hunt, coffee mornings, sponsored walks, a fashion show, concerts, golden oldies, Irish ballet dancing, by Patricia Mulholland's*

*school of dancing etc. A group of young men from Ballymurphy went on a sponsored cycle to Mount Melleray. Michael Mullan and Leo McCarthy did a sponsored walk to Rome. Children too ran their little functions. The people of Belfast and much further afield, continue their great generosity. Contributions have come to us from all over the country, especially from Cork and Kerry. People are eager to have their names enrolled in our special remembrance book, knowing they will always share the prayers of our community. Our Poor Clare communities in our Federation, have generously supported us also, very particularly the Dublin and Cork sisters. The Dublin community recently got a very large bequest, and were able to send us over £50,000. Cork community donated over £20,000. We ourselves were the recipients of some sizeable bequests, one being £57,000.*

The nuns were clearly very moved by the kindness of people:

*When our present committee started the fundraising last year we ourselves had about £150,000 collected, and now two thirds of the target have been reached – 'a marvel in our eyes.' People are so good – running all sorts of functions for us, and indeed giving private donations. It makes us feel very little. It's really for God they are doing it and how good to know He will amply reward them.*

In many ways, the whole project was a living example of the nuns living by trust in God by depending upon the goodness of their benefactors. This was clearly in the spirit of St Clare.

*Our brick campaign - £1 a brick is running successfully in the North just now. One of our Patrons, Jim Fitzpatrick, is owner of the Irish News, and he has been giving it great publicity in his paper free of charge. He also says the brick appeal will soon appear in the Republic. We've had donations from people from all over the country, especially in Cork and Kerry.*

The project of demolition and building was not without its worries. It took place whilst the Troubles continued in Belfast and was a source of concern for the nuns, fearful that some of the builders would be killed or injured as they worked on the building of the new monastery:

*Our ardent wish now is to see the building started. Please pray for that intention and also for the safety of the workmen. Building sites are notorious for murders.*

Again, prayer marked another important moment for the nuns:

> After long, long waiting, our new building to underway just after Easter. In a simple ceremony of prayers and Scripture readings, Bishop Daly, had blessed the site and dug the first sod on the 19th March, because we had set our hearts on making some sort of commencement on St Joseph's Day.

In the Divine Office, which the nuns prayed on a daily basis, they regularly prayed these words:

> If the Lord does not build the house, in vain do its builders labour; if the Lord does not watch over the city, in vain does the watchman keep vigil. (Psalm 126 (127):1)

The nuns recorded further key moments in the building project:

> The building contract was signed on the 10th April, (1990) the contractors being Kylen Construction and Development from Toomebridge. The foreman, Tommy Maguire from Magherafelt started his work early in Easter week. On the 25th April, the first foundations were dug, and concrete was poured in on the following day. Early in May the diggers came on a 40 foot well, which would have been in our outer yard, but all unknown to us, as there was a cement surface covering the whole yard.

Sr Assumpta's account in *Journal Two* gives more information on the progress:

> April 18th, 19th and 21st. The site was pegged out and as the monastery would be further back a few very tall inclining trees were cut down. Those on the larger lawn we called 'Erskines.'

She continues somewhat poetically:

> If trees could talk or hear or even see, gone forever are the stories they could have told and gone too are the days of raking dry, rustling leaves in biting cold. Gone is a field of snowdrops and crocuses in winter and in summer daisies likes snow. Gone the long walk filled with birds' song, the hum of traffic outside and the drowning sound – of silence.

In thinking about what it must have been like for the nuns during this time, the knocking down of the old monastery, which had become home for years for many of them, Sr Assumpta gives some insight into the pain of letting go but again relying on her faith to assist her come to terms with the loss; God, she believed, was present every step of the way:

*Much would be lost and God was holding in His Providence how it would be replaced.*

*April 25th – Things begin to move faster as the first of the foundations are dug and within a few days the first layer of concrete was laid, the first bricks laid. We had, as it were, our new house in embryo. God was on our side in blessing us with His best beautiful dry weather.*

*June 24th Liam (Sr A's brother) brought me another glimpse, on his video of how the work is progressing. How good to see the walls rising and to see the new little trees which will replace the old. 'Behold I make all things new.'*

When they were writing to the other nuns in the Irish federation, the small group of nuns who remained in Belfast gave some idea of what it was like to live in the gate lodge and how the building work was progressing:

*We were like fish out of water at the gate Lodge at first, but we gradually grew accustomed to the new situation, while always eagerly looking forward to the day we would be back in our enclosure. Dr Daly refers to us as 'living in tents,' on our way to our 'promised land.' We do not go outside any more than we ever did, except to make a retreat in other monasteries.* [some of the nuns went to Bothwell, Glasgow and to St Damian's, in Dublin] *We go to the chapel morning and late afternoon for Mass, the Divine Office, mental prayer etc. We do miss a lot not having our Eucharistic Lord under our roof here, but the chapel is only a matter of feet from us.*

The last entry in *Journal One* was another milestone and more prayer:

*A very important and happy day for us was the 27th September, when Dr Daly blessed and laid the foundation stone of our new monastery. By then the walls were already some feet high, but a niche had been prepared for the stone near the entrance.*

*The inscription for the stone had been beautifully carved by Mother Paschal's brother, Eoin, who specialises in stone work. Since then, the work has steadily progressed, under the capable hands of hard-working, conscientious builders.*

In *Journal Two* Sr Assumpta describes the day in this way:

*Sept 27th 'This is the day which the Lord has made.' Indeed and in truth it was a great and happy day, made more for me by the privilege of being present at the laying of the foundation stone. It was a short but very beautiful little ceremony or service, with readings, prayers and a short address by that great and holy man Bishop Cahal B. Daly. His Lordship spoke of our 'Lent before Easter' and our coming into the Promised Land. ... That very fine gentleman, Mr Tracey, the architect, gave me a guided tour. The rooms seem small but suitable to Poor Clare, Franciscan life. Lovely long, broad cloisters, places of special silence on 'per annum' days, yet holding the promise of times of fun and laughter. On those days when God and our Holy Mother Clare permit expression to 'other forms' of Enclosed Poor Clare Life. ... 'the promised land was in view.'*

As the work progresses, so also does the sense of excitement which the nuns felt as the day of coming together again as a community approached:

*Nov 1st Time has again being flowing swiftly. Mother and Sr Mary went upstairs and walked around – even danced – under the moon and – an overflying helicopter!*

In the uncertainty of life, with all its obstacles and its disappointments, the nuns continued to rely on faith:

*1991 A new year begins, one of hope and of expectancy. Hopefully it would bring New Beginnings of Poor Clare life in Belfast, God's beautiful Providence would unfold.*

Sr Assumpta charts the progress of the work:

*Jan 15th 1991 Snow and heavy sleet delayed work on the roof, but now things go forward again.*

*While one group of men work at the slates, another firm begin to put in window frames with safety locks and double glazing.*

*Jan 26th Mother came with 'tidings of comfort and joy.' The roof is almost complete, the slaters continue with a slow but beautiful job.*

The work, as in most things in life, did not proceed without its difficulties. The entry on 7 March 1991 records a setback:

*Over the previous two weeks the builders were robbed twice. The locks of their store house were cut and a lot of costly materials and equipment stolen. The phone was even taken from its little locked box.*

On 30 March as well as giving a positive update on progress, Sr Assumpta went on to reflect on the new and the old. She had placed two photographs in the journal, one of the last photographs taken of the old Dunowen House and community chapel as well as a photograph of the model of the new monastery. She then wrote:

*The beauty is in the eye of the Beholder, the Old had mighty power to draw those God chose, but now God speaks – Behold I make all things new.*

Whilst there is a sense of anticipation in the annual newsletter and in Sr Assumpta's writing, there is also some concern about whether the community would be able to attract new members. On 17 May 1991, Sr Assumpta wrote:

*Mother's feast day is a very joyful occasion in Poor Clare communities and no doubt it is so this year in Belfast for Mother Paschal as before and yet – there is a touch of sadness, a very big concern. A few months have gone by since the Federal Council asked for personnel and still there's no response. Have we drawn a blank card? Can it be that we hoped too hard, too high? And yet, God has blessed and is blessing the work. It goes ahead with gusto. … the house is in readiness, waiting for the Moment of grace, for God's visitation.*

The sense of excitement is palpable in Sr Assumpta's reflections:

*June 13th Meantime work continues on the inner fittings, the firm are moving to prepare a beautiful monastery. We trust that God is preparing a beautiful community. Our hearts long for confirmation but God says 'not yet.' All has been in faith, He will not let us down.*

*July 10th A lot of progress has been made since my visit a few weeks ago. The heating is on, the skirting is in place a lot woodwork done. ... There is a great 'army' of workers 'marching' towards August 25th and 26th.*

That sense of excitement also comes through in the annual newsletter:

*After all our waiting for our new Monastery, we can scarcely realise now that it is nearly complete. Our absent Sisters are patiently awaiting the day of our re-union, probably at the end of August. We are planning open days on the 24th and 25th, so that everyone can get a last peep before we close the doors behind us.*

The newly built monastery (photo courtesy of Tracey Architects, Derry)

# Monastery complete

Finally, the work has been completed and in August 1991, it was time to open up the monastery to the wider community.

*The 24th (August) was set aside for our patrons and for the Priests of our diocese and the Northern parishes of Armagh Archdiocese, who had given our fund raising committee permission to collect at their churches. Not very many Priests turned up, probably because it was a Saturday, and also the day on which the remains of Dr Philbin, our late Bishop, RIP, were brought back to Belfast. The following day, however, presented a very different scene. The doors were open from 1pm to 5pm, and throughout that time, a queue, four deep, stretched from the house, through the gate and down the road for about 50 yards.*

There were humorous moments:

*Mother and Sr Mary welcomed everyone at the door, and you can easily accept that by 5pm they are were getting hoarse from repeating: 'You are very welcome.' Now and again one of the helpers would make his way through the crowd with a beaker of water, so that they could lubricate their throats. A lady passing in, seeing a beaker in Mother's hand must have concluded that it was being held out for donations, and dropped two £1 coins into the water!*

After all the work and the worry, the building was complete:

*August 25th The Cliftonville Road holds a great stream of friends and well-wishers flowing towards '120!' Mother Paschal, Sr Mary and Denis Moloney stood at the front door for several hours welcoming each one. ... The day was crowned when towards evening we were honoured and O so happy at the arrival of that dear and holy friend – Cardinal Daly. His friendship and support have been great during the building process. And now the climax when he signs the book [visitors' book], we say Amen to his words – 'This is the day which The Lord has made.'*

Right from the first moment when the first group of nuns got off the train from Dublin in 1924 to begin their new lives and were greeted by the factory girls, the Poor Clares depended upon the support and generosity of others. This was certainly the case for the most ambitious project of their time in Belfast. The nuns wanted to remember those who had helped them:

> When we began to ask alms, we told our benefactors that their names would be recorded in the sisters' hearts but also in a special book.

The monastery was now complete and the nuns could move in. Then it was time to rebuild the chapel and the gate lodge:

> The second phase of our building project got underway when the workmen returned to prepare for the demolition of the choir, chapel and gate lodge. Anything of value in the buildings was removed before the real demolishers arrived with their machinery on the 22nd November. There seemed to be a note of sadness in the last peal of our bell before it was taken down on the 19th and stored away, until it would find a niche in the new chapel.

Sr Assumpta recorded it in this way:

> Nov 22nd 1991: The little Gate Lodge was demolished in twenty minutes, revealing how fragile and deteriorated the little house was. From my own few visits I've known it to be cold and damp. …Our little chapel was also demolished. There was a major problem with damp, ever since the big renovations a few years ago.

During the second phase of work, the community received a stone from San Damiano, where their founder St Clare had spent over 40 years as a contemplative. To be built in to the new wall of the passage between the house and the Choir, the stone had come via the Irish College in Rome and was brought to the monastery by a young couple who had been married in Rome:

> It will be close to the Choir as it was in San Damiano, and as we pass it day after day, it will remind us of our Holy Mother Clare and her sisters, whose eyes may often have rested on it; who may have touched it.

*It is a new link with them, and will be an incentive to us, to walk every more faithfully in their footsteps.*

The stone was accompanied with this text:

*This stone for centuries was part of the construction of San Damiano in Assisi, where St Clare lived with her Poor Clares from 1212 to 1253. When removed from the narrow stairway leading up from the ancient little choir where the nuns sang the Divine Office, the stone was seen to be chiselled carefully for some previous and more important use. Probably in the Twelfth Century it had been sculpted for an arch of a double window in the façade of the Church of San Damiano.*

Sr Assumpta records the completion of the new chapel in this way:

*Oct 4th 1992. This is the day which the Lord has made – has given and blessed. The day we'd longed, waited and prayed for. Were not our hearts full as we watched Mr Treacy hand the keys to Bishop Walsh and he present them to Mother Paschal who opened the doors leading into choir. That burst of clapping from the congregation also spoke for us as we entered our 'Promised Land.' Well might Deanby Choir have sung out: 'All the earth proclaim the Lord, sing your praise to God.' We were privileged and happy to have present Cardinal Cahal B. Daly who had initiated the work and had given his support these 3–4 yrs. … The large crowd heard and watched the ceremony on screens in a huge marquee erected outside our side of the Enclosure doors. Afterwards they all had refreshments. Let me not forget to say that the garden was decorated with yellow and white bunting. Everything was done to make our own people as welcome as we could make them. The chapel and monastery are their work – this was their day.*

On the Feast of St Francis of Assisi, 4 October 1992, Mass was celebrated for the 'Solemn Dedication of the Chapel of the Most Holy Trinity'. The beautiful new monastery and chapel were completed; a fitting conclusion after all the sacrifice and the hard work. The quality of the work was recognised not only by the regular visitors and neighbours of the nuns but further afield:

*You will have seen in Franciscan News that our monastery was granted one of the Healthy Building Awards this year. ...It was Mr. Tracey, our architect, who entered the building for assessment and we are delighted for his sake especially, that it merited the award.*

The text of the article in *Franciscan News* (1996) read:

Nuns of the Poor Clare Order have won a prize for their 'island of tranquillity' convent in North Belfast. The eleven sisters of the Order received a commendation in the Belfast Healthy Buildings 1996 Awards for their Cliftonville Monastery. Competition judges described the purpose-built convent as 'a simple but attractive building built around enclosed gardens and orientated to make clever use of light.' ... The Poor Clare sisters who maintain only a limited contact with the outside world were involved in the designing of the building. Judges were impressed by their healthy lifestyle which includes making their own compost and growing organic vegetables. They said: 'This island of tranquillity in a busy area close to the inner city has been designed and constructed for the particular needs of it occupants, the Poor Clare nuns and those people in need who may visit the convent.' The building was also considered to have 'minimal environmental impact' because it was built on an existing site using much of the fittings and material from the original monastery.

The completed monastery (photo courtesy of Tracey Architects, Derry)

Open Day Sept 1990. Front left-right: Denis Moloney, Sr Francis (Ennis), Sr Mary, Sr Paschal, Mother Marie-Céline (Federal President) Cork, Sr Miriam (Cork). Back: Fr Liam McCarthy, OFM, P.J. Geiger, Fr Fiacre O'Kelly, OFM

The public chapel (photo courtesy of Tracey Architects, Derry)

The nuns' chapel (photo courtesy of Tracey Architects, Derry)

# Chapter Nine

## The Long Struggle to Keep Going

New members join the community (Sr Gertrude, RIP, Sr Agnes (now in Poor Clares, Rome) Sr Marra, (now in Poor Clares Florida) Sr Helena RIP, Sr Joan RIP (Poor Clares, New York) Sr Paschal, Sr Mary, Sr. John, RIP (in wheelchair)

— 66 —

*We really need postulants urgently*

— 99 —

Within two years of the first community of Poor Clare nuns moving to Belfast, they were looking for a larger house because their numbers had increased. In the 1950s, the numbers of nuns in the community on the state electoral roll had gone up to 21. By contrast, in the last few decades of their tenure in Belfast the nuns struggled to attract new members. It was this issue of not being able to attract women to join the community that eventually put the closure of the monastery on the agenda. The concern about declining numbers went back to the 1970s. Around the time of the death of Sr Joseph in December 1978 there were signs even then that the community was getting smaller.

> *Life is also changed for us her little community of twelve – 11 solemnly Professed sisters and our little postulant…who entered on 22nd August 1978.*

By October 1979 the journals indicate that the community was having to adapt to this decline in numbers. There were rules in place for the different offices in the community such as the role and required number of 'discreet' nuns. When the numbers in a community were not sufficient as to provide for the various roles, special permission had to be sought to accommodate this.

> *Mother Michael was elected, by postulation, for a fourth term and Sister Catherine Vicaress, Sisters Mary and Paschal discreets. Because of the small number of our Solemnly Professed Sisters (10), it was decided, in consultation with Fr Cassian, Religious Assistant, to ask Rome for an indult allowing only 2 discreets with the Vicaress.*

In May 1981, the journal entry reads:

> *We are only eleven now in Community – ten Solemnly Professed and one novice and with Sisters Assisi and Thérèse ill, we really need postulants urgently. Mother (Michael) put an advertisement in 'Ireland's Own,' 'The Irish Catholic' and a few other Papers. It would be a blessing if even one of them brought some interested and suitable young women.*

Instead of the numbers increasing, the numbers continued to decrease when 'Sister Death' – as the nuns referred to death – visited the community on four occasions between October 1981 and October 1982. This is how it is described in the annual newsletter:

> *It was the 9th of October, the eve of Mother Michael's first anniversary, which meant that four of our Sisters had been called to eternity in one year. What big vacancies they left in our little community!*

It was becoming clear that the community needed help. Something had to be done and so three nuns, Sr M. Paschal, Sr Marie-Céline and Sr Mary Conception from St Clare's Monastery in Galway wrote to the Irish Federation President, Mother Francis, on 29 September 1983 asking for help for the Belfast community. They were hoping that 'one or two Sisters would be willing to go to Belfast for a period of at least two years. …The sisters in question should, obviously, be in good health, having regard to the over-all situation that prevails in Belfast and in the North of Ireland. They should be between the ages of 30 and 60.'

Their letter continued:

> *Belfast Monastery, without any question, needs the help for which it is now seeking…We would therefore ask you to give this matter your most sincere and prayerful attention, mindful of the spiritual bonds of sisterly unity which should prompt us, in circumstances such as these, to come to the assistance of one of the monasteries of our Federation which is in genuine need…*

The appeal for help was well received, as these entries from the community journal reveal:

> *Nov 6th 1983: After Mother Mary C.'s visit, it was decided to appeal to the federation for personnel for our community. We are only seven now, there being several deaths in the community during the last twelve years, or so. As Mother said, the result has been 'magnificent.' And so we welcome five wonderful new sisters, who have volunteered to come to Belfast for three years. The first to arrive is Sr M. Gertrude Purcell from Drumshanbo, accompanied by Mother Angela whom it was our great pleasure to meet.*

*Nov 21st Sr Francis and Sr Paschal came from Ennis. Sr Paschal's name is written as Marie-Paschal to avoid confusion with Mother.*

*Nov 29th Sr Dominic came from Carlow to Dublin where Sr Patrice joined her. And now we are one family, twelve of us. 'How good and pleasant it is…'*

The presence of the additional five nuns was a considerable boost to the community. It was however a short-term measure and did not resolve the issue of the slow decline of the community in numbers over the years. It was decided to make another appeal, which came from Sr Marie-Céline, St Clare's Monastery, Galway in 1985 and was supported by the bishop of the diocese, Bishop Cahal Daly. Little came of it, however.

In July 1986, during a visit from Fr Seán Collins, a Franciscan priest, whose role was to support the nuns, the issue of community sustainability was surfacing:

*July 26th–29th 1986: Our new Religious Assistant Fr Seán Collins made his first Visitation. Father was to have a meeting with Bishop Daly, concerning the future of our community – we are only seven and Sr Veronica on loan from Bothwell. It was Jan 31st '87 before the meeting took place.*

As we saw in the previous chapter, the decision to proceed with the major building project had been made in January 1987. But with the issue of the smaller size of community looming in the background there were always going to be implications for the nuns. Indeed, they were unable to meet the full requirements of the constitutions of their Order and had sought permission from Rome to allow for their changed circumstances. There were no issues in obtaining this permission:

*December 1988. Due to unforeseen circumstances pertaining to our Bishop, our elections did not take place until the 9th December. Mother Paschal was elected Abbess by postulation. Because of our small number in community, an indult had been obtained from the Holy See, for the re-election of the discreets, if they had obtained the required number of votes. They did. Sr M. John was elected Vicaress and Sr Mary the discreet.*

The nuns, relying on faith, which was the bedrock of their lives, had proceeded with the rebuilding project while having some concern about whether they would attract new vocations to the community. Towards the end of 1991 the community was still holding out hope that there would be other nuns willing to come to Belfast from within the Irish federation:

> *Nov 28th 1991: …even yet the Irish federation may come to our help before poor Mother Paschal has to appeal for personnel outside Ireland.*

As the weeks rolled on in 1992, Sr Assumpta acknowledges that no help is coming from within the federation. The new monastery was now completed and they were planning for the opening of their new chapel later in October. These were anxious times:

> *Jan 23rd 1992: The building is going well, but I begin to wonder – there is still no hope of more personnel… Were we wise to rebuild – could our faith and hope have been too great, but without grounds? 'Fall down before the presence of God now and He will raise you up at the appointed time.'*

Sr Lorette pictured behind the grille in the parlour, a well-known image of the Poor Clares (courtesy of Brendan Murphy)

# The first Filipino nuns

Despite the requests for personnel from the Irish federation, no one was forthcoming. The community had been hugely successful in generating funds to rebuild the monastery, the chapel had been dedicated on 4 October 1992, but eventually Mother Paschal had to look beyond Ireland for help. Finally, a breakthrough was found when the nuns were able to secure members from the Philippines:

> *Jan 20th 1993 …Mother also confirms that we will be receiving two Filipino sisters in a few months, when the weather gets warmer. The Sisters hope to make a permanent transfer but will begin with three years temporary stay first, in accord with the General Constitution regarding transfers from outside the federation. We walk in faith, O God direct us. The Irish federation don't feel in a position, personnel-wise, to help us so what is poor Mother to do? We have a duty to our community and to our benefactors who built this beautiful monastery for our future.*

It seemed that at last there was some hope of the community surviving in Belfast thanks to help from thousands of miles away on the other side of the world:

> *April 27th 1993 A day of grace, blessing and happiness. We are joined by two beautiful little Filipino sisters, Marra (34 yrs) and Agnes (32 yrs). How strangely and beautifully God's will unfolds for us.*

This was a very important event which the Belfast community was delighted to communicate to the other communities in the Irish federation:

> *You all probably know by now that we have two lovely Filipino Sisters here, since 27th April, Sisters Agnes and Marra. They are a great boon to our community, and we love them. …They have settled in very well here and are full of enthusiasm for their 'mission,' as they term it.*

Within a few months of their arrival, the two Filipino nuns were making their own distinct contributions to community celebrations:

*On the evening of St Anthony's feast [celebrated annually on 13 June], we had
a most enjoyable concert in our parlour, provided by some very musical friends
from Portglenone and Randalstown. There were four violinists, a flautist, a
cellist, three Irish dancers in traditional costumes, and two little girls, aged
five and seven, who sang. The elder of the two also played a keyboard. Mother
played the violin and we chimed in with some songs. Sisters Agnes and Marra
gave a rendering of their native hymns and songs.*

There was more good news for the community when agreement was reached
for two religious sisters from another order to come to live in the gate lodge
as 'care-takers.' After the dedication of the new chapel on 4 October 1992
it had been suggested that some Sisters of St Clare (who were not confined
to the enclosure as were the Poor Clares) be invited to fill the caretaker post,
which the community had advertised.

*Negotiations went on for some time and happily resulted in Sister Maria's
and Sister Jacinta's coming to take up residence in the gate lodge, henceforth
termed 'Portiuncula,' on 30th June last.*

*July 1st The sisters were welcomed officially at evening Mass, celebrated for
them. …After Mass the sisters invited Fr Diarmuid and ourselves to a house
warming party. After our repast there was much talk, singing, music and
'interpretive dancing' by our two little Filipino sisters and in true Franciscan
simplicity Fr Diarmuid also danced to our singing of 'Brother Sun.'*

The community began to grow again. They were even joined by another Poor
Clare nun from the USA, Sr Joan:

*Our last three transferred sisters, Sisters Joan, Agnes and Maria, are now
fully incorporated into our community, having met the requirements of Art.
91 of our Federal Statutes, concerning transfers. We are very grateful for that.*

For all the world then, by 1997 it looked at last as if the community had
turned a corner after the years of concern that they would not be able to
survive.

# Under pressure

Unfortunately, by 2001, however, it is clear the members in community are declining again and putting the small number who were left under pressure:

*Early August saw Sr Joan bound for New York to see her elderly brothers and sister who could not visit her. While there she felt drawn to rejoin her community of origin, and remain close to her own people. Needless to say, we miss her good community spirit and willing hands, but we pray and hope that she may always have contentment and joy in her chosen location. Our community was then reduced to seven, and not all of these were on the work list, so we realised that we needed help from outside, in order to be able to keep up our prayer life. On three days a week, two ladies come in, one to cook our dinner and the other to do necessary cleaning, hoovering, dusting, polishing, etc. They are both mature and conscientious ladies, who cause no disturbance whatever.*

More change was soon to come, as the 2002 newsletter related:

*November also brought us the surprising and sad news of the recall of the Sisters of Clare, Srs. Jacinta and Mairéad, from their Belfast ministry. Sr Jacinta left on Christmas Day, and Sr Mairead remained until we got replacements. The Franciscan Missionaries of the Divine Motherhood eagerly accepted our invitation to continue the role of caretakers in 'Portiuncula' and were warmly welcome to our diocese by Bishop Walsh.*

As the numbers shrank there was a greater awareness of when a community member was away, as was the case when Sr Marra went back to the Philippines for a three-month holiday in 2003, although she returned in January 2004.

*The absence of even one Sister from a small community like ours, makes a big difference, as many of you will easily understand. There's an empty space in many places, choir, refectory, recreation room etc. and all that implies. A familiar voice is not heard.*

*Willing hands are not available, a sharing of experiences, an input into discussions, a sisterly caring, and much more that is part of community life, is missing. It could almost be likened to someone's having gone on the 'long vacation,' as it is sometimes called, except that it is not so final, and the Sister will return.*

With the decline in 'willing hands' re-emerging, this time the nuns looked for help to Fr Gerry Raftery from the Franciscan Order to assist them in their decision-making:

*A meeting of the Poor Clare Community, Belfast took place in the Monastery on June 24th 2003, the Solemnity of the Birth of Saint John the Baptist. The purpose of the meeting was to make a decision about the future of the Poor Clare presence in Belfast. In attendance were Sisters Mary, Paschal, Gertrude, Helena and Marra. The meeting was facilitated by Fr Gerry Raftery, O.F.M.*

In this meeting, those present considered the history of the community in Belfast and broke it into different key stages. They considered how in the early 1990s there were attempts to re-found and begin again in Belfast. The monastery, after an extensive fundraising campaign, had been rebuilt. Yet the community was now facing its third 'crisis' – the word used at the meeting – and the factors were described as follows:

*…The federation was unable to supply sisters, the community grew older and more feeble and there were a number of deaths.*

For survival and a new vibrancy the following would be needed: A minimum of eight sisters who are well integrated contemplatives and reasonably healthy. Sisters who live the life of prayer and contemplation in a simple setting, giving witness to the goodness and compassion of God to all who come. The community needs an Abbess, a Vicar, Discreet(s), Portress, Sacristan, Cook, Infirmarian, Gardener and other house workers. All of these be involved primarily in the life of prayer and contemplation.

The meeting went on to consider 'interested parties' namely people who would be directly affected by the nuns' presence or more to the point their 'non-presence.' One such group was described as the 'People of Belfast and Northern Ireland.' The meeting then considered a number of options including:

- Re-founding and renewing the Poor Clare presence in Belfast which would require 'Vision, Vibrancy and Vocations.'
- Moving to a smaller house.
- Giving the monastery to other Poor Clares.
- Survival i.e. maintain presence which would require at least four healthy and well integrated sisters.
- Keeping going until the last two remain.
- Dissolution and dispersal, this would involve the closure of the Belfast Poor Clare monastery and the sisters being transferred elsewhere.

Further discussion alluded to the fact that the nuns were feeling the expectation of benefactors and that the large number of callers to the Monastery was putting pressure on the core life of the community, fidelity to prayer and contemplation. The nuns felt that they should provide the same service that was given by a much bigger and younger community in the past. The danger of reaching 'breaking point' was recognised. To avoid breaking point the following three options were then considered:

- Closure of monastery and dispersal of sisters.
- Cutting back on work and contact with people from outside the monastery.
- Bringing in healthy transfers.

After a period of prayer, a vote was taken among the five community members. There was no consensus, so after further discussion a proposal was put to the Conventual chapter to 'transfer the present community to other suitable Poor Clare Monasteries.'

# An appeal for help abroad

As the struggle to keep the Poor Clare monastery in Belfast continued, the next correspondence in the Poor Clare files details a meeting in November 2003 when the community met with the Sr Bernadette Coughlan, President of the Poor Clare Colettine Federation in Ireland and Great Britain, and Sr Francis Collins, Federal Secretary. The following was unanimously agreed upon:

> Sister Bernadette will write to the Delegate General for the Poor Clares to explain the entire situation requesting his assistance and direction so as to ensure continuity of the Poor Clare way of life in the Belfast Monastery. It is important for the Sisters to look for a group of Poor Clares, ideally from the same Community, with a knowledge of the English language, and who would join them with the possibility of assuming future responsibility for the government of the Monastery.

Sr Bernadette Coughlan wrote a very moving letter on 11 December 2003 to Fr Enrique Gongales OFM, the Delegate General for the Poor Clares, explaining the situation in their Belfast community:

> …At present, there are just five Sisters, with one Filipino Sister on a three-month break in the Philippines. The Sisters are also burdened with ill health. However, they are availing of help from outside cleaners and a cook, in order to keep up their life of prayer. And I find their faithfulness to Clare's Form of Life admirable, given their present circumstances. But they know, that they cannot continue as they are doing for too much longer. I know this is cause of great pain for them, and this is my reason for coming to you for help. …

> Their greatest desire is to retain the Poor Clare presence in Belfast. Unfortunately and sadly, our federation is unable to offer assistance by way of personnel, due to lack of numbers and ill health in most of our monasteries. But this little group of courageous Sisters are now prepared to look, in hope, to other Poor Clare Sisters from abroad for help. Let me share their request/dream with you:

Ideally they would hope for a group of Sisters from the same Community with knowledge of the English language, who would join them with a view to assuming responsibility of the government of the monastery.

I promised the Sisters that I would do everything possible to keep the light of Clare burning brightly in this troubled part of our country. I am aware that Lady Insecurity, companion to Lady Poverty, is walking closely beside them, and has been doing so for some years now. But there is a wonderful spirit of joy among these Sisters! …How wonderful if a little group of Sister could be a source of 'new life' to this group of Clares in Belfast?

The people of Belfast and all of Northern Ireland have always had a great reverence and love for the Sisters, and have most generously supplied their temporal needs since their establishment in the city in 1924. In 1992 the Sisters built a new monastery on the original site.

Her letter ended in this way:

Help us to keep the spirit of Clare of Assisi alive in Belfast for these good Sisters, and for the people who appreciate so much their lives of prayer and dedication.

Fr Enrique replied candidly, saying that a proposal to seek 'the importation of religious' was not realisable. After receiving this reply, Sr Bernadette wrote back to clarify the request she was making on behalf of the federation:

Given the location of the monastery in Belfast which is a deeply divided city, in need of the witness of women living a sisterly life in common and in need of prayer for reconciliation; given the fact that the monastery is quite a new building [1992]; and given the fact that English is the spoken language there would you know of any Poor Clare monastery interested or able or willing to make a foundation in Belfast? The proposal is not to seek a temporary solution, but to offer the possibility to others to come to Belfast to live the life.

The sisters who are currently living in Belfast are willing to join any such community that might be established.

In essence, Sr Bernadette on behalf of the Poor Clares was inviting another monastery in another part of the world to establish a new foundation in Belfast, which the nuns living in Belfast would join.

This request was supported by the bishop of the diocese of the time, Bishop Patrick Walsh, who in view of the existing Filipino connection also wrote to Mother Marietta, the Federal President of the Order of the Poor Clares in the Philippines, to express his regret at the declining numbers in Belfast, the grace and spiritual comfort the nuns had provided to the city and his warm welcome for a potential Filipino foundation.

At this time the nuns' annual newsletters chart the comings and goings of community life – with more going than coming:

> *A Poor Clare community in Florida appealed to the Philippine Federation some time ago for Sisters to boost their community. A Sister in the Philippines encouraged Sister Marra to transfer there. At first she seemed to struggle with the idea, but eventually she felt God was calling her there, so she went on the 10th of May, and seems to have settled in there.*
>
> *On Ash Wednesday, the 9th of February, Sister Agnes transferred to the Poor Clare Monastery of San Lorenzo in Rome. She seemed to fear that we would have to close down, so she wanted to secure a place for herself in a larger community. Thank God, she seems to be happy there.*

Praying for light in darkness, line drawing from *Tel-A-Vision*

# A re-foundation

It has to be said that the Belfast community tried very hard to sustain the community and attempted various ways to keep going. Help was not available, until the Philippines stepped in to bring some much-needed good news. In a letter dated 19 May 2005, Sr Bernadette wrote to Mother Clare Marie and Sisters:

> As you all know, Mother Marietta, President of the Filipino Federation, accepted the invitation from Mother Paschal to establish a Community in Belfast. Mother Marietta has arranged to visit Belfast from 15-30th June. On Tuesday 21st a meeting will take place with Bishop Walsh and Fr Aidan [McGrath] and I have been invited to attend. …it will be of vital importance for the continuity of the Forma Vitae of our Mother St Clare in this beautiful monastery so crucial to the people of Belfast in these times of suffering and unrest.

Negotiations took place with the diocese and in due course a memorandum of understanding was drawn up in 2005. This transferred ownership of the monastery to the Trustees of the Diocese of Down and Connor. The nuns would remain as long as they wished in the monastery. If they decided to leave the monastery, the property would revert to the Diocese of Down and Connor and its trustees.

It was clear from the minutes of the negotiation meeting that the Franciscan Curia Delegate, Fr Enrique Gonzalez, based in Rome but who was present at the Filipino Federation where the decision was made with regard to nuns going to Ireland, was in favour of a re-foundation of the monastery 'rather than just individual insertion of a sister from a different culture to another community.' It was also very clear that Bishop Patrick Walsh was very supportive of Filipino Poor Clare nuns coming to the diocese. He had already written to Sr Marietta to assure her of his support. He also agreed to write to each of the nuns who had volunteered to come to Belfast, something which could be used as supporting evidence for their visa application. The meeting also covered the issue of obtaining long-term visas to the United Kingdom.

The minutes recorded unanimous agreement of an idea put forward by Sr Mary that it was:

*Not only the Filipino sisters who must study the culture of Belfast but she and Mo. [Mother] Paschal as well must exert effort to study and know the culture of the incoming group.*

The news of the re-foundation was announced via a press release. The headline read: 'From the Philippines to North Belfast…A Message of Hope' and it set the context for the plan to establish a Filipino Poor Clare community in Belfast:

As with other religious orders in Ireland, this 800-year-old contemplative order of nuns has been faced with difficult challenges in recent years. Numbers have been in decline due to a dramatic fall in vocations, and an increasing age profile.

The press release continued:

Help…and a solution…has arrived from an unusual quarter. …The Poor Clare Sisters in the Philippines are sending a community of their own Nuns to live and work in the North Belfast Monastery!

Speaking in Belfast, Mother Marietta, Federation Abbess of the Poor Clares in the Philippines, said: "It is an honour for our sisters to come and serve in Ireland. For many of us, we do this in gratitude for the hundreds of Irish missionaries who came to devote their lives to our people. Indeed, I myself was baptised by an Irish Columban priest."

Mother Marietta added: "Our first sister, Justine, has already arrived. Plans are underway to increase this over the coming months. Five of our Filipino Poor Clares have now volunteered to come to Belfast, and will be in residence in the Cliftonville Monastery by the end of the year. They are all most excited and enthusiastic about their challenging new ministry."

Sister Paschal emphasised: "Regardless of our country of origin, we're here to pray. That is our primary role. We pray together seven times a day. We each have our time of private adoration in chapel. We also have our times of spiritual reading and meditation. That takes precedence over everything.

We have Mass together every morning, most importantly, we share daily Mass and the Liturgy with the local lay community. For generations, we have been blessed to enjoy a close and loving relationship with the people of Belfast. We also provide a listening ear, and as much practical support as we can."

The enthusiasm of the local people was clearly evident; "we've never witnessed anything quite like it," commented parishioner and neighbour Patricia Walsh. The announcements by Sisters Paschal and Marietta were loudly applauded by the whole congregation.

There is a feeling of real relief and gratitude that the future of the Monastery is now secure. We salute the great courage and commitment of the Filipino Sisters. They are assured of a warm Irish welcome and the love and prayers of the local community."

The press release ended on a humorous note from Sr Marietta:

"Finally, we look forward to challenging all our comfort zones, not just spiritually…but also physically from our point of view, with especial regard to your famous Irish food and, of course …your weather!!"

Perfect Joy. Line drawing from
*Tel-A-Vision*

# A Filipino Poor Clare community

After all the deliberations, a Filipino Poor Clare community in Belfast was to be set up which would include the Irish nuns who had been members of the monastery for the last 60 years.

In her letter to Sr Francis, Federal President, dated 4 July 2005, Sr Bernadette Coughlan confirmed that at the meeting on 21 June it was agreed by those present that the Belfast monastery be 're-founded by transfer' meaning the continued existence of a Poor Clare community in Belfast. The letter went on to explain how the process was developing:

> Eight volunteer Sisters have already formed a community in the Philippines for three months and from this group will emerge the four or five sisters who will form the new community in Belfast. …As you already know Sr Justine has arrived in Belfast, Sr Magdalen hopes to be there at the end of this month and Sr Immaculata in October.

Her letter also gave details of an amalgamation of three Poor Clare monasteries, thus indicating that declining numbers was a problem for other communities:

> Another event has taken place in the federation which must also be shared with you. The question has arisen of **Amalgamation** for our three monasteries: Donnybrook, Southampton and Neath. …Early in June Mother Brigid and her sister very kindly issued an invitation to Southampton and Neath to amalgamate with them. It was explained that all three communities would form a whole new entity with a restructuring of the life, and elections.

In the 2005 edition of *Tel-A-Vision*, there were real signs of hope that the Poor Clare presence in Belfast could be sustained:

> *By the time she left Belfast, Mother Marietta had definitely decided to send Sisters to Belfast. After a Council Meeting, when she got back home, she nominated three former Abbesses, to come here as a pioneering group.*

*Two of them, Sisters Justine and Magdalene are already here, and we await the arrival of Sister Immaculata. That will bring our number to five. We have an organist again and good singing voices to boost our choir. Other Filipino Sisters are preparing to come later. We have good reason to be continually thanking and praising God.*

On 31 October 2005, Filipino Poor Clare Federation President, Sr Marietta wrote movingly to Mother Paschal and Sr Mary:

We continue to pray for our sisters there, for the I know that adjustments and adaptation will really cause inevitable discomfort, both for you and the new-comers. How are things going? Please widen up the spaces in your hearts to accommodate their inadequacy and limitation while they are on the process of finding their comfortable places in such new community. I am sure that they too are undergoing some stretchings and bendings to fit into the new situation. For these, I accompany everyone with my prayers and sacrifices.

The 2006 edition of *Tel-A-Vision* gave an update on how the Filipino nuns were settling in:

*In our newsletter last year, we informed you of the arrivals here, of Sisters Justine, Magdalene and Immaculata, in June, September and October respectively. Having them actually here with us was as significant step forward in the process of forming a Philippine-Belfast Community. Much prayer, inside and outside the monastery, frequent communications, ups and downs of all sorts, but always an ever-growing trust in God's goodness, compassion and love, led up to this rewarding situation.*

*The three Sisters came with one-year visas, to experience Poor Clare life in Belfast, and discern whether or not they had a call to remain here permanently. Sr Justine had already returned, as her community needed her. In July Sister Immaculata will take a break of two months in the Philippines, when she will celebrate her Silver Jubilee of Profession, and Sister Magdalene will leave for home in September, not to return, in the near future, anyway. On the 19th March, we had the joy of welcoming Sisters Lorette and Florence, who came to stay permanently, God willing.*

*They were accompanied by Mother Marietta, and for a while we numbered eight again. It was great. More sisters will come later. D.V.*

Once again, it seemed as the community in Belfast could survive. The early signs were very positive:

*Living together, sharing our cultures, getting to know one another, planning and deciding our future, was a very enriching experience. All the Sisters sing, three of them play the organ and all play one instrument or another, so, our liturgies have got a great boost, and we have some very lively recreations.*

But, as in life, there were further setbacks which inevitably tested the faith of the community:

*The 5th November was a sad day for us, as early in the morning, Sisters Bee and Michaela slipped away from 'Portiuncula,' all the goodbyes and tears having been previously expressed. We were extremely lonely, but they and we had to let to, as their superior recalled them, due to shortage of Sisters.*

The reality of closure must have been on the minds of the community:

*Our prayers and thoughts are very much with our dear Sisters in Neath, Southampton, St Damian's and Bothwell as they prepare and plan for the demanding and painful steps that lie ahead. May God and Our Lady let them experience at all times, their closeness to them, caring for them and loving them.*

There was also the sadness of the departure of the Capuchins from Belfast and an acceptance that for other religious orders similar decisions would have to be made:

*A matter of concern for us here is the fact that our Capuchin Brothers will be leaving the city within a few weeks. …We joyfully welcomed the Friars minor twenty three years ago, and the Capuchins some years later. With two fraternities of Secular Franciscans here then, there was a strong Franciscan witness throughout the city. However, the tides have turned.*

*Soon only the Secular Franciscans and ourselves will be left to keep the Franciscan flag flying. With Job we must say: 'The Lord gave, the Lord has taken back. Blessed be the name of the Lord.' (Job 1:21) It is probably only a matter of time until other religious communities here will also leave, due to shortage of vocations...'*

With three Filipino nuns having officially transferred to Belfast in 2007, there were sufficient numbers to complete the process of the re-foundation of the Poor Clare community by holding 'elections' to fulfil the various posts and roles necessary to run the community. On Thursday 20 September 2007, the elections took place and Sr Immaculata was elected as Abbess, Mother Paschal as Vicaress and Sr Mary as 2nd Discreet. In a letter to the other communities in the federation Sr Bernadette described it this way:

*Belfast has now been officially 'Refounded,' and we give praise and thanks to the Father of Mercies, for making this possible through the great kindness and generosity of Mother Marietta and the Philippine Federation. ...The brilliance of Clare of Assisi will now continue to shine brightly on the City of Belfast, and on the Northern part of our country! Praised be God.*

Following the election, at the community meeting on 26 September 2007 at which there were six nuns present, a minute of the meeting recorded:

*Sr Immaculata thanked the sisters for the trust and asked for cooperation in fulfilling her office as the new servant-leader Abbess of the community.*

In the next meeting at the end of October 2007, the nuns were exploring the idea of another nun coming from the Philippines to become a member of the Belfast community. Whilst there, she would make her solemn profession in the community chapel 'in order to attract new vocations.'

There were signs the two cultures in Belfast were blending well:

*Sr Florence, having completed three years here, left for her home visit on 3rd of March. The absence of even one Sister from a small group, such as ours, leaves a void, but we kept going, with God's help, and before we realised it, we were already preparing for her return, which was on the 19th May.*

*She came laden with very practical and welcome gifts. In the Philippines, such gifts are called 'pasalubong.'*

There was hope the community would continue to grow:

*Early in August DV, Sr Lorette will have her home visit, so she is making remote preparations already. By then, Sr Frances will be here, from the Philippines. She has had to wait a long time for her Visa. She is a blood sister of Sr Margaret, who spent almost two years here...*

Unfortunately for the community, Sr Margaret did not stay and at a community meeting on 26 August 2008 this was an item on the agenda:

*Sr Margaret's farewell and final decision on leaving Belfast community. Sr Margaret submitted letter of her final decision to leave our community for good.*

Even though there were positive signs of community growth, the departure of even one member made a significant difference. The minutes of 25 November 2008 note the concern about the lack of numbers:

*Father, Aidan, Father Tom Leyden inquired if we have any plan for the future of the community. They suggested to ask for help from our own communities: Cabuyao and Isabela. ...We would be asking Cabuyao and Isabela communities to assist us in our need of personnel.*

It was a mixed response to this appeal. The minutes of 15 January 2009 record responses from the Poor Clare monastery at Cabuyao in the Philippines explaining that they were unable to send anyone, whereas another Poor Clare monastery at Isabela also in the Philippines approved the application of a nun called Sr Frances to come to Belfast.

By the following March 2010 there was an item on the nuns' agenda which was now presenting more major issues – the Sponsorship License Scheme. This was a UK Border Agency scheme that dealt with applications and certificates related to residing in the UK for a period of time, and it included restrictions on who could come and how many.

In the minutes of meeting, it is clear this was becoming more and more burdensome and expensive, leaving the nuns at times unsure of whether they would be able to obtain a visa for a new member of the community.

Once more, the community was facing into difficulties, compounded also at this time by monastery maintenance issues such and painting and gardening, windows needing replacement and growing financial pressures:

> *Garden – one hour or 30 minutes a day could really help. We can't afford to pay additional workers as our resources decrease.*

There was yet further disappointment for the community when Sr Frances returned home. The issue of obtaining visas was becoming a recurring problem:

> *Sr Frances returned to the Philippines on the 27th May 2011. Her visa had almost run out. The original arrangement made by her community was that she would return home, when her two years would have expired. We miss her a lot.*

Community prayer (courtesy of Brendan Murphy)

# The decision to close

As another community member, Sr Florence, went back to the Philippines for health reasons, it was becoming clear that the community could no longer keep struggling on. Something more radical had to be done. No doubt there was considerable soul searching, prayer and conversation, but it led eventually to the difficult decision to close the monastery after 88 years.

On Sunday 27 May 2012, the four nuns still remaining in the community met with Bishop Noel Treanor the bishop of diocese. Sr Bernadette Coughlan, the federation president was also present. In the report of the meeting, drawn up by Mother Immaculata, were the following details:

> The meeting was to inform the Bishop of their decision for the closure of the Monastery, made after much prayer and discernment, and to discuss with him the reasons for the closure. Over a period of time, the Belfast Community has been experiencing difficulties regarding their inability to fully live the Poor Clare way of life. This is due to decreasing numbers and lack of vocations. The Sisters of the Monastery in Cork have been generous in sending two Sisters from time to time to assist them; but it is the only Monastery in the federation that can offer support. However, this situation cannot continue as the Community in Cork are also short while their Sisters are away. There is also the problem of a financial situation.

> It was a very pleasant and informative Meeting with all present freely contributing to the discussion. Bishop Noel was most understanding of the many difficulties the Sisters were experiencing and agreed with their decision to close the Monastery.

Bishop Noel Treanor's letter of 1 June 2012 brings together his understanding of the circumstances which led to the closure of the monastery, including 'the efforts which the Poor Clare federation in the Philippines had provided and the hope that native Irish vocations might have been forthcoming.'

He also acknowledged 'the difficulties for the federation in the Philippines in identifying Sisters capable and willing to undertake this Mission and the further problems posed by the UK Border Agency Control in the matter of acquiring visas.'

His letter concluded in this way:

> I realise that you and the Sisters living in the Community have prayed and deliberated about this matter for some time. I know that this has been a difficult and painful time for you all. I trust that whatever decisions are taken in respect of provision of care for Sister Paschal and Sister Mary will be in their best interests.
>
> As you proceed with this matter, please know that I am available to you and the Sisters at any time.

In the evening of 1 June 2012 there was a meeting of the Conventual Chapter at 6.45pm involving the four members of the community. The following is an extract from the minutes:

> Re: The continuation of our Poor Clare life in Belfast
>
> With a great deal of prayer and reflection, the members of the Chapter have been seriously considering the continuation of the Poor Clare life in this monastery in Belfast, taking into account the small number of sisters in the community and their ability to continue to live the life to the full.
>
> Over more than twenty years, the monastery has benefitted from the assistance of temporary transfers from other monasteries. ...The arrival on a stable basis of sisters from the Philippines Federation almost ten years ago was a source of hope. However, it has become increasingly difficult, time-consuming and very costly to renew visas for these sisters.
>
> The members of the Chapter are aware of a statement from one of the past Federal Assemblies to the effect that repeated calls from a monastery for the loan of sisters from another monastery of the

federation will not solve these problems: there are too few sisters who are able to leave their own community. Most of the communities are already bearing the responsibility of many sick and very elderly sisters.

The Chapter then moved to face the option to close the monastery and disperse. With faith and in prayer, a secret vote was taken. The result was unanimously in favour of requesting the Holy See to suppress the monastery. (Although not present, Sr Florence was informed of the matter and has written back, expressing her deep sorrow but wishing us all well in the decision that needs to be taken). The Abbess will make contact with the President of the Federation to see which of the other monasteries would be willing to receive the remaining Irish sisters, and with the Philippine Federation to do the same for the Philippine sisters.

All four nuns signed the extract from the minutes.

On 13 June 2012, Sr Mary Louise Gretchen OSC, the Abbess of the Poor Clare Monastery of Our Lady of the Eucharist, Guibang in the Philippines, wrote to Mother Immaculata and Sr Mary Lorette in these words:

When you called us up and informed us of the forthcoming closure of your Monastery for the main reason of no vocation since your arrival there almost seven years ago, we had a Conventual Chapter at once in the evening of May 31, 2012. We realized during our discussion that no matter how you do in terms of vocation promotion and living the life so as to build the community in Belfast with love and joy the dying process of the community keeps on. Maybe God has other plans for you and so while you expressed your desire to return here, your original Monastery, you are most welcome to come back and be with us again.

On 25 June 2012, the four remaining Belfast nuns wrote to the Prefect of the Congregation for Institutes of Consecrated Life & Societies of Apostolic Life, Cardinal João Bráz de Aviz, to confirm the closure of the monastery.

*Following much prayer and reflection, it is with deep sadness that we, the undersigned Sisters of the Poor Clare Monastery, in Belfast, Northern Ireland, humbly request the consent of the Holy See to close our monastery.*

*For more than 20 years, this monastery has benefitted from the assistance of temporary transfers from other monasteries. The arrival, on a more or less permanent basis of stability to the life of the monastery, and has been a source of continuing hope.*

*However, it has become increasingly evident in the past few years that our numbers do not permit us to live the Poor Clare way of life as fully as is envisaged in the Constitutions; nor do they permit us to meet the ever-increasing demands of our chapel, monastery and residential retreat facilities. We are now only five sisters – three Filipino (one of whom is on extended leave in the Philippines), and two octogenarian Irish sisters. The number of suitable volunteers from the Philippines has reduced over the years and the costs and the increasingly difficult and time-consuming challenges of obtaining Visas to live in the United Kingdom have brought added pressures to an already over-worked community.*

*Faced with this reality, in a spirit of faith and after much prayer, our Chapter met to discuss the issue; at the end of the discussion, the Chapter voted in secret, and the result was unanimously in favour of requesting the Holy See to suppress the monastery and disperse. …*

*While this request is a matter of some sadness, all of the Sisters wish to give thanks to God for the many graces and blessings that He has wrought in Belfast during the 88 years of the Monastery's existence. The Sisters have remained in this place during the most turbulent years of Northern Ireland's history, praying with and for the people, and suffering alongside them in the decades of sectarian discrimination, division and violence. We wish to thank God, too, for the lives of those Sisters who lived and died in this Monastery over those long decades, and whose memories we will bring with us. We wish to thank God for the loving care and attention which the Monastery has received from successive Bishops of the Diocese of Down and Connor, as well as from the clergy, religious and people of the Diocese.*

The nuns also issued a public statement confirming their decision to close the monastery owing to the scarcity of numbers and the demands of the 'chapel, the Monastery parlours and the Retreat facilities.'

They acknowledged a decline in volunteers from the Philippines and:

*…The UK Border Agency regulations in respect to non-EEC nationals making the task all the more challenging.*

Their statement also acknowledged very clearly the following:

*In this process of discernment, the Sisters have been accompanied by the Most Reverend Noel Treanor and the President of the Poor Clare Federation of St Mary of the Angels in Ireland and Great Britain. However, it must be understood that the decision to request the closure of the Monastery comes from the Sisters of the Monastery and not from any outside authority. In respecting the Sisters' decision they ask people to continue to accompany them in prayer and in their contemplative life for the reminder of their time in Belfast.*

On 16 July 2012, the Congregation for the Institutes of Consecrated Life & Societies of Apostolic Life 'suppressed' the Monastery of Our Lady and St Michael, Belfast.

On 20 July Sister Immaculata wrote to Bishop Treanor to request permission to transfer the remains of 21 Poor Clare Nuns buried in the Monastery's garden cemetery. The bishop duly gave that permission and offered the assistance of Fr Eugene O'Hagan to help in any way possible. In the press release on behalf of the diocese Bishop Treanor said:

I pay tribute today to the Poor Clare Sisters who take leave of their monastery after 88 years of dedicated service to the local community, the city of Belfast and the Church. The Sisters leave behind an invaluable legacy of prayerful support and a sense of the closeness of God, especially in turbulent times. Their presence and spiritual guidance were both sought and received well across the communities. They will be sadly missed. Their departure is a profound loss to Sacred Heart parishioners, to the Diocese and to all who have come to know and love the Sisters over the years. From within the enclosure of their monastery they have constantly reached out in support of those who came to visit them.

The press release continued:

> The Sisters have modelled a spiritual joy and sense of peace which are the fruits of a life of contemplative dedication. I join with all those who visited their monastery over the years, the parishioners of Sacred Heart and beyond, priests and religious, as I wish them every blessing for the future and as they transfer to other monasteries in the Philippines and in Ireland.

Bishop Treanor also thanked the priests and people who had supported the nuns over the years:

> …I also pay tribute to the Franciscan Friars, and in particular to Fr Aidan McGrath OFM, and to the Vincentian Fathers, under Fr Perry Gildea, who ministered to the Sisters throughout several decades in providing Chaplaincy services to them and to the people who attended morning Mass with the Sisters. Together with the Sisters I thank all those, who over the years, have supported them in numerous ways and especially in more recent weeks. I would like to publically thank them for their care, kindness and practical help to the Sisters.

Belfast's Deputy Lord Mayor at the time, Councillor Tierna Cunningham said: "The people of this parish and further afield will be heartbroken to see the Poor Clare convent finally close on August 29."

There was indeed great sadness that the Poor Clare presence had after all the years now come to an end in Belfast.

On 29 August, the nuns left the monastery in Belfast – Srs Immaculata and Lorette returned to the Philippines and Srs Paschal and Mary went first to Dublin and then on to Carlow.

In September 2013, the building was rededicated to become St Malachy's Seminary the residence for students studying for priesthood in the Diocese of Down and Connor.

The annual newsletter which the nuns write for their fellow nuns within the federation included these poignant words:

*This is probably our last Newsletter from '120,' so we very sincerely thank you all for all you have meant to us down the years, for all your sharing, all your prayers and your goodness. You will always have a special place in our prayers. Wishing you all countless blessings and graces every day of this jubilee year. Your Sisters in Belfast.*

Congregation at the farewell Mass (courtesy of Ann McManus, *Irish News*)

Friends say goodbye on the final day of the monastery (courtesy of Thomas McMullan *North Belfast News*)

Sr Mary (left) and Sr Paschal surrounded by friends (courtesy of Thomas McMullan, *North Belfast News*)

The last farewell. From left: Sr Paschal, Mother Immaculata, Sr Mary and Sr Lorette
(courtesy of Thomas McMullan, *North Belfast News*)

# Chapter Ten

## The World Outside

*Irish Catholic* coverage of Pope John Paul II's visit to Ireland, 1979

> ❝
>
> *They seem to have departed enriched by the knowledge*
> *that we are normal human beings*
>
> ❞

The Poor Clare way of life in Belfast may have ended with the closure of the monastery in 2012, but the nuns' story does not. For as well as recording the 'principal events' of the community over its 88 years in Belfast, the nuns' well-worn community journals reveal much about how they got on with and how they related to the world outside their monastery. Though in theory cut off from the world and never leaving the confines of their contemplative life without good reason, in practice the Poor Clares were able to establish a wide network of contacts, make a multitude of friends and over the years welcome a great many guests and visitors.

One of the greatest gifts the Poor Clares gave the 'outside world' of the city of Belfast was the gift of relationship and friendship. Those who came to see them were always warmly received and affirmed – indeed it was said that the nuns were among some of the best-informed people in Belfast despite being enclosed. The welcome the Poor Clares gave was a much-appreciated side of their time in the city, and during the course of their presence in Belfast the community welcomed many visitors and friends. Countless people, some in great distress, made their way to a parlour in the monastery where they would have time to sit and share their story. The nuns heard many tales of sadness in these parlours.

Local people young and old from various parts of Belfast and beyond called to visit the nuns. Years later, people can still recall visits they made to the nuns as children. Others remember visits at significant moments in their lives such as exam times, interviews, relationship breakdown or the sickness of a family member. Through the nuns' warm welcome and prayerful presence many people found peace in their troubles. Comfort was always found in the reassurance that the nuns would be praying for their intentions.

Right from the very start when the first Poor Clare nuns arrived in Belfast in 1924, the monastery was a place of hospitality. Even on the very first day they moved in they welcomed their first visitor, the bishop of the diocese, Bishop MacRory. Though he had been less than enthusiastic when the Order first approached him in March 1923, the journal describes his visit in this way:

*Later in the evening His Lordship called and gave us a most hearty and fatherly welcome; he had appointed a chaplain – Rev Father Greaven – so that we had Holy Mass the very next morning and the Divine Master took possession of His new Home. So closely did we stand round Him singing His praises in our tiny choir that we could almost touch Him.*

An amusing moment from a later visit from Bishop MacRory and a Mrs McCann from Dublin is also recorded. When they called, the community at that point was clearly not geared up for visitors:

*She [Mrs McCann] and his Lordship [Bishop MacRory] arrived one evening for tea; as yet we had very little in the way of china for visitors' tea; the nearest approach to a sugar-bowl was the sacristan's best flower vase, so out the flowers had to come until after the Bishop's tea. However, our generous friends, the factory girls, whose first thought seems to be always for Our Hidden Lord in the Blessed Sacrament, brought us some beautiful vases and in time some other benefactor brought us a sugar bowl so the famous vase/ sugar-bowl was returned to the sacristy and still serves as a Holy Water Stoup for the Asperges* [The act of sprinkling of Holy Water].

In addition to the great many people whose names were not in the public domain there were also very well-known individuals who came to visit the community as the years went by. One such person in Catholic circles in the 1950s was Father Patrick Peyton who was known as the 'Rosary Priest'. He was most associated with the line: 'the family that prays together, stays together'. Both his visits in June 1954 are recorded in the community journal:

*In this year 1954 our 40 hours began June 11th, Father Peyton the rosary priest came to Belfast the Thursday before to have 3 Rosary rallies – Belfast – Ballymena and Downpatrick. He stopped with the Bishop – we had been joking about his paying us a visit – to our surprise and delight he appeared at the Grille on the Saturday morning – we all went to the parlour for ¾ hour. He came back in the afternoon and said he would like to make a Holy Hour with us. He knelt on the altar steps and gave out the rosary – we answered and sang Hymns in between.*

Fr Patrick Peyton (photo provided by Family Rosary, Massachusetts)

*The rallies were a great success. He gave us his rosary which he always had round his hands at night…He also gave Mother [Mother Abbess, the superior of the community] his rosary manual. …The following Saturday just as we were going to bed David (the caretaker) came over to say that Father Peyton would be there shortly. He came and remained until 10.15. He told us all about his crusade – 95% of the Catholics in the north signed to say the daily family rosary.*

The Rosary Rallies referred to took place on 17 June 1954 in Ballymena, with 15,000 people attending. On 19 June 1954 over 100,000 people attended a Rosary Crusade in Belfast, 80,000 were in the grounds of Our Lady's Hospice, Beechmount, several thousand mothers with young children were in MacRory Park and over 1,000 sick and elderly people in Broadway Cinema. On Sunday 20 June 1954, the final rally took place in Downpatrick. In all, 162,561 Catholics in Down and Connor signed the Rosary Pledge.

Over the years the community received visits from many priests including Fr Stefano Gobbi the founder of the Marian Movement of Priests, Fr Slavco Barbaric OFM from Medjugorje, Fr Gabriel Harty OP the Irish Rosary priest, Fr John Burdyszek OFM Conv who had known St Maximilian Kolbe personally. Regarding the support they received from priests in the area the nuns had this to write:

*Priests are really wonderfully good to us – coming daily and so punctually – nearly all of whom are at the same time busy with some special active work in their various Parishes – even the Religious Orders have to help with Parish work more than formerly – as Priests are fewer and much more work to be done.*

One particularly well-known visitor was Mother Teresa of Calcutta, whose visit was joyously noted in the journal entry dated 9 November 1971:

*We had the great joy of a visit at 7pm. Mother Teresa from Calcutta came with Sr Frederick from London & Sr Regina – a real Indian. We were overjoyed at meeting in person this world famous Religious – Foundress of the Missionaries of Charity. She was humble & simple as a little child – full of fun & more full of holiness. May her first Foundation in Ireland bring many Blessings.*

Mother Teresa of Calcutta (courtesy of Hugh Russell, *Irish News*)

As it happened, the foundation of the Missionaries of Charity did not last. The sisters stayed only a short time in Belfast and then left. There is no single undisputed explanation for their departure from the city.

There would be no surprise that people like Fr Peyton or Mother Teresa visited the Poor Clares. It may be surprising to discover that a former boxer Barry McGuigan regularly visited over the years. It's hard to imagine contemplative nuns being interested in boxing. The annual newsletter explains it like this:

> *You are probably not interested in boxing, neither are we but we are interested in a boxer, the now famous Barry McGuigan, who comes here for prayer before all his 'fights' as he calls them. He trusts more in prayer than in his boxing ability. He's just a big boy, very simple and humble. A priest fan of his says 'he's a fine character' and success doesn't go to his head. Once the fight is over, his little son seems to claim all his attention. He himself told us that after he had won the European title, he, his wife Sandra and the baby were at a function held in his honour in the Europa Hotel, and while the bands were playing and everyone calling out for Barry, 'here was I' he said, 'feeding the baby.'*

In his autobiography, *Barry McGuigan Cylone My Story*, the boxer acknowledges the esteem in which he held the nuns. He wrote about them in a chapter that described a fight with a Nigerian fighter called Asymin Mustapha, who boxed under the name of 'Young Ali.' Barry described the experience of the fight which left Young Ali fighting for his life; in the end the young fighter did not recover. Barry described the time Mustapha was unconscious and struggling for life as a 'very lonely and isolating experience.' He described how he coped:

Barry McGuigan (courtesy of Hugh Russell, *Irish News*)

> I went to church and prayed a lot. The people that I always had faith in were those at the Poor Clare Monastery in Belfast because of their amazing dedication – they had given their whole lives to God. Some of them have been in there sixty years. I visited them a lot during this difficult time, and their words were a great support. 'There is nothing you can do, Barry,' they told me. 'Just leave it in the hands of God, and just hope by some miracle he will recover.' (McGuigan, pp. 100-101)

Even after Sr Paschal and Sr Mary, the only Poor Clare nuns from the Belfast community remaining in Ireland, moved to Carlow, Barry still went to visit them.

Another well-known public figure who visited the nuns was North Belfast man, Frank Carson. The nuns got to know him away from his public persona:

> *Some of you at least may have heard of Belfast born Frank Carson, the comedian. A one time plasterer, he worked on our house here in the early fifties and since then has often sought the help of our prayers. Mother seems to be one of his special friends. He rings or write occasionally to give her the family news. Now on his way to international fame, it is gratifying to see how he appreciates his faith and lives up to its demand.*

*One evening he, wife Ruth, and daughter Majella paid us a visit. He entertained us with some of his T.V. show pieces which we enjoyed immensely. 'It's the way I tell 'em' he says.*

The fact that the nuns were prepared to appear on television gives some idea of the esteem in which Frank was held by them:

*A few days previously we had been asked to make a few minutes' contribution to Frank Carson's T.V. show 'This is your life,' and because Frank is such a good friend of ours we consented to do so, as a mark of gratitude to him.*

Frank Carson at the barber's (courtesy of Bill Smith, *Irish News*)

It is clear from the many visits and support the nuns received that they were highly regarded. One of the first visits Bishop Cahal Daly made after he was appointed Bishop of Down and Connor in 1982 was to the Poor Clare community:

*It was not a complete surprise for us that Dr Daly was appointed to succeed Dr Philbin as our bishop, as rumours to that effect had been abroad anyway. Dr Daly's first visit in his new diocese was to us, half an hour, he said, after handing in his letter of appointment to the diocesan chapter. His last visit in his former diocese was to our sisters in Drumshanbo – enough to show that the Poor Clares mean a lot to him. He contacts us quite often and has come for Mass on three occasions already, the last being the anniversary of his ordination, the 16th July.*

Bishop Cahal Daly

Another of the people who would have known the nuns over the years through her own family connections, particularly her mother, was Mary McAleese. Mary, who served as President of Ireland from November 1997 to November 2011, grew up in North Belfast. She visited several times over the years, including once, in 2007, when she was President. The journal recounts the visit as follows:

The community meets the President and her husband. Back row: Sr Paschal, Sr Lorette, Sr Immaculata, Sr Florence, Front row: Mary McAleese, Martin McAleese, Sr Mary

*The 10th of December brought us a treat we had hopefully awaited for a long time – a friendly visit from the President of Ireland, Mrs. Mary McAleese and her husband, Dr Martin. She wishes us to call her just 'Mary' as we had always done. A Belfast lady, she was one of our Patrons, during the construction of our Monastery and chapel, and she and Martin were outstanding fundraisers. We spent a delightful forty five minutes together, sharing lunch in our refectory, while reminiscing on earlier days and sharing the present day happenings. Mary was particularly glad to meet our Filipino Sisters, and know they are part of our Belfast community. Needless to say, with our farewell, we promised them a daily place in our prayers, which they really had already.*

In the same way as some people may have been surprised to read that the nuns were friendly with an international boxer, so too it might not be expected they would be visited by a police chief. The visit can however be explained by the fact that Matt Baggott, who was the Chief Constable in Northern Ireland from 2009 to 2014, was a committed Christian. In the 2011 edition of *Tel–A-Vision*, there was a brief account of his visit and the time he spent with the nuns:

*Matt Baggott an English man, is Chief Constable of the PSNI here in Northern Ireland. He is not a Catholic, but it is evident that God is very much a big part of his life. One day he confided to Denis Moloney, a good friend of ours that he would like to spend some time in prayer with us, being very conscious of his need of powerful help from God. Denis and he organised the visit. ...*

*After a cup of tea, we prayed some of the Divine Office together, and before they departed, we sang the blessing of St. Clare for them. They seemed to be well pleased with the visit. So were we. Thanksgiving to God filled our hearts, for placing such good and conscientious men in high places, where they could have only a positive and Christian influence, on all with whom they worked.*

Former Chief Constable Matt Baggott (image courtesy of PSNI Corporate Communications)

Over the years, from the beginning of the foundation in Belfast, the nuns became friends with a wide range of people including those who worked closely with them. Their records indicate these friendships such as the deaths of a former caretaker and his wife who had been with them for years:

*September 3rd 1976 The death of Mr David McCorry. David and his wife Nellie were our faithful Lodge Caretakers for 30 years, having come shortly after the Foundation of the Monastery. They retired November 4th 1955 and lived in St Agnes' Drive, Andersonstown. We owe them a great debt of gratitude; they remained our best friends by constantly getting Masses offered for the Nuns on occasions of Receptions - Professions - Jubilees etc even though they never knew some of the sisters, and for the Community in general they prayed day and night - they knew where we were at each hour and joined us in spirit with their own Prayers at the time of the Divine Office.*

*August 16th 1981. Our dear 'Nellie' died, in Musgrave Park Hospital, where she had been for the last few years. Nellie was in her early nineties. R.I.P.*

As in life, the nuns had to deal with the deaths of good friends, one such being neighbour Arthur Speight:

*Our good friend, Arthur Speight was found dead in bed one Sunday morning early in January. Though he suffered from various ailments and had been to hospital after Christmas, he seemed in the best form just then. That made his death all the greater shock for us. It was a a great loss also, because he had given invaluable help at the lodge some months previously, and had served our Mass every morning. This he counted a great privilege.*

*He was always near to lend a hand when we called on him, and he was most reliable.*

The ordination of a former neighbour and friend brought joy to the community:

*March 8th 1986 Our former altar boy Mark Nolan, who is a Benedictine Monk now, was ordained to the Priesthood.*

*On the 8th of March we felt a sort of sense of achievement when Brother Mark Nolan, O.S.B. was raised to the priesthood, because he had been an altar boy here from the time of his First Communion until he joined the Benedictines in Le Bec, Normandy. His community made a foundation in this diocese a few years ago. It looks as if the Lord brought Fr. Mark Ephrem … over to Le Bec, so that he could send him back again as one of the 'foundation stones' of his Order in Ireland.*

There was more good news with the ordinations of the nephew of Sister Paschal, Fr Donal McKeown as a bishop, and the nephew of Sr Petronilla, Michael Murtagh as a priest:

*A very special occasion for us all was the 29th of April 2001, the Sunday on which Sister Paschal's nephew, Father Donal McKeown, was ordained Auxiliary Bishop of Down and Connor, replacing Bishop Dallat, who died last year, R.I.P. Bishop Walsh had invited Sisters Paschal and Mary to the ordination ceremony in St Peter's Cathedral, and they said it was an unforgettable experience.*

*Last December Sister Petronilla's nephew, Michael Murtagh, was ordained as a Redemptorist. For two years previously he had been a member of the community here in Clonard, and used to come to see his Auntie occasionally. We got to know him quite well. After ordination he was re-assigned to Clonard.*

*A nephew of our late Sr Petronilla, RIP Fr Michael Murtagh CSsR, was elected as Rector of Clonard Monastery last year. A native of Lanesbro, Co. Longford we have known him for a number of years.*

*He worked in Clonard for a year, as a student, came back again after ordination, and took his share of priestly work, until he was transferred to Dublin to be Novice Director. A few years later, a Provincial Chapter assigned him as Rector to Clonard community, a daunting task, but God and Fr Michael can work wonders!*

Sr Paschal with her nephew Bishop Donal McKeown and Sr Mary (courtesy of Brendan Murphy)

Sr Petronilla and her nephew Fr Michael Murtagh

## Visitors from other denominations

Even though Belfast had experienced two trying years of sectarian violence from 1920–1922, within a short time of arriving in Belfast the little community had begun to develop some very positive cross-community relationships.

One such relationship was that of Francis Joseph Bigger, who, unlike other evangelical preachers who wanted to 'convert' the nuns, was calling to befriend them. Bigger was born in Belfast in 1863 to a Presbyterian father and Church of Ireland mother. He worshipped at St Peter's Church on the Antrim Road. He had a lifelong interest in the Irish language and learned to speak it.

The journal indicates how the community appreciated his kindness to them:

> *But all the non-Catholics were not of the same mind; that great patriot, Mr Bigger, who was a great admirer of Our Holy Father, Saint Francis, was most friendly and as far as I can remember tried to make us have a Xmas turkey for dinner – he was very kind to us any way and he was only one of the many non-Catholics, rich and poor who come in goodly numbers since we came to Belfast, to ask for prayers and bring their little offerings.*

Bigger was known as a 'Protestant with Franciscan leanings,' which explains the reference to being 'a great admirer of Our Holy Father, Saint Francis.' There are pictures of a grotto depicting the scene of St Francis of Assisi preaching to the birds in Bigger's garden in his home. From his high Anglo-Catholic background and his love of St Francis, Francis Joseph Bigger would have been keen to support the Franciscan prayerful presence of the Poor Clares in North Belfast.

At various points throughout their journals and correspondence, there are references to visits from other Christians to the community. In simple, unassuming ways, these relationships were a prophetic sign in the midst of the chaos which at times overwhelmed the city. The Troubles in Belfast were particularly ferocious during the 1970s when to many people looking in at the city from various parts of the world it seemed there was sectarian warfare going on. Although the world looking on might have been thinking that Belfast was riven with sectarianism, in places like the Poor Clare Monastery relationships with Christians of other denominations were quietly continuing. When it came to celebrating the Golden Jubilee of the Belfast foundation on Tuesday 29 May 1974 the community journal records this:

> *May 29th 1974: Father David OFM and Fr Cassian OFM were unable to come from Dublin owing to the train stoppage threat, and the very 'tense' condition of the City during the Big Strike set going by the Ulster Workers Council. However, their absence was 'made up' for, by the presence of 3 Anglican Franciscan Brothers wearing their holy Habits and one had a beard!*

The nuns as members of Order of the Poor Clares were greatly influenced by the person of St Francis. In turn, they resonated with that Franciscan spirit whenever they met it including in their Anglican brothers and sisters. Their journals and correspondence indicate regular friendly regular contact with the Anglican Franciscans:

> The Anglican Friars have changed house and are now quite near us. Their provincial, Fr Michael, was over from England for the opening and blessing of the new abode. He and Br. Eric came to see us. We all met them in the parlour, and Fr. Michael said we were just like his own community of Anglican Poor Clares in Oxford.

The accounts of the visits of the Anglican friars indicate a very relaxed relationship with regular visits to the nuns:

> Three of the Anglican Friars up the road dropped in on the Feast of the Holy Innocents. Brother Eric, with all the surprised joy of a schoolboy, told us he had got an electric razor from Santy. Not long ago we noticed a photo of him sporting a beard in their magazine 'The Franciscan,' so he must have offered up the razor.

The beginning of a new year was marked by a visit from their Anglican brothers:

> Then on Jan. 1st 1979 we all went to the parlour to meet four members, or Friars, I should say, of the Society of St Francis. Although they are Anglican, we are very happy to have them in Belfast. They are truly Franciscan and very gentlemanly. They very simply and very gratefully accepted the potatoes and all Mother offered them.

The annual newsletter of 1984 gives some detail about the monthly contact across the denominations on the common ground of a Franciscan spirituality:

> For some time, the Franciscans in Belfast, that is the Sisters of Holy Cross, the Franciscan Missionaries of Mary, the Anglican Friars and Sisters, and of late, the Friars, have been having 'Franciscans Together' every month, that is, some members of each community assemble in one of their houses and pray together

*for about an hour and a half for 'peace and the healing of this land.'...Soon
they will come to us so that we can join in.*

The following year's newsletter offers some more information:

*In last year's Tel-A-Vision, we made reference to Franciscans Together in
Belfast. As there are six Franciscan houses here, the meeting is held in each
one twice a year. We take part, physically anyway, only in our own two. An
hour is spent praying together 'for peace and the healing of our land.' Then we
have refreshments and a chat together. It's inspiring to hear the other religious
speak about the great work they are doing, often under many pressures and
difficulties.*

The inter-Franciscan group later develops to move into the area of inter-faith
contact as the 2004 *Tel-A-Vision* records:

*The S.F.O. groups here arranged for a Muslim, a senior doctor in the city, to
come to our meeting room on the 16th June, to speak to them and us on what
Muslims are all about, especially in the field of religion. He and his friend
showed some interesting slides. Then he gave us run down on the contents of
the Koran. It was very enlightening.*

These meetings were very important for the nuns:

*An Inter-faith meeting, organised by the SFO groups here, has become an
annual event in the autumn. A special feature of last year's one, was the
presence of Fr Gerry Reynolds CSsR, from Clonard Monastery. He spoke
of his role behind the scenes, during the 'Troubles,' in bringing Protestants
and Catholics together, in the cause of peace. Resulting from that is the now
well established custom of a group of Catholics from Clonard Church, joining
a Protestant community in their church for their Sunday Service, and the
roles of the two groups being reversed on another Sunday. Barriers are being
broken down, and a spirit of acceptance, understanding and love is growing.*

As well as visits from Anglican Franciscans, the nuns also enjoyed visits from
people of other denominations.

When they met it was on the common ground of their shared Christian belief influenced by a common interest in St Francis. One such visit took place in early 1977:

> Towards the end of February two German Lutheran contemplative Sisters called to see us. They belong to the Evangelical Sisterhood of Mary, and have a house in England. Deeply interested in prayer they draw inspiration from the mystery of the Incarnation and the presence of God in nature. They claim O.H.F. Francis as their guide. We were deeply impressed by their manifest love of God and total dependence on His Divine Providence.

The references to Christians of other denominations indicate the willingness of the nuns to meet and learn from others as can be seen by a visit in 1994:

> In May this year, a group from the Irish School of Ecumenics, with their leader, the Rev. John Morrow, a Presbyterian Minister, came one evening to learn something about us. We had a meaningful sharing, and all agreed that we broke down barriers, as we recognised and acknowledged better than before, our oneness in Jesus.

The nuns clearly appreciated these visits:

> One of the ladies who comes in to assist Sr Assumpta, belongs to a Presbyterian prayer group. She bought the whole group, four couples, and two other ladies, to our parlour one evening for a shared prayer experience. It was very rewarding. The group were wonderful people and so prayerful! We sang hymns, read scripture, prayed together, and concluded with a cup of tea.

In 2001 *Tel-A-Vision* their yearly newsletter recorded this visit:

> Sybil McGahey, a Protestant lady, an exemplary Christian, and a treasured friend of ours, called with another friend on the 9th May, and we enjoyed the visit immensely. She is most interesting, very close to God and broad-minded. It puzzles her, as it does many others, how Protestants and Catholics here, all children of the same Father, can be continually at each others' throats.

In the 2003 edition of *Tel-A-Vision* it was very clear that the community had very high regard for the longest serving female Presbyterian minister:

*You may know, or at least have heard of the Reverend Ruth Patterson, an ordained Presbyterian Minister, who is now full-time Director of Restoration Ministries, based in Dunmurry. Invited by a branch of the S.F.O. here, she came with them to our chapel on the 3rd April to talk about the situation here, her ministry and her vision for Ireland, especially N.I. May her tireless work bear much fruit for a better future.*

## Franciscan visitors

It is no surprise to discover the importance the nuns attached to visits from other members of the Franciscan family. As a community, they appreciated time spent with them by other Franciscans. There are many references to Fr Theodore Crowley OFM who was Professor of Scholastic Philosophy at Queen's University. They were particularly sad when he left Belfast in October 1975. He had been a very supportive Franciscan priest and friend of the community:

*After 25 yrs. Professor of Philosophy in Queen's University Father Theodore resigned* [In fact he was Professor of Scholastic Philosophy, a separate department from the department of Philosophy]. *We were very sorry at his going away as he had been a wonderful and much appreciated friend all through the years.*

They clearly appreciated his friendship:

*On the 10th February 1990, our good friend of thirty five years, Fr. Theodore Crowley O.F.M. died in hospital here. R.I.P. On most Sundays, he used to come for Mass at 9.30 a.m. People who knew him, spoke of his capacity for friendship as his outstanding trait. We wholly endorse that opinion.*

Fr Theodore Crowley OFM

There was particular delight when the nuns heard about the arrival of Franciscan priests and brothers in Belfast after a long absence from the diocese:

> *Jan 19th 1984 Fr David and Fr Fiacre had a long meeting with the Bishop, they called with us later. But t'was only on 31st we had had definite confirmation that two Friars would be up to Belfast to stay, in less than two months D.V.*

> *Feb 6th Our first visit from our two friars. Father Liam McCarthy and Father Diarmuid O'Riain.*

The arrival of fellow Franciscans was a very important milestone in the life of the community:

> *March 16th 1984: The Friars came to Belfast to stay. D.G. History is made!*

The short phrase 'history is made!' which is underlined and with an exclamation mark gives some idea of the importance the nuns attached to this development.

> *Perhaps we were like the importunate widow persisting in asking God to send our Brother Friars to Belfast. At any rate He granted our request and now, after a lapse of about 200 years, they are back in Down and Connor. As Father David said: 'History has caught up with us. 1984 will go in the history and annals of the Franciscan Order and Poor Clare community as a Holy Year of reunion, and for the Diocese of Down and Connor, a year of Reconciliation.'*

There are many references to the Franciscans in Belfast which indicate the special role they played in the community's life:

> *On the 16th March [1984] the two 'Foundation Stones,' Fathers Liam and Diarmuid arrived at their new home attached to St. Joseph's Church in Pilot St. in the Docks area. This is in St Patrick's parish, St Patrick's being the parish Church.*

*From experience they had over the years, they are very conscious of the fact that Providence has led them here to establish a House of Prayer. Their 'house shall be called a House of Prayer'… In the house itself there is a special Prayer Room where the Blessed Sacrament is exposed for some hours every day. People come and join them in adoration and the Divine Office. Straight away they won a place in people's hearts. Some call them the 'new missioners,' others, the 'Flour Mill Fathers' because there is a flour mill on either side of them and probably to harmonise with the Mill Hill Fathers who had come to St Mary's some months before they arrived.*

*March 18th [1984] They visit us and promise to be on duty as soon as Bishop Daly gives leave. We are happy to help our brothers in every way we can.*

*April 2nd [1984] Fr Diarmuid said our first Mass by our Belfast Friars. In the weeks ahead we were to be visited by several visiting friars including Fr David on 19th.*

*June 25th [1993] Our dear Fr Liam left Belfast to take up a new assignment in Rome and today he was replaced by Fr Martin Wright.*

*Aug 14th [1993] Our celebrations began with a little Pageant, Drama of scenes from the life of St Clare. The Pageant was the brainchild of Sheila Hughes T.O.S.F. and the cast included members of our three orders. Our two little Filipino sisters did an interpretative dance 'You have chosen life.' Fr Diarmuid was St Francis and Dr Sean Donnelly G.P., T.O.S.F. was Br Silvester.*

*Our newsletter last year was written in the aftermath of the Friars' Chapter, when they were assigned their new locations and roles in the Province. Before you could have read our news, Father Diarmuid had taken up residence, with Brother Salvador, in their house of prayer in New Barnsley, in the Ballymurphy area of the city and was replaced in St Joseph's by Father Florian. We missed his lovely Masses with his pithy homilies.*

*July 9th [1993] The Friars began a new project – a new house in New Barnsley, Belfast is a 'Franciscan city.' Fr Diarmuid is the first Foundation Stone, with Br Salvador to help until, hopefully, another friar comes.*

*Oct. 10th* [1993] *Fr Diarmuid bade his official farewell to the public as he takes up his new appointment. We welcomed Fr. Florian. Poor Father found St. Joseph's a big challenge, it would be interesting to hear how quickly he learned to love Belfast and her people.*

They followed in some detail developments for their Franciscan brothers based in Belfast:

*The Friars' Chapter in July* [1999] *seemed to result in major changes in the Province. Belfast witnessed the departure of Father Richard to Rossnowlagh, and the arrival of Father Aidan and Father Joseph. When both Friars are at home, we enjoy the luxury of a concelebrated Mass every morning. Home for them now is 'Greccio,' Hughenden Avenue, the suitable house they procured after much head ache and heart ache. Nothing worthwhile can be got in this life, without a touch of the cross, as we all know.*

The Friars left Belfast in 2004. Owing to the shortage of personnel they were not in a position to appoint anyone to the city.

Br Michael, Fr Liam and Fr Diarmuid (courtesy of Fr Liam McCarthy)

# Watching the world

In addition to recording their contacts with friends and visitors the nuns' journals also yield a timeline of milestones, occasions and highlights from the outside world that were significant and important to them over the course of their 88 years in Belfast. Mind you, watching the world wasn't easy for the nuns in the early years – there was no incoming contact at all from radio or television until the time of the 1932 Eucharistic Congress.

Hosted in a different international city each year, this was the first time that Dublin, and Ireland, had been selected to hold this huge international gathering of Catholic clergy, religious dignitaries and laity. The climax of the Congress was on Sunday 26 June 1932 and the celebration of Solemn Pontifical High Mass in the Phoenix Park. Over 20,000 stewards marshalled the crowd, estimated at between 500,000 and one million people. The Mass included the singing at the offertory of 'Panis Angelicus' by Count John McCormack, the famous Irish tenor and papal knight, and a radio address from Pope Pius XI, broadcast live from the Vatican.

Such was the importance of the occasion, the Poor Clares managed to gain access to the media in the form of a 'wireless' as Journal One records.

> *In the year 1932 the year of the Eucharistic Congress in Dublin she* [Mother Colette] *managed to get the 'wireless' installed where we all could hear and follow each day all that was being done at the Congress. She got it on several special occasions afterwards.*

The nuns took an interest in and recorded other worldwide events, naturally including the deaths and elections of every Pope, except Pius XI (1922–1939), who served during the Poor Clare tenure in Belfast.

Regarding the election of Pope John XXIII, for example, Mother Colette, who was recording the events, wrote about the 'coronation' of the Pontiff as it was called in those days.

*28th October 1958: Pope John XXIII was elected 76 years old. He was crowned on Nov 4 (my birthday) so it was lovely getting His first blessing as Pope. Mr McAlinden of the Glen Road brought us his brother's T.V. set and we got leave from the Bishop. We had a wonderful morning. M. V. and myself were in the Chapter room before ¼ to 8 and the ceremonies had begun when we turned on the T.V. It was not over until ¼ past 12.*

The journal also contains some detail about the death of the Archbishop of Armagh, Cardinal Conway in 1977:

*April 17th 1977: Cardinal Conway, Primate of Ireland died. He had not been in good health on and off. Heart trouble – was advised by his Doctor to rest but managed to get to Rome for the Canonization Ceremony of St Oliver Plunkett – he had an operation – gall bladder removed and was better but then suddenly we were told he was really very ill and died shortly afterwards – he knew well himself and wrote a very nice parting letter to His good Bishops.*

That same year, the appointment of Monsignor Tomás O'Fiaich as the new Archbishop of Armagh is recorded with some detail in the journal:

*2nd October 1977: …we had the great joy of seeing the Consecration of Monsignor Tomás O'Fiaich (Fee) President of Maynooth College from 1974 as Bishop in Armagh's Cathedral – he has been chosen by our Holy Father Pope Paul VI to succeed the late Cardinal Conway as Primate of All Ireland. …He is the 113th successor of St Patrick in his home diocese of Armagh. Native of Crossmaglen where his brother is a Doctor; married with wife and family – these were present – with hundreds of people from here, there, everywhere and of all denominations. The President of Ireland Mr Hillery and all leaders of the Government present and former. Mr Mason from the North and leaders of the Non-Catholic Churches. Archbishop O'Fiaich gave the impression of being a very holy, humble man, with a great sense of humour and a great man whose aim is Peace and Brotherly love, Unity among all.*

*Aside from Church matters in 1977, the Poor Clare community kept up to date with developments within Northern Ireland, such as the visit of Queen Elizabeth II to celebrate her Silver Jubilee.*

Their sense of appreciation for their own calling comes out very clearly in this reference from *Tel-A-Vision*:

*'Heiresses and queens of the heavenly kingdom' – that is our glorious title, confirmed by our Holy Mother Clare. On her feast last year, we could not refrain from contrasting our fortunate lot with that of Queen Elizabeth, who was then in Northern Ireland, rounding off the cycle of her Silver Jubilee visits. What most impressed us about the visit was, that Her Majesty had a security guard of 32,000, while we, in our royal capacity, but for self-imposed enclosure, might roam the world, carefree, joyous and untroubled. Compassion for the Queen was uppermost in our hearts, while in all humility we thanked 'the Giver of all good gifts' for his choice of us. We had reason also to thank Him for keeping the 'bad boys' quiet during those days. So many things might have happened to put us all in a sorry plight. Only one bomb exploded when the Royal yacht was already homeward bound.*

In 1978, there were also accounts of the election and installation of Pope John Paul II, followed by some details of the preparation and excitement as the community undertook extra prayers and devotions for the success of Pope John Paul II's visit to Ireland in 1979.

*Oct 15: The nine days of morning and the Cardinals, 100 of them are in Rome for the Conclave to elect a successor to John Paul I…they shall meet today Sunday 15th to begin the Conclave with two Ballots in the morning and two in the afternoon.*

*17th On the second day another surprise awaited the world 'Karol Wojtyla – 58 Archbishop of Cracow, Poland was elected – the first non-Italian for 300 years.'*

*22nd Sunday We saw his instalment in the open in St Peter's Square at 10 o'clock in the morning – he wished it early – not to upset Television Programmes set for the evening and other Sunday enjoyments of people everywhere – thus showing a real human heart.*

*24th-28th September: We had a 'Holy Week,' as Mother called it, in preparation for the visit of Our Holy Father the Pope to Ireland.*

*27th September: The refectory decorated with yellow and white bunting and the large framed picture of Our Holy Father was brought down from the Portress' Room and hung above Our Lady's Altar in the Refectory. ...In the antichoir, just under the crucifix was a large – almost life-sized picture of Our Holy Father.*

*29th September–1st Oct: All our preparations were rewarded as we watched Our Holy Father the Pope, for those three memorable days, on a beautiful new coloured television – obtained for us by our dear friend and Father, Canon McAllister P.P*

Cardinal Conway (courtesy of the Cardinal Tomás
Ó Fiaich Memorial Library & Archive, Armagh)

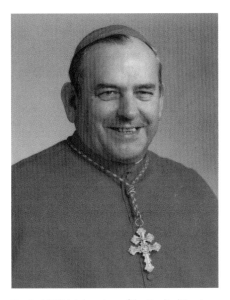

Cardinal O'Fiaich (courtesy of the Cardinal Tomás
Ó Fiaich Memorial Library & Archive, Armagh)

Later, Pope John Paul II's visit was acknowledged in this way: as the 'wonderful influence and spiritual renewal it has caused in our country.'

*We got the Holy Father's addresses on a tape and record and play them on special occasions, such as, St Patrick's Day and 29th June* [Feast of St Peter and St Paul]. *It is really lovely to hear his living voice again but so sad to realise that his earnest plea to the men of violence has fallen on deaf ears, if indeed it ever reached their ears.*

After the Pope's visit, Bishop Philbin came to see the nuns and told them of some of the impact of it had made. The journal contains the following:

*Better relations had been formed all round. One non Catholic lady had sent him £50 to help defray the expenses of the visit. He said the whole point of his referring to all this was to bring out the power of prayer. A whole nation had been praying beforehand for the success of the Pope's visit, and its prayer had been answered. That highlighted the value of our lives of prayer and was a confirmation of the validity of the contemplative life.*

The attempted assassination of Pope John Paul in 1981 was also recorded with a sense of helplessness:

*That brings us to that memorable day, the 13th May. Can we ever forget it? People were ringing from all directions to tell us that awful news of the Holy Father's attempted assassination. We almost needed that to make us realise that it was a reality. It seemed unthinkable, unacceptable. Everything in us and around us seemed to go limp – we felt so helpless. However, we tried to pray for the dear Holy Father, as we anxiously awaited each news bulletin. We prayed too for the poor unfortunate man who used the gun. When in Ireland, the Holy Father, you remember, asked us contemplatives to be with him, close to him. Can we not hear his plea again from his sick room? May we not fail him.*

The appointments of bishops and cardinals was always something the nuns would comment on and record. Bishop Cahal Daly's appointment as Bishop of Down and Connor and subsequently as Archbishop of Armagh following the death of Cardinal Tomás O'Fiaich was noted.

Further demonstrations that the nuns were paying attention to what was going on in the outside world as shown by their thoughts on three major events in 1997:

*We shared the sorrow of millions on the deaths of Mother Teresa (5th September) and Princess Diana (31st August), R.I.P., and we watched their funeral services on T.V.*

*26th September 1997: What a shock to learn of the earthquakes in Assisi at the end of September! Our hearts went to our Sisters, Brother Friars and so many other people afflicted with such a disaster. It's hard to imagine the extent of it. We know God is with them. This must be a very significant time in their lives, as they share so deeply in the Cross. I wonder would our holy Father Francis call it 'perfect joy!'*

The funeral of Pope John Paul II and the subsequent election of Pope Benedict in April 2005 brought these remarks:

*2nd April: We were able to view most of the T.V. coverage of the events surrounding Pope John Paul's death, lying in state, Requiem Mass and final departure. We shared the sadness of practically the whole world. It was as if everyone had lost a very dear and personal friend. So also we shared the gratification and elation, of witnessing such outpourings of love, respect and admiration of the Holy Father – a great, good and holy Pope, Mary's Pope. What a compelling example he has left us!*

*24th April: Having heard Cardinal Ratzinger's eloquent homily at Pope John Paul's Requiem Mass, his election to the Papacy, was no great surprise for us. We eagerly watched the programmes, surrounding his first days as Pope and his inauguration on the 24th April, as we thanked God, for such a worthy successor to Pope John Paul. May God continually bless our Holy Father.*

Among other big events that drew the notice of the nuns were the wedding of William and Catherine in 2011:

*29th April: We watched most of the Royal Wedding of William and Catherine, having taken our dinner with us to the Community Room.*

That same year, the year before the closure of the monastery, the visits of President Obama and Queen Elizabeth II are written about as 'feasts for the eyes':

*23rd May: The visits of President Obama, and (17th to 20th May) Queen Elizabeth to Ireland, also captured our attention for some time.*

*There were feasts there for the eyes, the mind, the ears, and the memories will be with us for a long while. However, one could almost heave a sigh of relief, when they got back home safely, and thank God for his goodness yet again.*

4.

All's well that ends well. Four days later Father Duffy could scarcely believe it, when notified that his car was in University Street. It had been driven from here and abandoned there. He found it intact, minus only a packet of books and a ten pound note. Because of that the case was not pursued any farther as it was very trivial in comparison with the major ones the police have to cope with every day.

We get quite a lot of news about El Salvador. Father Pat Hudson, while in St. Joseph's some months ago, gave us two long talks. He had worked for many years in El Salvador and Bolivia. More recently, Father Michael Lenihan, who is home on holidays related to us many of his experiences with the poor, suffering people there. Our holy Father Francis must be truly proud of these sons of his, who so generously leave their homeland to serve these needy people and try to alleviate their hardships.

We often hear of candlelight processions but rarely, if ever, of candlelight collations. That's what we had, one dark November evening, when the electricity failed for no apparent reason. Candles and candlesticks had to be unearthed from most unsuspected places, and when all was in order, we really enjoyed the diversion. There was a touch of Christmas about it. Nothing more serious than a fuse in the mains had afforded us the pleasure, we learned afterwards.

Early in December the Friars held a Draw in St. Joseph's to raise funds to buy a large statue of St. Anthony. Sr. Veronica was the lucky winner of one of the prizes, a black and white portable TV, her ticket having been drawn by Brother Michael. There was much rejoicing and teasing when we got the news, and to share Sister's joy, we watched something – can't remember what it was – on the screen.

Our beloved Bishop, Dr. Daly, came in good time with his Christmas greetings. It was the 23rd December. He offered Holy Mass for us and as usual shared with us some of his deep spirituality in his homily. It was a lovely prelude to our Christmas liturgy and celebrations.

A Taize group, consisting of adults and children, has been formed in our parish. They made their debut in our chapel, with beautiful music, singing, Scripture reading, intercessions, and silent prayer before a cross laid on the floor. It all began in darkness, except for dozens of little night lights aglow throughout the sanctuary, on the floor, altar, altar rails and pedestals. At the conclusion, about half a dozen children rushed into the sanctuary to put them out, and in their fervour blew the grease in all directions. It was fascinating to watch them. The group has promised to come again and they will be heartily welcome.

"Perfect joy" someone was exclaiming as I came on the scene. It was bedtime. Water was seeping through the ceiling on the third landing, while a few buckets, a small bath and a mop were posted here and there in an effort to catch the falling drops. An engineer, a good friend of ours, had been working on the heating system during the day, but knowing his efficiency, we could not accuse him of having done something amiss or of having left something undone. However, there was nothing to be done now except to contact him to see if he could throw any light on the situation.

Page 4 from 1986 edition of *Tel-A-Vision*

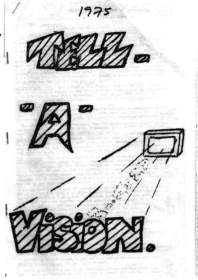

First edition of *Tel-A-Vision*, the inter-monastery annual newsletter

# Chapter Eleven

## The World Inside

Sr Paschal and Sr Lorette singing the responsorial psalm, 2012

—— 66 ——

*Do we sleep in our coffins and wear hair shirts?*

—— 99 ——

Behind taking an interest in Church, world and local community affairs, the nuns lived quietly and unobtrusively in their enclosed community life, and nothing defines the Poor Clares' true gifts to the city of Belfast more than their contemplative spirituality.

The Poor Clares were women of faith who believed in God the Father, Son and Holy Spirit; they loved and lived out of their Catholic faith deeply; they were people of personal and community prayer.

The minutes of a community meeting give some idea of the timetable for these times of prayer including their very early start:

> We start our morning vocal prayers at 5.45am. Sr Margaret goes out to prepare breakfast at 6.20pm. The community goes out at 6.25am.

> We will add the prayer before meditation before starting the Lectio Divina. Lectio Divina, dating back to the early traditions of monastic life, was a structured, prayerful reading of a scripture passage.

As well as the community prayer of the Liturgy of the Hours, the nuns had their own personal prayer time which the minutes record as:

> Meditation or mental prayer should be 30 minutes in the morning, 30 in the afternoon.

As Poor Clares, they were rooted in their Franciscan way of life with special devotion to St Clare of Assisi. All of this was rooted in a Biblical spirituality:

> Of late we have launched out on a Scripture comprehension course with Father Joseph enlightening and guiding us. Two hour sessions may seem rather long but it is so very interesting and helpful that we rarely think of the time factor. We are blessed in having such a golden opportunity of learning so much more about Jesus and the Good News…

As people of prayer, they knew of the need to trust God:

*'Lord, help me to remember that nothing is going to happen to me today that you and I together can't handle.'*

They knew difficult times:

*In our darker and more difficult days, when our two octogenarians, Sisters Gertrude and Helena, were ill and dying, when our number was down to two and our future so uncertain, the awareness of our Best Friend being the third Person in our home, as he had been with the Apostles in the boat on the stormy lake, was our comfort, our strength, our reassurance and our trust.*

They continued to trust in uncertain times:

*14th September (2010) Bishop Treanor returned to supervise the elections. With only five votes to be counted every time, the whole business was completed very quickly, with results similar to those of three years previously – Mother Abbess, Sr Immaculata, Vicaress, Sr Lorette and Second Discreet, Sr Paschal. With hearts full of gratitude to God for his unfailing kindness, we launch out into the deep in faith, trust and abandonment.*

The influence of St Francis was also a very important part of their spirituality:

*May 1981: As a preparation for the 8th centenary (Oct. 4th '82) O.H.F. St Francis – each month for our Chapter of Renewal, we are taking Franciscan themes.*

## The influence of St Clare

There were special celebrations to mark St Clare's life:

*Aug 11th '93 began our celebration of the 8th centenary of the birth of St Clare. The year will run until Oct. 4th '94.*

Her life was central to Poor Clare spirituality:

> *In preparation for our holy Mother Clare's feast, we had a triduum in our chapel, conducted by Father Martin. On each of the three evenings he spoke of our holy Mother at a different stage of her life – her childhood, 'conversion' and life at San Damiano, her last years and death. That prepared the way for a very fruitful celebration of the Transitus. The new form of the ceremony with various people taking part, was very expressive, and our congregation loved it. We had notified a few of our neighbouring parishes of the triduum, through their Sunday bulletins. Even though our new chapel seats more than twice as much as our old one, there was not enough seating room for all who turned up, so we had to send out all available chairs to the chapel.*

The nuns believed that by imitating her example they would be better examples of living the Gospel:

> *We are having a shrine to our holy Mother Clare erected in the 'Garden of Reflection' – our architect's term. This is a small garden for the public at the end of our chapel. Hopefully we will all get to know our holy Mother Clare better during the year, and mirror more of her spirit to the world.*

Their focus on St Clare of Assisi was to help them live the Gospel more fully:

> *…while we prepare for our Holy Mother Clare's feast, may she pray for us and help us to walk ever more faithfully and lovingly in the way of the holy Gospel.*

The community was clearly delighted in 1989 when Agnes of Prague a 'spiritual daughter' of St Clare, and to whom Clare had written four letters, was declared a saint:

> *The 12th November was a very happy day for us, when Blessed Agnes of Prague was canonised. In preparation, we had a triduum of evening devotions, and on the day itself we had solemn Vespers, with Fr Liam O.F.M. delivering a beautiful homily on the saint. We felt very close to our origins that day.*

# Sacrifice

An important part of their spirituality was sacrifice. The nuns had left everything to follow Jesus, including their families:

> Next came word that Sr Mary's mother was very low and as our revised constitutions allow Sisters in case of the death of their very close relations to go home for a week. Sr Mary went to Sligo to see her Mother, where all the Family were awaiting the end – after twenty -five years enclosed, she must have felt strange to be home again.

There is a record of the death of Sr Mary's mother and then Sr Mary's return to the convent; she did not attend the funeral:

> Our Sr Mary was due home on the 18th – all the family had gathered as the Mother was very low. She died that morning at 7 o'clock so it was easier to leave – she had had a really very good visit – the Mother knew her when she saw her early in the week but when she got near death she failed to recognise her. She got home on the evening of the 18th very satisfied with everything.

There are many examples of the nuns' self-sacrifice, such as the care for an elderly sister:

> 18th Sister Assisi's night nurse came back. Sister is keeping well D.G., [Deo Gratias – Latin for thanks be to God] but wakes a few times during the night which is very difficult for Sr Paschal, who looks after her, as Sr Paschal likes to come to Matins a few nights a week and so never gets a full night's sleep.

# Fun and humour

Even though they lived a very austere life the nuns were able to see and appreciate lighter moments in community life.

> In a video entitled Silent Light some of the nuns are filmed riding bikes, digging the garden, mowing the grass and playing tennis.

In the 2003 *Tel-A-Vision*, the newsletter describes some maintenance work on the paths with a positive finished result:

> *The job completed, the paths looked and were as good, as when they were treated. Now, our more agile members can cycle comfortably round the whole perimeter of the garden, without having to look out for 'potholes' and the like.*

A photograph dating back to the early 1980s shows four nuns getting ready for a game of tennis!

Some lovely moments of humour are recorded in the journal such as the entry for October 1976:

> *A lovely Electric Cooker arrived to the great joy of the Cooks. On the day of its arrival, the Aga went out unexpectedly; this was a cause of merriment at Recreation. However next day Aga's heat would have cooked an Ox so I expect they will live happily ever more.*

They were able to see a funny side to life in the horrors of Belfast at that time:

> *'Burn all the Irish Catholics.' That command issuing from Belfast in this troubled era might not surprise you until you hear that it came from no less a person than Rev. Mother Abbess. Yes, 'Burn all the Irish Catholics.' She said just that. It was bonfire day and Sr Catherine called at Mother's room to see if there were any contributions for the fire. 'No,' Mother said. Someone else had emptied her wastepaper basket earlier. Then as if on second thoughts she said: 'Burn all the Irish Catholics.' … We realised then that she was referring to newspapers and we laughed and laughed and laughed.*

There is a sense of enjoyment in a community picnic in the rain:

> *Our Holy Mother Clare's day provided the next lovely outing and then Our Lady's Assumption. Though the sky was overcast that evening we were not daunted, but prepared the tables and proceeded with the meal. Soon it began to rain but we could not accept the fact that it would disturb us, so we ate on and drank, chatted and laughed.*

*The rain however, wasn't going to be ignored. It began to pour, but as we were beside the house, we fetched umbrellas and rain capes, and most of us stayed to eat as much as we wanted, to the accompaniment of the rain pelting on our plastic canopy. You may conclude we were crazy but it was fun. That was the last of our pic-nics.'*

There was also a reference to a widely known blessing of animals ceremony in 1985:

*The Friars made history in Sailortown on the 6th October, when they held their first ceremony of the Blessing of Animals. ... There were animals there by the score – dogs 'of all denominations,' cats, mice, budgies, a porcupine, a pony, a white rabbit, which Father Liam 'took to his heart,' ...Music, singing and bunting added to the joy of the occasion, and proof of its success was a resolution to make it an annual event. The press gave it wide publicity. One report on it was entitled: 'Religion gone to the dogs.'*

When the weather allowed, the nuns held religious processions in the monastery grounds. One such procession in 1986 was led by a duck at one point:

*Ducks in our garden! There they were, a lady and two gents, waddling round the lawn where we opened the door on the first of the Rogation days, to see if weather permitted an outdoor procession. .... The last of the Rogation mornings was fine so we went outside for our procession and Lady Duck led the way for about fifty yards. She looked altogether unsure of herself and at last changed course and let us humans follow our own bent.*

There was great amusement for the nuns when one of the community confused many in the neighbourhood by ringing the Angelus bell at 5.20am one morning:

*On the two days following Christmas, our Mass was at 9am, so Mother said we could indulge in an extra sleep. However someone had to ring the angelus bell. On awaking, Sister Mary looked at the clock and thought it was 7.10am. She reasoned that although late for the Angelus, she should nevertheless ring the bell, as some of the neighbours might be depending on it.*

Anyone for tennis? Sr Gertrude, Sr Paschal, Sr Patrice and Sr Dominic circa 1983

Br Michael at the blessing of animals in 1985 (courtesy of Brendan Murphy)

Sr Paschal and Sr Mary in the old chapel before demolition (courtesy of Brendan Murphy)

Table fellowship (courtesy of Brendan Murphy)

*Back in the house, she peered at the clock again before returning to bed, and with eyes now wide open, she read 5.20am! …You should have heard the comments and questions after Mass! One woman said she got up and checked all her clocks, even the cuckoo one! Others wondered had it been a distress call, others simply didn't understand what was up. They know now for sure that Poor Clares can make mistakes!*

Some of the lighter moments in life were recorded by in the annual newsletter such as an encounter with a Jesuit priest called Fr Quinn:

*Enough to set Mother thinking. She had heard of a priest of that name in Edinburgh. 'Could he be the same James Quinn, S.J.' who translated so many of the hymns in our Breviary and hymn books?' She enquired of him and he said: 'yes.' …In some reference to his Jesuit brethren, Father said: 'All Jesuits are cast in the same mould but some of them are mouldier than others.'*

There is a sense of mischievous fun in the following extracts when two of the nuns to fly for the first time:

*5th August 1976: Mother Abbess and Sr Paschal made history to-day when they travelled by jet plane to Shannon Airport. …In Ennis, Mother Abbess had been given some plants – house and outdoor ones. They succeeded in smuggling this real Irish soil over the Border…*

*It was a new experience for both Mother and Sr Paschal – the Mistress of Novices – newer too was the experience of being searched even personally (which of course is the usual thing these desperate times in Ireland). It would seem unthinkable that Poor Clares would travel in such an expensive way but the cost of travel by train or car would even have been more so and then the difficulty of changing and would take so much longer. It only took about an hour by the Plane to get to Shannon Air Port and then on to Ennis to our Convent…*

The nuns also enjoyed time for singing and light hearted amusement:

*Unexpectedly on the 24th of March Fr Liam McCarthy OFM on vacation from Zimbabwe, arrived at our door, which was hastily opened for him.*

*We had a pleasant time together, sharing our news and views since his last visit. ….After Mass and breakfast next morning, he suggested a mini-concert, a sing-song; always a must. He sang some songs, and the inevitable one always requested, the 'Motor Bike.' No one else sings it as he does! He enjoyed the instrumental music supplied by our Filipino Sisters. Then it was time to leave. It was great getting first hand news of our Poor Clare Sisters, whose monastery is not far from the Friars. We admire and keep them in our prayers.*

Over the years, various school groups visited the monastery. It was very clear from these visits that the pupils had some very strange notions about life in an enclosed monastery which no doubt made the nuns laugh. The nuns sometimes kept a note about some of the questions they were asked by the young people:

*They seem to have departed anyway enriched by the knowledge that we are normal human beings. They had asked some of the usual questions: Do we sleep in our coffins and wear hair shirts? Etc.*

*On another occasion a group from the Dominican College at Fortwilliam came to the parlour, equipped with note-books, in which they had all their questions jotted down. These covered a wide range; one might almost say: 'from the sublime to the ridiculous.' 'what do you see as your role in Belfast at the present time?' 'what do you wear at night?' Curiously enough they didn't include the age-old ones about digging our graves with a spoon and ringing the bell when we are starving…*

The nuns made the most of an opportunity to dispel some of the myths:

*On the 26th October, (1982) the Irish News, THE Catholic paper in the North, carried an article on the Poor Clares. We had submitted it in response to an invitation from the Down and Connor Vocations Commission to all the communities of religious women in the North, to contribute a paper on their own history and work. The idea which inspired it was to dispel the bizarre notions some people have about us religious, and thus, perhaps, to prepare the way for vocations.*

New members from the Philippines also brought their own unique ways of relaxation including Sr Immaculata and her saxophone!

Mother Immaculata relaxing with a saxophone (courtesy of Brendan Murphy)

# Enclosed nuns have 'a precious vocation'

We continue our occasional series on religious orders in the North today with a glimpse into the history of the Poor Clare Order. This article is based on a feature supplied by a member of the Order.

ST. FRANCIS OF ASSISI, the eighth centenary of whose birth we celebrate this year, together with St. Clare, founded the Poor Clare Order.

It had been revealed to Francis that he should live according to the holy Gospel. Adopting the apostolic life of preaching, he strove to follow Christ in total poverty, humility and simplicity, giving all his love in return for the Divine love so manifest in the mysteries of Christ's infancy, Passion and sacramental life.

Clare's way of observing the holy Gospel was to live a life of prayer and penance, in solitude and silence, occupied mainly with God. In this way, she would give witness to Christ, praying on the mountain and living His hidden life at Nazareth, while sharing in the most universal way the hardships, miseries and hopes of all mankind.

Like Francis, she had grasped the meaning of Christ's total emptying of Himself to become a slave, so that, through His poverty, we might become rich, and her response was a life of complete poverty, not only the renunciation of earthly possessions and comforts, but the entire giving of self.

Many women came to join her way of life, and other monasteries soon sprang up in Italy, throughout Europe and other continents. Their form of poverty was not always understood. Pope Urban IV permitted some communities to have goods in common and these became known as Urbanists.

St. Clare pursued her ideal of poverty to the end, and it was only on her deathbed that she obtained confirmation of her rule. Only, when Pope Innocent III offered to release her from her vow of poverty, she said to him: "Holy Father, never do I wish to be released in any way from the following of Christ."

## Had to flee

By the 15th century, relaxations had crept into the Poor Clare Order, and God then raised up St. Colette of Corbie in France to restore it to its first fervour. She had been a humble recluse, and it was only after several revelations and chastisements from God, that she undertook the work of reform. She restored the observance of the early rule in several monasteries and founded many others. For these, she wrote new constitutions and all who accepted them were known as Poor Clare Colettines.

After Vatican Council II, new constitutions were drawn up for the entire Poor Clare Order, and approved by the Holy See in 1973. These bring Poor Clare life into line with modern reforms in the Church, and up to date for 20th century living.

The earliest recorded date of Poor Clares coming to Ireland is 1629. In that year, a group from Belgium settled in Dublin, where their numbers soon multiplied. Due to the religious persecution of the period, they were driven from one place to another and suffered untold hardships. Many of them had to flee to the Continent.

A community of Poor Clare Colettines was set up in Carlow in 1893. Since then, other foundations have sprung up. There are now seven monasteries in the country, but one on Cliftonville Road, Belfast, is the only one in Northern Ireland.

Poor Clares have a well-balanced life of prayer, work, study and recreation. The legacy of Eucharistic devotion left them by their bold Founders, finds expression in daily worship of the Blessed Sacrament exposed. The chanting of the Divine Office both day and night is their sacred and privileged duty. All the sisters engage in simple household duties. Those with special talents for printing, music and other arts have ample opportunity for using and developing them.

"The Church is both zealous in action and dedicated to contemplation." (Sacrosanctum concilium). "It is, therefore, both legitimate and necessary that some of Christ's followers should give expression to the contemplative character of the Church by withdrawing into solitude to lead this particular type of life." (Venite Seorsum I). That is why Poor Clares freely and lovingly make a solemn vow of enclosure, not as an end in itself but as a support for their prayer life. They do not run away from the world but answer a divine call to do something very positive, namely, to worship God.

When you specialise in one thing you must of necessity bypass many others. "It must not be thought that . . . nuns . . . separated from the rest of mankind are aloof from them. On the contrary, they are united with them in a more profound sense in the heart of Christ." (Venite Seorsum III). Sometimes, when a young girl enters a Poor Clare monastery, people say: "What waste of a young life! What a waste of talents! She could have done so much for people in need!"

## Fruitful

That remark echoes the one made by Christ's disciples on His feet: "Why this waste? This could have been sold at a high price and the money given to the poor." (Mt. 26: 8-9). Note that Jesus did not agree with them. While not denying the needs of the poor, He upheld the propriety of the woman's action.

Anything given to God cannot be wasted because He has absolute right to the highest service we can give Him.

In the time of St. Clare, the needs of humanity were as pressing as they are to-day. To mention only two: leprosy was rife in Italy and illiteracy was common, especially among women. Yet, under Divine inspiration, she founded an enclosed contemplative Order. The Church approved than and has always done so. Countless passages might be cited from allocutions of Popes and Vatican II documents in proof of this. To quote only two: Pope John XXIII said: "In all truth, it is these souls (contemplatives) who . . . exercise in silence within the Church, the apostolate which is the most universal and the most fruitful." At Maynooth in 1979, Pope John Paul II said: "Never was the contemplative vocation more precious or more relevant than in our modern restless world."

The many religious, who so generously devote their lives to works of the external apostolate, and enclosed contemplatives, complement one another. All are members of Christ's Mystical Body and fulfil their own distinctive functions to fulfil.

The value of a vocation to the Order of the Poor Clares, *Irish News* article 26 October 1982

# Community life

There are countless references to the various aspects of community life including one to the different offices which made up a Poor Clare community:

> *Abbess, Vicaress, Discreet, Mistress of Novices, Portress, Infirmarian, Sacristan, Refectorian and two cooks.*

The journals and newsletters reveal a fairly simple life style. It was thanks to a generous benefactor that they were able to buy new beds:

> *June 1977: As it is now almost impossible for us to get Straw suitable for our Beds and likewise hard to get mattresses to fit our old-fashioned four posters – it was agreed to get modern beds and mattresses combined – it was a big item but our great Benefactor together with 3 friends of his donated 14 such beds – the old ones have been turned into presses for the cells, where the new beds are. The old beds had a box attached to them at the foot to hold one's clothes etc. so the Press now does duty for that – the beds alas were each broken up and Jack and his hand men converted them into Presses. A few of the old beds are still intact, one of which we hold in great respect as it was our dear Mother Colette's for many years while she was Vicaress. … These beds cost £25 each – thought cheap as Prices are nowadays.*

Community life was clearly very important:

> *17th Nov Srs Francis and M. Paschal returned to their own community in Ennis, having given themselves previously to us for two wonderful years. Our sorrow was turned into joy that night when Sr Veronica from Bothwell came for two years. Sister is a gem!*

> *Nov. 9th Dear Sr Gertrude returned home to her convent in Drumshanbo. We were happy for her having been away for three years, but what a loss for us!*

They lived an austere life. It was only in 1981 that the whole house had warm water:

> *July 1st 1981. An Immersion Heater has been installed in the Novitiate Pantry. Until now the novitiate sisters only had cold water.*

During the rebuilding of the monastery, three of the nuns remained on in the gate lodge. The 1989 annual newsletter describes their life:

> *You may wonder what kind of life we live here at the lodge. It was very strange at first, but we are getting more and more accustomed to it. We get up as usual at 5.30am and go over to choir for Lauds and mental prayer, then back to the lodge for breakfast. Our Mass is at 8am and we have exposition until 9.30am. We cannot have midday office together in Choir as only one of us would be free to go there at that time, but have it together in Choir as only one of us would be free to go there at any time, but have it together in the lodge after dinner. Two of us go over together in the evening for office for the dead, mental prayer and Vespers, and we have exposition during that time.*

There was clearly a sense of excitement in being introduced to some 'modern' technology:

> *Jan. 1st 1981: Father Michael Duffy O.F.M. cap. Visited us and showed us scenes of their ... Open Chapter ... It was our first experience of Video Tape and an experience it was.*

There was a simple appreciation of any work done on the monastery:

> *June 1978 During the past few months we have had Painters, electricians renewing the cells and made a very convenient and compact cell for any sister disabled like dear Sr Thérèse on the ground floor – all cells were painted – the choir is now nearly finished. White and apple Green everywhere – looks so fresh and bright.*

Even though the community was attracting less members than in the earlier days, there was still considerable interest and fascination about their life in the enclosure:

*Dec. 2nd 1982: In June Mr Delargy from U.T.V. had asked permission of Bishop Philbin to make a short Documentary Programme on the life and role of our community. So for the last few months, teams from the studios have come in a few times to film and interview the sisters. At last, after very much prayer and work, it was shown and we have received many letters of gratitude and appreciation of the programme and ourselves. Next day U.T.V. sent a beautiful bouquet of flowers. They had already given Mother a money gift, towards the expenses of electricity, used on Sound and Lighting.*

The Ulster Folk and Transport museum even borrowed a habit for an exhibition:

*Early August last year (1990) saw us involved in a very unusual affair. …the Ulster Folk Museum is running a three-year exhibition on married and religious life in Ulster, over the past few hundred years, and we, among other religious, were asked to co-operate. At first it seemed only a matter of supplying a few data of information. Then it advanced to a tape recording and some old photos. By then it would appear that our interviewer, Lynda Ballard, had gained enough confidence to request a habit, and we supplied it, secretly hoping that the sight of a fully-clad 'Poor Clare' in the Museum, would arouse the interest of some of the many young people who go there.*

Celebrations such Jubilees marking years of religious life were very important to the community:

*August 1978: We had a big Jubilee beginning on August 2nd, Feast of Our Lady of the Angels. 'Portiuncula' Sr Assisi a Diamond Jubilarian – Mother Vicaress Sr Catherine her Golden and Sr Mary of the Angels – her Silver Jubilee. There were great preparations – practising singing Mass and Hymns, Decorations, little plays etc. Our good Canon McAllister came as chief celebrant of the Mass and there were 6 with Him. It was lovely & the Jubilarians renewed the Vows after the Gospel. Fr McAllister made the Ceremony very impressive by delivering a fine Homily on the Poor Clare life and congratulating each sister separately. Sr Assisi from Dublin, Sr Catherine from Meath and Sr Mary from Sligo. There followed a week of enjoyment – music and Plays and songs etc. etc. which all seemed to enjoy well.*

*July 1st: We celebrated with Mother Paschal, the Silver Jubilee of her Holy Profession.*

One of their rare appearances outside the monastery was to vote:

*Westminster elections took place on the 6th of May, and so, bright and early on that morning, Srs. Paschal and Mary, walked to the school, a few yards up the road to cast our vote. It was just an in-and-out affair; just one X was all we had to write on our paper. Previously, we could have had two more choices.*

They have a fascination with the world around them:

*Like so many others, we watched the total eclipse of the sun on television on the 11th August. Happening on the exact second predicted, it gave a good lesson in punctuality! Sister Marra demonstrated for us how some Filipino Sisters handle such an event. She placed a basin of water on the ground in the garden, and there you could clearly see the eclipse without any threat to your eyesight. Try it next time!*

Whilst they are living a simple life, they are also keen to use modern means of communication:

*A very kind benefactor provided us with a computer, printer and scanner in March, last year, and we are trying to build up our computer skills, in so far as time allows. With only eight of us here, and some of these off the work list, there isn't much spare time available.*

They were open to learn new things:

*Of late there seems to be a great renewal of interest in icons, especially in this part of the country. Sr Paschal here has found a new outlet for some of her hidden talents. She attends one of the two classes, held in our Conference room every Monday, except during recess. None of the rest of us feels that way inclined, but some items of information trickle through to us now and then, like the fact that you write an icon, not paint it, and you read it, when completed. The tutor, Philip Brennan is an excellent tutor. The work is done in a prayer context, prayer at different paints of the session.*

*Sr Paschal has completed one icon, and it is a masterpiece.*

In essence, the nuns whilst being people firmly rooted in prayer, relying on their faith, loved people and joined with them in their joys and sorrows.

*Our letters to you may be few and far between, but we often visit you in spirit, especially in times of celebration, and when grief and sorrow knock on your doors. Then we pray specially for you.*

The importance of silence – *Journal Two*

The farewell Mass: Sr Mary, Mother Immaculata, Sr Paschal, Fr Perry Gildea CM, Michael McCann, Sr Lorette and Mother Encarnation

Celebrating the Feast of St Clare: Jim McEldowney, Sr Immaculata, Angela McCann, Deirdre Fearon, Sr Mary, Sr Lorette, Brid McEldowney, Sr Paschal and Michael McCann

# Chapter Twelve

## Resting in Peace

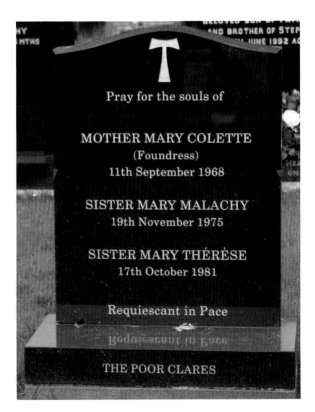

One of the seven headstones in Milltown cemetery where the Poor Clares
are buried (courtesy of Rev Elizabeth Hanna)

—— 66 ——

*She calmly and peacefully waited for Sister Death*

—— 99 ——

Anyone looking back over the 88 years of the existence of the Poor Clare community in Belfast, can only admire and appreciate the unique contribution the nuns made to the lives of so many people. Although enclosed and dedicated to a life of contemplation and prayer, their influence clearly extended far beyond the walls of the monastery. It is impossible to quantify the solace people found in one of the parlours in the monastery on the Cliftonville Road. The monastery church was a very special place, even a 'thin place' to borrow a phrase from Celtic spirituality where the veil between heaven and earth was especially thin.

It was with a deep sadness that people bade the nuns farewell in August 2012. Whilst it is true that the monastery may have closed at that time and the remaining members of the community dispersed back to the Philippines or to Carlow, the legacy of the nuns' life of prayer, worship and ministry of listening remains – most especially in the memories of the people who were helped by them.

At the time of writing, several people who became friends of the nuns regularly visit Sr Paschal and Sr Mary in Carlow. Many of the people who went to Mass in the monastery when the nuns were still there, continue to worship at Mass in Sacred Heart Church to where the Mass was transferred in September 2012. The nuns' 'invaluable legacy of prayerful support and a sense of the closeness of God', to quote Bishop Treanor's press release on the closure of the monastery, are still appreciated and remembered. The Poor Clares were indeed a compassionate presence in the wounded and wonderful city of Belfast.

In their journals the Poor Clare nuns often spoke about and made many entries related to 'Sister Death'. They recognised that dying was a part of living, and of course there was a certain amount of joy that in being called to their Heavenly Father they would be at their journey's end. A happy and holy death was often the nuns' greatest wish.

Due to the way the community's records were kept over the years, it would be impossible to be exact about every nun who lived in the Belfast Poor Clare community over its timespan in Belfast. In its heyday in the mid 1950s, there were 21 members of the community on the electoral rolls.

Over the 88 years, some of the nuns stayed for a short period of time in the community but then went on to live in other communities or indeed left the order. Others were in in the monastery as a visitor, on a temporary basis or for just a short stay.

In the end 'Sister Death' ensured that 21 nuns came to be buried in the cemetery within the monastic enclosure, and after the closure of the foundation were later reinterred in Milltown Cemetery in Belfast or in other cemeteries according to the wishes of their families. Of the five founding nuns – the 'foundation stones' – as they are called in the journals, only one, Sr Mary O'Connor, was not buried in the monastery's cemetery. She was buried in St Damian's in Donnybrook, Dublin because the monastery cemetery had not been established at the date of her death.

Death must come to us all, and throughout my researches I have been deeply conscious of the dedication of these women to their vocation, their witness to Jesus Christ and their willingness to embrace and even welcome 'Sister Death'. The purpose of this closing chapter and these following short obituaries is therefore to pay tribute to the nuns' vocations, their Poor Clare way of life, and the legacy they left behind in Belfast. May they rest in peace.

## Sr Mary O'Connor

Sr Mary was born Eileen O'Connor around 1894. She was received into the Poor Clare Monastery of St Damian in Donnybrook, Dublin on 16 June 1915 and was given the name of Sr Mary of the Sacred Heart. She made her final profession on 22 August 1916. Sr Mary's name was included amongst the names of the five nuns in the initial request which  Mother Genevieve made to the archbishop of Dublin, Archbishop Edward Byrne. She was one of the original community who arrived in Belfast in 1924. Sr Mary was part of the community when they moved to Dunowen on the Cliftonville Road in 1926. After only 10 days in her new home, Sr Mary, who had been ill for some time, died on 14 June 1926.

Her death is recorded in this way:

> *Poor Sister Mary's condition now became serious, and we were only ten days in our new Convent when God called her to Himself. R.I.P. She had been well purified by suffering and having received the Last Sacraments was ready to meet the Divine Bridegroom. She was the first Victim of the Foundation – having joyfully made the sacrifice of her beloved Monastery – St Damian's. It was June 14th. As we had no cemetery, her remains were taken to Donnybrook where she was buried in the Convent where she had received the Habit of Our Holy Mother Saint Clare, and made her Holy Profession. Although we missed her more than words could tell, we were happy for her sake, and knew she would be our special intercessor in Heaven.*

In 1959, Mother Colette Egan after attending a meeting in the Poor Clare Monastery in Galway travelled back to St Damian's in Donnybrook where she stayed overnight before travelling back to Belfast. She wrote movingly about her visit to Sr Mary's grave:

> *I had a unique privilege there to visit the grave of Sr Mary. R.I.P. She came to Belfast with us in the foundation in 1924 and died in 1926 shortly after we came to the Cliftonville Road. One of the Sisters took my photo standing at her grave – it was 35 years since I had been to Donnybrook.*

## Sr Paschal Hughes

Sr Paschal was born Bridie Hughes around 1892. She was received into the Poor Clare Monastery of St Damian in Donnybrook, Dublin on 19 August 1918 and was given the name of Sr Paschal of the Blessed Sacrament. She made her final profession on 8 Sept 1919. Sr Paschal was one of the first nuns of the group of five who came from Dublin to form the community in Belfast in 1924. She wrote the initial entries in Journal One which told the story of the first contact with Bishop MacRory and the setting up of the new foundation in Belfast. Another nun takes up the story:

> *The foregoing pages were written by Sister M. Paschal (Hughes) - one of the Sisters who had come from Donnybrook in 1924. They were written a few months before her death. She had been in poor health for many years. She*

*was always an exemplary Religious and had a wonderful devotion to the Blessed Sacrament and the Holy Sacrifice of the Mass, and an ardent love for the Divine Office. She was Mistress of Novices for several years before her health failed. Her death came as a great shock to us on Christmas Eve 1949 RIP. She was the first to be buried in our Cemetery.*

Sr Paschal died at the age of 57. The entry in the journal described her death in this way:

*1949, Dec 24! Sister Paschal (Hughes) died. R.I.P. She had been an invalid for years but took suddenly worse the middle of the day on the 24th. We got the Doctor & priest – she became unconscious shortly after & died just before mid-night Mass – she died of a cerebral haemorrhage. She was one of the Foundation Stones of this Foundation. She celebrated her Silver Jubilee a few years before.*

## Sr Patricia Ward

Sr Patricia was born Nellie Ward in 1884 or 1885. She was received into the Order of the Poor Clares on 23 January 1911 and was given the name of Sr Patricia of the Seven Dolors. Her profession took place on 6 March 1912. She was another of the original five who came to Belfast in 1924.

In the entry describing the arrival of the five nuns, she was referred to as 'Mother Ward' which would indicate she held a position of responsibility in the monastery in Dublin.

The following details were recorded about her Jubilee celebrations:

*…Mother Patricia another Foundation stone whose Silver Jubilee followed that of Mother Colette in 1937 – she was then Mother Vicaress – such a simple generous soul – a real Franciscan. Prayerful, mortified – a marvellous worker and full of fun too. Like all other Jubilees hers was marked by the usual celebrations and decorations …and little plays which she opened herself in the morning at our 'Bit' as we called the fasting Breakfast in those good old days. I'm sure that morning we had perhaps a hot bun to make the occasion and of course Recreation when quite unexpectedly in came the Jubilarian (who was from Kilcock) by the way. She was dressed as a 'Duck' and walked in just as any duck would do. She had some very funny verses. Though from Kilcock, she was just a duck – such a 'dear little duck too.' She had hoped to have an egg for each dear sister for her Breakfast but that could not be – all she could give was a spiritual one for each – she had a string which was unnoticeable hanging from the ceiling – when she gave it a pull down came a great green bag with a gift for each – it was the unusual that made us laugh and enjoy it so much. That kind of thing was characteristic of her; and she was full of charity and service for others. She was also Cook and Infirmarian in the early years of the Foundation. She was the third of the Foundations stones to die (1959).*

Sr Patricia died on 2 September 1959 at the age of 75. She was the second member of the community to be buried in the cemetery within the monastic enclosure. Her remains were later exhumed and reburied in Milltown Cemetery.

## Sr Magdalen Power

Sr Magdalen was born Bridget Power in 1906 or 1907. Details of her life and profession of vows are scant, however a reference to her in Journal One offers this background information:

*This year 1937…Fr Evangelist OFM gave us a Triduum* [A three-day time of talks and prayer services] *and sent us a Postulant (Sr M. Magdalen afterwards), another of his children* [spiritual children] *who had entered two years or less before – both of these were in the 3rd Order Merchant's Quay Dublin…*

The next reference to Sr Magdalen comes in a letter, written a few days after the Belfast Blitz by Mother Colette:

> *The first night Sr Magdalen and myself got up at the siren and went down to the parlour with the community – they were hammering away at their aspirations to the Sacred Heart.*

This was a reference to another community of religious sisters living on the Glen Road in Belfast, where some of the Poor Clares stayed for a short time during the Blitz before going on to Newry.

In January 1966, there was a severe outbreak of flu when nine of the community had to stay in bed for two weeks. Sr Magdalen died unexpectedly at that time, aged only 59. The community journal records:

> *…on 9th February, we got a great shock. Sister Magdalen (Power) who was the cook at this time died suddenly as a result of Thrombosis. She was a most generous Sister & during all the time of Flu she never spared herself. Indeed it can be said her death was simply the result of her great charity; how many times she went to the top of the house and down again during these days is known to God alone. When found stretched out on her bed in her cell she was still warm and Fr Tronson who was hearing Confessions at the time came and Anointed her. It was a dreadful shock for Mother Abbess (Paul), as it was she who found her. … She was buried two days later.*

After describing the Requiem Mass for Sr Magdalen and naming all the priests who were present at it, the journal notes that Sr Magdalen was 'an exemplary and self-sacrificing religious.'

# Mother Colette Egan

Mother Colette was born Colette Egan on 4 November 1884. She was received into the Poor Clare Monastery of St Damian in Dublin in 1909. She made her final profession on 24 February 1910. Mother Colette was one of the original five 'foundation' nuns who came to Belfast in 1924. Owing to the important part she clearly played in the life of the community, Journal One devotes a large amount of space to her life and death:

*11.15am on 11th September 1968 – the death of Mother Colette*
*Mother Mary Colette. Colette Egan was born in Dunleary, on November 4th 1884. These few notes are not a Biography – I leave that to a better hand, so I pass over her early years. She entered the Poor Clare Colettine Monastery, Donnybrook August 15th 1909. In 1924, she was sent as Abbess, along with 4 other Nuns to make a new Foundation in this City, and so we gave her the Title of Mother Foundress, though Mother M. Genevieve (Stead) Abbess in Donnybrook at that time was responsible for bringing all the arrangements to a successful issue.*

*Mother Colette all though her life in the Monastery, was an excellent Religious; very particular about The Divine Office and all the Spiritual exercises and a staunch upholder of our Holy Rule of Constitutions, in the kindly spirit of St Clare and St Colette, but always very firm in these matters. She did not indeed pass over faults but, at the same time she was very kind and considerate. The sick were a special object of her great charity and she saw to it that they received all necessary attention, spiritual and temporal. Always a very hard working religious, and blessed by God with great health and strength, she gave of her best to her Community as long as she was able. Her last illness came on her on the Anniversary (56th) of her Holy Profession, Feb. 24th 1967 – heart failure, with complications.*

*Two days later she was Anointed, and the Doctor did not expect her to live beyond 48 hours. But, thank God the holy Anointing revived her. Between that time and her death in Sept. '68, she received the great grace of Anointing several times.*

*She was full of kindness, patience, and good humour – always ready to enjoy a joke. On the 10th Sept. she received Holy Communion for the last time; during the day it became evident the end was coming. She was quiet and peaceful and was able - in a muffled voice – to let us know she was quite happy. On one occasion, a short time before her death a Sister was speaking to her on that subject; she told the Sister she was quite happy about it 'but' she added, 'if only I could take you all with me!' Those words speak volumes! She passed away peacefully at 11.15 a.m. on Sept. 11th (Wednesday).*

Mother Colette was 83 when she died. She was buried in the community cemetery.

## Sr Oliver Feeney

Sr Oliver was born Kathleen Feeney in or around 1895 in Kilcock, Co. Kildare. She was received into the Order of the Poor Clares on 12 May 1921 according to the records from St Damian's monastery in Dublin. She made her solemn profession on 21 May 1922. She was given the name Sr Mary Oliver of Jesus Crucified. Sr Oliver arrived in Belfast in 1925, a year after the establishment of the first monastery, to provide additional support to the fledgling community:

*When Mother Genevieve came to visit her little Foundation on the 23rd July 1925, Sister M. Oliver who had made her Final Profession in St Damian's on the 21st June accompanied her - Sister Mary had become seriously ill, so Mother thought it well to have another Sister in Belfast.*

Sr Oliver was considered as one of the 'foundation stones'. She died on 17 September 1970 in St John's Nursing Home, beside the Mater Hospital in Belfast and was buried in the community cemetery. Her remains were later exhumed and reinterred in Milltown Cemetery.

# Mother Paul Hobbins

Mother Paul was born Teresa Hobbins in or around 1889. According to the records kept in St Damian's Monastery in Dublin, her reception ceremony into the order took place on 24 July 1913. She was given the name of Sr Mary Paul of Jesus. She made her solemn profession on 12 August 1914 in St Damian's. Ten years later she became part of the original five nuns who went to Belfast to set up the new foundation.

She was evacuated to Newry during the Belfast Blitz and wrote to the community in Dublin about the experience, as we saw earlier. Mother Paul was the last of the 'foundation stones' to die. The community journal records her death in this way:

> *November 18th 1972 at 9.30pm. Our dear Mother Paul died a holy and happy death after six months of illness very patiently borne. She was a native of Kerry & also lived for some time in Limerick. She entered in Donnybrook and was there for some years before being sent on the Belfast Foundation. The many Mass cards received show how well she was known & loved throughout the North & beyond it. Good & generous, she could never see or know of anyone in want without trying to help them. May she rest in peace.*

Mother Paul died in 1972 at the age of 83 and was buried in the community cemetery. Her remains were later exhumed and then buried in Milltown Cemetery.

# Sr Malachy McHenry

Sr Malachy was born Kathleen McHenry on 23 September 1912 in Portaferry, Co. Down. Sr Malachy had trained as a nurse and been nursing in the Mater hospital before joining the monastery in Belfast.

There are several references to her in the correspondence including the time of the Belfast Blitz. When the community left the monastery during the Blitz, Sr Malachy along with other nuns stayed for two days in a convent in the Glen Road before going on to stay at the Carmelite convent in Newry until they returned to Belfast.

The journal records that she had been in hospital earlier in 1975 but had recovered. *Journal One* recorded her death in this way:

> *Sister Malachy McHenry (Portaferry) was an invalid for 34 years with multiple sclerosis. All during those long years she did her best to 'keep with' the Community at all the Spiritual Exercises and Recreation. She was an exemplary Poor Clare. Died 19th Nov 1975.*

The 1975 edition of *Tel-A-Vision* notes she died on the Feast of St Agnes of Assisi. St Agnes was St Clare's sister and was also in community with Clare. Also noted is that in a community ballot to have a patron saint for the year, she had drawn St Agnes of Assisi. Sr Malachy was 63 when she died.

Pray for the souls of

# Sr Francis Bryce

Sr Francis was born Frances Bryce on 28 April 1898 in Portaferry, Co. Down. She died on 2 February 1977 at the age of 79 as recorded by the 1977 edition of *Tel-A-Vision:*

> *Perhaps our most important visitor this year was Sr Death. Twice she came - or rather sent by the Lord: that makes all the difference to the kind of reception she gets in a community. She stole away two of our gems, Srs Francis and Anthony.*

The community journal records her death as follows:

> *Sr Frances died in the Mater hospital – she had been there following a heart attack a week before – this had been a second time for her to be brought out after a similar attack. She had been Portress for twenty years almost – so the people will miss her – we were expecting it as she has been failing for some time – her death will bring us many graces and blessings – not least the remembrance of her virtuous and saintly life. Our good Bishop found time to come to the Funeral and officiate at the Graveside after a concelebrated Mass... Many of her relatives were able to be present, and be inside for the Burial and carried the Coffin.*

The yearly newsletter acknowledges Sr Francis in this way:

> *Her death left a void, not only in the community, but also in the hearts of the countless friends she, as portress, had made in the parlour; the people who say such things as: 'I could tell all my little troubles to Sr Francis,' or 'I still have the last letter she wrote to me, and I'll treasure it.' Their tears and the countless Masses they had offered for her, witness to their esteem for her and the comfort and help she must have brought them.*

# Sr Anthony Lloyd

Sr Anthony was born Gwendoline Margaret Mary Lloyd on 6 March 1906 in Dublin. She died on 20 May 1977 aged 71. The yearly newsletter and community journal records the lead up to her death:

*St Anthony's health had been declining for some time, though she had been under doctor's care. Even before she went to hospital she was longing to die, 'to rejoin Sr Francis' as she used to say, but she had to wait ten long weeks before her desire was granted. That was on the feast of St Bernardine, with whom she shared a great devotion to the Holy Name of Jesus.*

*May 20th Our dear Sr Anthony died in the Mater after suffering much. Doctors decided after much testing that her case was malignant and finally decided not to operate to give her all that would mean and [then] mean nothing. She was so happy to die and edified everyone by her virtue and holiness. We feel her loss but are glad God took her as she desired so much to go to Him. She was a most lovely character – so very charitable and understanding – very cultured and so well informed about everything especially historical – wrote so many martyrologies and make Poetry while you wait; so to speak. She was sacristan for years and never spared herself in this lovely duty which she dearly loved – keeping everything spick and span till she was no longer able to keep going. We all remarked that she died on a Friday; the funeral could not be till Monday – so she had a longer while before Him in our choir than would otherwise have been – it was just a sentiment of course as we all hoped and believed she was already enjoying the Beatific Vision.*

*She had been sacristan for years, so you can understand how we miss her about the choir. One of the Sisters paints this personality pen portrait of her: 'she was a praying nun, holy and fervent, poetess, playwright, linguist, a most interesting and enjoyable conversationalist at recreation, and silent and prayerful during the day.'*

# Sr Clare Gaynor

Sr Clare was born Mary Gaynor on 24 April 1892 in the Republic of Ireland, as indicated on her death certificate. The community journal records her death in this way:

*November 18th: Sr Clare died at about 10 o'clock. Mass during the Retreat was at 12 o'clock each day so the Priest gave her from a spoon the Precious Blood which she was able to swallow – she quietly and sweetly passed off a short time after. She had been in St John's Hospital some time earlier in the year and came hime very well but had to be careful and looked after - she had had 2 bad Heart attacks. She just got sick several times – she was able to come to the Retreat but just got another attack and though somewhat conscious, did not seem to recognise us. Sisters stayed up with her that one night and next day the Lord came for her. She was always and everywhere so bright and cheerful, ever full of fun - she had a great sense of humour - at the same time very prayerful and devoted to the Choir and the Office. She loved the Blessed Sacrament spending long spells with our dear Lord. She was in her eighties and had had several operations early in life so was not latterly able for much about the House but was always ready for Prayer. RIP.*

The newsletter gives some further details of her death:

*Our lovely retreat in November… had a dramatic ending with the death of our dear Sr Clare R.I.P. She had taken part in the retreat with the rest of us on the first three days. Then she began to feel unwell.*

*On the sixth and last day, about twenty minutes after receiving Holy Communion, she slipped away imperceptibly, surrounded by us all. … The chants of the Mass that day were most appropriate, especially the Communion verse. It ran: 'The bridegroom is here; let us go out to meet Christ the Lord.'*

Sr Clare died on 18 November 1977 aged 85 was buried in the community cemetery. Her remains were later reinterred in Milltown Cemetery.

# Sr Joseph Grogan

Sr Joseph was born Mary Grogan on 12 March 1894 in Belfast. She came from Orient Gardens in Sacred Heart Parish, the neighbouring parish to where the nuns set up their foundation in 1924. Sr Joseph became the first novice in the community in September 1924.

*Our first Reception Ceremony was on the 5th August 1925 - Mother's choice of name for the first Novice gave evidence of two of her special devotions - Saint Joseph and the Holy Spirit.*

The annual newsletter records a celebration to mark her 50 years as a nun:

*September 4th 1976. Sr Joseph, one of our Golden Jubilarians, had the joy of welcoming her sister, Sr Margaret Mary, a P.C. Extern Sister in Ellesmere, for the Jubilee celebrations. The home from which Sr Joseph stepped, so many years ago to become a Poor Clare nun, was then just across the road from here, so you can guess what memories they had to share. Sr Joseph was the first postulant of the new foundation and has rendered invaluable services to the Community down the years as cook, Novice Mistress, gardener and general 'handyman' with several sturdy proofs of her skilled carpentry through the Monastery.*

Sr Joseph had also been responsible for writing the community journal. Her last entry was on Sunday 22 October 1978. She died on 31 December 1978.

*Jan 1979: The writing has changed, so also has – 'life has changed not ended' for our dear Sister Joseph who went home to God on December 31st. It was very fittingly the feast of The Holy Family and the community were down at Mass, which was transmitted up to Sr Joseph in the Infirmary. She had received Holy Communion the morning before. It was after Mass when Sr Paschal Joseph (Infirmarian) went up to prepare her for the same privilege that she found Sr Joseph who must just have expired.*

*We wonder was she still conscious to hear the Gospel being read 'Now Master you can let Your servant go in peace.' RIP. Life is also changed for us her little community of twelve – 11 Solemnly Professed sisters and our little postulant Linda, who entered on 22 August 78. Being the first postulant to enter in Belfast and while the little band of Pioneers were still living in Mossville, Sr Joseph proved how true her Poor Clare Vocation was when she persevered through all the difficulties and hardships of a new foundation. She was an inspiration to her sisters during the next fifty four years when she served the community as Discreet, Novice Mistress, Gardener, Cook, Portress, Sacristan and many other duties. So life indeed must be different without her, whom we all loved and thought of as one of our Foundation Stones.*

*Sr Joseph was eighty-five and had failed greatly over the last year and then she got the bad 'flu which struck Mother (Michael) and several of the sisters before Christmas. Poor Sr Joseph got so weak, she just couldn't pull up.*

Sr Joseph was aged 84 when she died in 1978. She was buried in the community cemetery. Her remains were later exhumed and reinterred in Milltown Cemetery.

## Sr Bernadette McGrenra

Sr Bernadette was born Mary McGrenra on 10 March 1919 in Letterkenny, Co Donegal. She was aged just 59 when she died in 1979. The journal records her death in this way:

*On Jan. 27th Sister Death again visited our little community and took our dear Sister Bernadette. Sister Bernadette had been suffering for many years but only a few months ago we were all shocked at the diagnosis of Cancer. She was altogether three months in hospital this time, a few weeks in Montgomery House – now called Belvoir Park Hospital and then back to the Mater, here in Belfast, where she died.*

*The chaplain had just left after giving General Absolution and saying all the prayers for the dying. Mother and Sr Paschal (J) were with her, also two Sisters of Mercy. Sr Bernadette was just 60 years of age, 35 yrs in Religion. … Fr Cassian gave the homily and spoke about our Poor Clare vocation and though we greatly miss a deceased sister, still with St Francis, we welcome Sister Death. RIP.*

Sr Bernadette was buried in the community cemetery. Her remains were later exhumed and reinterred in Milltown Cemetery.

## Mother Michael Sheridan

Mother Michael Sheridan was born Brigid Mary Bernadette Sheridan on 7 March 1915 in Belfast. From a reference in the journals, it would seem that Mother Michael made her solemn profession in 1935 and would have celebrated the Silver Jubilee of her profession in 1960 had it not been delayed until the following year:

*July 1961 when we kept 3 Silver Jubilees – Sister Malachy McHenry and Mother Michael Sheridan –were really due the end of 1960 but we thought it was enough for the Community the Golden one in the year so we waited until 1961. This was Sr Anthony's real year.*

Whilst the nuns did not suffer directly during the Troubles, they were brought close with the impact on some of their family members. Mother Michael's sister had her bar bombed. Two people were killed in the explosion.

The community journal records Mother Michael's death in this way:

*At last Mother went to God RIP, having been fully conscious and lucid up to the last. As Mother died early in the morning – about 8.30, her precious body was brought home before dinner time the same day and we had the consolation of seeing her and praying by her open coffin until just before the funeral Mass on 12th October.*

Mother Michael died on 10 October 1981 in the Royal Victoria Hospital, Belfast and she was buried in the community cemetery. Her remains were later exhumed and reinterred in Milltown Cemetery.

## Sr Thérèse Hoey

Sr Thérèse was born 13 July 1902. Before entering the monastery in 1926, she had trained as a nurse:

*When she entered originally, our other Jubilarian and infirmarian Sr Thérèse, was a trained nurse from the Mater hospital and she had been a Godsend to the little Community in those early days. She had nursed us all whenever we had aches or pains, but her outstanding work was her loving care of our dear invalid, Sr Malachy who was herself a nurse from the Mater hospital.*

The last part of Sr Thérèse's life was marked by sickness. She had fallen in 1978 and broken a leg requiring an operation which took place in the City Hospital. Journal One contains details of Sr Thérèse becoming ill in February 1981 and requiring the doctor. This must have been a difficult time for the community as a number of the nuns were also very ill. It is clear however that the courageous way in which she and Sr Assisi dealt with their illness inspired other members of the community:

*Sr Thérèse got a bad turn a few days after Sr Assisi took ill and has been as far as the Pearly Gates a few times since. St Peter has evidently said: 'not yet'. As her doctor said: 'she has a few more rosaries to say' before she goes on the long vacation. At present she is able to be at Mass most mornings. Both she and Sr Assisi are our treasures, an inspiration to us all. Always cheerful and contented, they portray the ideal Poor Clare at the end of a life of total and loving dedication to God. A sister said recently: 'that's what I'd like to be when I reach the end of my life.'*

Sr Thérèse died in the Mater Hospital on 17 October 1981 aged 79, another death which impacted the rest of the community:

*'Welcome Sister Death.' So would have spoken our dear Sr Thérèse R.I.P. and so we also speak. Sr Thérèse's departure is a very big sacrifice and cross, for our little community, so soon after Mother. (We are only 10 now.) but having suffered so much and been near death so often we must be happy for her.*

Sr Thérèse was buried in the community cemetery. Her remains were later reinterred in Milltown cemetery in 2012.

## Sr Assisi O'Neill

Sr Assisi was born Mary O'Neill on 31 December 1890. Journal One indicates she had been in Belfast since 1939 and had been 66 years in religious life. The latter part of her life was described in this way:

*On the night of the 5th February Sr Assisi got a slight stroke. Her right side was partly paralysed and her speech impaired. With the aid of physiotherapy and careful nursing, she has improved somewhat since then, though she will probably never regain her full power of speech. She loved having visitors to her room in the Infirmary, so we call in as often as possible.*

*On Sunday evenings we all spend part of the recreation with her and it is she who really recreates us, singing some of her old favourite songs. Strangely enough, she has the airs perfectly, though she cannot get the words out properly. ... The requests for various songs usually get the same response - most often 'John Brown's body,' or rather her version of it!*

Sr Assisi suffered another coronary attack and was taken to the Mater hospital where members of the community went to visit her:

*Before Mother left her she was singing: 'when Irish eyes are smiling' and calling out for her tea. This improvement was short-lived. ... God called her home at about midday on the 7th. Now ninety-one she had been sixty-six years in religion. Each of us could write her own 'volume' of memoir of her holiness and wit. Let it suffice to quote one of her more serious requests: 'I'm an old woman; ask God to show me the way home soon.' He did.*

Sr Assisi died on 7 June 1982 aged 91. She was buried in the community cemetery. Her remains were later reinterred in Milltown cemetery in 2012.

## Sr Catherine Fagan

Sr Catherine was born Catherine Fagan on 24 July 1904 in Mullingar, Co. Westmeath and made her first profession in 12 August 1929, which was the Feast of St Clare until the revision of General Roman Calendar in 1969 when the feast was changed to 11 August, the day of St Clare's death in 1253.

*Journal One* notes that Sr Catherine celebrated her Golden Jubilee in August 1978. The 1983 annual newsletter records details of her growing infirmity:

*... The consultant told her she had about a year to live, though he told Mother she would go very quickly, perhaps within six months. The fact was, she survived only ten weeks. She accepted the news with her accustomed calm and simplicity and went about her work as usual.*

*We noticed how carefully she packed away and labelled such things as materials for veils and cords, telling us where she was putting everything, so that we would have no trouble finding them. This was just another instance of her characteristic self-forgetfulness, or more positively, her concern for others.*

The newsletter then goes on to record this about the last part of her life:

*On Mother's return from the Assembly on the 25th, she noticed how Sister had failed in her absence. 'Thank God I was able to keep up till you came back,' was all Sister wanted to say about herself. Mother got in touch with the hospital immediately, and Sr Catherine was readmitted the following day. There she spent the remaining fortnight of her life, edifying everyone by her simplicity and contentment. When we used to ask her did she want anything, her invariable answer was: 'I have everything I want; I'm alright.' She was able to receive Holy Communion every day. …on Friday 8th…that night just as we were going down to Matins, a call came from the hospital, saying she was extremely weak and might not survive till morning. Mother and Sr Mary went out immediately and stayed with her…The nurses said she revived when she saw them and then she had some restful hours. She was very conscious and alert all day on Saturday. Some cousins came from Dublin to see her. She recognised them at once and was able to converse with them. In the evening the chaplain sat by her bed and said the rosary with her. When she became too weak to articulate the words her lips continued to move, showing that she was still joining in the prayer. Mother and two of our good friends were with her during the late hours of the night. …While the three prayed for her, holding her hands, at 11.15, she simply stopped breathing, and slipped away to eternity. It was the 9th of October, the eve of Mother Michael's first anniversary, which meant that four of our dear Sisters had been called to eternity in one year. What big vacancies they left in our little community. We still miss them a lot, though we know they are not forgetting us.*

Sr Catherine was 78 when she died in the Mater Infirmorum Hospital, Belfast on 9 October 1982. She was buried in the community cemetery. Her remains were later reinterred in Milltown Cemetery.

# Sr Assumpta Horner

Sr Assumpta was born Sylvia Teresa Horner on 2 November 1951 in Aghalee, Co. Antrim. Even as a young girl aged 14, she wanted to join the Poor Clares. She was accepted by the Order when she was 17.

From 1989 onwards she kept a journal referred to as Journal Two in this book. It describes community events such as the knocking down of the old monastery and rebuilding of the new one. During her time in Belfast Sr Assumpta was diagnosed with suspected Multiple Sclerosis. As well as charting developments of the knocking down and rebuilding, she journals about some of her own reactions to events as well as coming to terms with her illness. She writes candidly and gives a fascinating insight into her own journey.

*Community life – is also something usually challenging and demanding. Even though we do grow to love our sisters very much, we are still human, still women; deprived of this mutual support, I appreciate more, not only Community Life but our community – my sisters.*

*How important too is our Prayer. These sisters and all active sisters have their good works and they are no doubt great but our Prayer is our first and greatest work, without it we have nothing. Here at Nazareth it is a challenge to foster my personal prayer…many helps are missing. I'd love a good Franciscan Retreat.*

*A distraction becomes an inspiration. Two old ladies saying the Rosary together, both deaf, each announces different mysteries. So difficult at first – but then the lights come on and this is so good.*

For someone dealing with a condition like Multiple Sclerosis her courage is clear:

*Dec 21st 1993: God sent Fr Michael to bring me tidings of peace, confirmation and holy joy. Father asked me to name, what made me so happy, one word, what comes to mind?*

*I surprised myself, but had to say – acceptance. God knows …and would I go back to green pastures and sunny days if I could? No, not back, even to have the experience. I long for it, but the present too has its graces, no less real for being in the shade.*

She continued to write in the journal, her handwriting getting gradually more difficult to read until this last entry:

*June 1994: Nineteen years solemnly professed. Pain in neck, swollen, pain in arms… Dr Martin Donnelly came, sent for X-rays, God would speak. Since I let go in June, things began to happen. In the past all my efforts only brought me so far and then the door slammed closed on me, I hope I've learned now, I only want to sit back and watch. The Lord works – 'I am defenceless, utterly.' It is over to you now, what would be now? God knows!*

These lines were the last Sr Assumpta wrote. Details of her dying and death are recorded in the annual newsletter:

*Sr Assumpta had suffered from M.S. for over twenty years. During her last two years her condition had deteriorated quite rapidly. She had been to hospital ten times within that period and each time was at death's door. …She had always prayed that she would die here at home. When at the beginning of November last year, she could no longer swallow, the doctors said nothing more could be done for her in hospital, so she calmly and peacefully waited for Sister Death, who came for her on the morning of the 8th. That was just six days after her 46th birthday. For about a week before she died, she had not been able to speak, but a few days before she died, she lifted her head off the pillow, and looking straight ahead of her, called out: 'Daddy, Daddy,' and then lapsed into silence again. She must have had some contact with her daddy then. He died twenty years ago, RIP.*

Sr Assumpta died on 8 November 1997 in her beloved monastery. She was buried in the community cemetery. Her remains were later reinterred in a cemetery in Aghagallon not far from where she was born.

# Sr John Heaney

Sr John was born as Susan Bernadette Heaney on 6 August 1915. The nuns' records yield little details about Sr John until the last stages of her life. Various newsletters give the following information about her:

> *6th December 2000: St Nicholas' Feast, witnessed Sister John becoming the possessor of a brand new wheelchair – a 'Santy' from the Health Service having brought it along. At recreation Sister John glided into the company dressed as 'St Nicholas,' sporting a brown curly wig and presented each of us with a signed prayer to 'herself.'*

> *…the third week in May 2002, Sr John was hovering between life and death. …On the 15th, it became obvious that Sr Death was round the corner, so we made sure that someone with her all day and night. At 2.15pm, on the 20th, she slipped away, with all of us praying around her. Her sister-in-law, Clare Heaney, a niece and two nephews were able to come from Dublin for her funeral. …We miss her a lot, not least for her kindness, her generosity and her great sense of humour. Through her work as portress for several years, she had endeared herself to many people, who regard her passing as a personal loss. They tell of the many occasions on which she helped them, and how her wit was often a tonic to them.*

Sr John died on 20 May 2002. She was buried in the community cemetery and later her remains were reinterred in Milltown Cemetery.

## Sr Petronilla Murtagh

Sr Petronilla was born Brigid Murtagh on 2 April 1919 in Lanesboro, Co. Longford. On 8 September 1951, along with Sr Helena Forsythe, she made her final profession as a Poor Clare nun. On 12 March 1989, shortly before the old monastery was demolished Sr Petronilla left for the Poor Clare monastery in Drumshanbo. She came to the Belfast community when the monastery was completed.

*Jubilee bells, Golden bells rang out here on the 8th September, as Sisters Helena and Petronilla celebrated their fifty years of vowed life. The Mass of thanksgiving in the early afternoon was celebrated by our Bishop, Dr Walsh, with Father Rooney, assistant Vicar for Religious, Father Michael Murtagh, C.Ss.R., Sr Petronilla's nephew, Father Kenneth, C.P., and Father Senan, S.J., concelebrating. Deanby Choir from our parish, supplied the music and singing,*  *which were beautiful. Large numbers of the Jubilarians' families travelled from Coleraine, Larne, Longford and other parts of the country to be with us.*

The annual newsletter gives detail of Sr Petronilla spending the last few years of her life in a nursing home in Belfast:

*The Sisters of Nazareth have built a new nursing home, having sold the old Nazareth House. The new one is known as Nazareth House-Care Village, and it is laid out in Streets. Sister Petronilla is in No. 2 room, on 6th Street. Hasn't it a New York touch about it? It is up to date, but simple and very spacious; has a large recreation hall, a beautiful chapel, a small shop, a coffee room. …In April, the Sisters and nurses organised an Easter Bonnet party and parade for the residents. It was a Sunday, and our Sisters, who had gone to visit Sister Petronilla, were invited to share the fun. There was a pianist, a violinist, and young Irish dancers there to provide entertainment, and some of the residents, aged up to ninety five, were able to sing 'Put on your Easter Bonnet' which they did. Sister Petronilla sent hers home to add to our store of 'costumes' for concerts or plays.*

In 18 months' time, Sr Petronilla's time on this earth came to an end as reported by the newsletter:

*October 22nd was a sad day for us. At 1.20p.m. our dear Sister Petronilla slipped off to eternity, to we hope, Heaven, which had been the focus of her longing for years.*

*Though she had spent the last few years of her life in Nazareth House, she was very much a part of our community. Our weekly visit to her was always a happy occasion. Her remains were brought home to our Choir on the evening of the 22nd. …Many of her relatives, including her only surviving sister, and priests, came from various parts of the country and beyond, for her requiem Mass and funeral on the 24th. We hope she is now interceding for us in Heaven.*

Sr Petronilla died on 22 October 2002 aged 83 in Nazareth Care Village, on the Ravenhill Road in Belfast. She was buried in the community cemetery and her remains were later reinterred in Milltown Cemetery, Belfast.

## Sr Helena Forsythe

Sr Helena was born Margaret Forsythe on 23 January 1922 in Coleraine. When she entered the Order of the Poor Clares she was given the name of Sr Mary Helena of the Passion in religious life. On 8 September 1951 alongside Sr Petronilla she made her final profession as a Poor Clare nun. The annual newsletter gives details of her eightieth birthday:

*Sr Helena celebrated her eightieth birthday on the 23rd January. It was a special family occasion as her brothers, sister and sister-in-law were able to join her in the parlour that day, and share the birthday cake.*

Her sudden death is recorded as follows:

*Due to heart failure, Sister Helena was in the Mater Hospital, from the 30th September to the 15th October. On being discharged she was admitted to Our Lady's Nursing Home in Beechmount, as with only two of us 'keeping the home fires burning' we could not give her the daily nursing care she required. She was very happy in her new surroundings, and appreciated the care and attention that were lavished on her. …The morning after she left the Nursing Home, Sister Helena died very suddenly. Seated at table in the dining room, with the other residents, as they waited for breakfast, 'she just put back her head, gave two little sighs, and was gone,' according to the lady who sat beside her.*

Sr Helena died on 4 March 2005 in Our Lady's Nursing Home in Beechmount, Belfast at the age of 83. She was buried in the community cemetery. Her remains were later reinterred in Milltown Cemetery, Belfast.

## Sr Gertrude Woods

Sr Gertrude was born Margaret Woods on 12 May 1921, in Lowton near Manchester. She joined the Poor Clare monastery in Liverpool in England. When that monastery closed she then joined the Belfast community in 1992.

The annual newsletters recall the stoic side of Sr Gertrude:

> Sister Gertrude, one of our octogenarians, gave us all a fright on the 1st February. In choir in the early afternoon, she slipped off the sanctuary step, banging the back of her head against the marble surround. She was alone with the Lord. A lady in the extern chapel, who had heard the bang, hastened round to Sister Paschal in the parlour to alert her. ... Sister Paschal came along to find that blood was pouring from Sister Gertrude's head. Soon we were all around her, doing all we could to help her. Sister Evelyn a nurse, came in from Portiuncula, and was able to control the bleeding until an ambulance arrived to take Sister Gertrude and herself to casualty in the Mater Hospital. Sister Gertrude had to get four stitches in her head. X rays proved that no interior damage had been done, for which we were thankful to God. We know Sister Gertrude must have had a lot of pain, but of course, she did not complain, and was soon 'back to her old self,' as we say.

It would seem that she was ready to let go of her life:

> On 9th November 2004, Sister Gertrude went to the Mater, for a routine check-up and was kept in. By the end of the month, a consultant informed her that she had developed cancer and asked if she would avail of chemotherapy. She declined, having learned that it could length her life only by a few months. On the 3rd March, she transferred to the Northern Ireland Hospice, where she was lovingly cared for as her condition worsened.

She was ready to meet and waiting for Sister Death:

*Sister Gertrude almost felt cheated. She thought Sister Death would have called her first, and besides, Sister Helena would be taking her 'spot' in the cemetery. Just three days later, on the afternoon of the 5th April, she slipped away peacefully, while her only sister, Josephine, the Hospice Chaplain, Father Sean, O.F.M. Cap., Sister Bee F.M.D.M. some nurses and ourselves, surrounded her bed, supporting her with prayer. She was buried on the 7th, two days before the Holy Father's interment.*

Sr Gertrude died on 5 April 2005 in the Northern Ireland Hospice on the Somerton Road, in Belfast. She was buried in the community cemetery before her remains were exhumed in 2012 and reinterred in Milltown Cemetery. Both she and Sr Helena were remembered by trees planted in their memory:

*Some of you may remember that our late Sisters, Helena and Gertrude, RIP, spent some months in Our Lady's Home, Beechmount, on the Falls Road, before Sr Death Called for them. The Sisters of Mercy, who run the home, and the staff arranged for two trees to be planted in the garden in memory of the two Sisters.*

Milltown Cemetery, the final resting place of the Poor Clares (courtesy of Rev Elizabeth Hanna)

# Timeline for the Poor Clares in Belfast

| | |
|---|---|
| March 1923 | Poor Clare Superior in Dublin seeks permission to set up in Belfast |
| May 1924 | First nuns establish a convent on the Antrim Road |
| September 1924 | First postulant, Sr Joseph enters |
| June 1926 | Nuns move to the Cliftonville Road |
| November 1930 | Dedication of the new chapels |
| November 1930 | Cemetery now in use |
| June 1932 | Eucharistic Congress in Dublin |
| February 1939 | Death of Mother Genevieve, the Foundress of the Belfast foundation |
| September 1939 | Beginning of World War II |
| April 1941 | Monastery damaged during Belfast Blitz, evacuation of nuns |
| August 1953 | 700 years since the death of St Clare |
| June 1954 | Visit of 'Rosary Priest' Fr Patrick Peyton to the monastery |
| March 1960 | Request for a nun to join the Poor Clare Monastery in Ennis |
| October 1962 | Opening of Second Vatican Council |
| July 1965 | Agreement on re-ordering sanctuary according to new liturgical rites |
| December 1965 | Closure of Second Vatican Council |
| August 1966 | Change to white veils, long enclosure veils no longer used |
| September 1968 | Concelebrated Mass for the first time in the Monastery |
| August 1969 | 'Serious riots in Belfast' (Journal One) Beginning of 'The Troubles' |
| November 1971 | Visit of Mother Teresa of Calcutta |
| March 1974 | Golden Jubilee of Foundation |
| September 1976 | Death of David McCorry, former caretaker |

| | |
|---|---|
| 29 Sept-1st Oct | Visit of Pope John Paul II to Ireland |
| December 1982 | Broadcast of UTV documentary on life and role of the Poor Clare |
| February 1983 | Extensive renovations to the choir |
| November 1983 | Appeal to the federation for personnel for the community |
| November 1983 | Arrival of new nuns as members of the community |
| March 1984 | Arrival of Franciscan Friars in Belfast |
| December 1984 | Dedication of the monastery chapel altar and sanctuary |
| February 1986 | Discovery of damp in the monastery |
| October 1986 | Peace Day in Assisi |
| December 1986 | Recognition of major deterioration of the monastery |
| January 1987 | Decision to rebuild monastery |
| August 1987 | First parish collection taken up towards building costs |
| April 1989 | Demolition of the monastery |
| April 1990 | Building contract signed, first foundations dug |
| August 1991 | Open days for people to visit the new monastery |
| November 1991 | Demolition of choir, chapel and gate lodge |
| February 1992 | Foundation stone of new chapel laid |
| April 1993 | Arrival of first Filipino Nuns |
| October 1992 | Dedication of the monastery chapel |
| April 1998 | Good Friday Agreement signed |
| May 1998 | Referendum on the Agreement |
| April 2005 | Meeting with Philippines Poor Clare Federation President |
| August 2012 | Closure of the monastery |

# Bibliography

Adamson, I., and *Belfast Telegraph*, 2011. *Bombs on Belfast. The Blitz 1941.* Colourpoint Books, Newtownards.

Armstrong, R.J. OFM, Cap. 2006. 'First Letter to Agnes of Prague' and 'Third Letter to Agnes of Prague', in *Clare of Assisi*. New City Press, New York.

Armstrong, R.J. OFM, Cap., ed., 1988. *Clare of Assisi. Early Documents.* Translated from Latin by R.J. Armstrong. Paulist Press, New York.

Bardon, J., 1982. *Belfast: An Illustrated History.* Blackstaff Press Limited, Belfast.

Barton, B., 2015. *The Belfast Blitz. The City in the War Years.* Ulster Historical Foundation, Belfast.

Boyd, A., 1987. *Holy War in Belfast.* Pretani Press, Belfast.

Cliftonville Cricket Club. Official website. Our History. [Online] Available at www.cliftonvillecricketclub.co.uk/wordpress/ourhistory [Accessed 18 June 2016].

Conlan, P. OFM., 1992. 'The Franciscan Family: Poor Clares in Belfast'. *The Brief*, Oct/Nov 1992. Irish Franciscan Province OFM, Dublin.

Cunningham, N., 2013. 'The Social Geography of Violence during the Belfast Troubles, 1920-1922,' in *Journal of Historical Geography* Vol. 40. 52-66.

Daly, C.B., 1984. 'Rededication of Church in Poor Clare Monastery, Cliftonville Road'. *Addresses to Religious, Vol.3, 1982–90.* Archives, Ara Coeli, Armagh.

Delio, I., 2007. *Clare of Assisi: A Heart Full of Love*, St Anthony Messenger Press, Cincinnati.

Egan, C., 1941. Unpublished letters. Archives, St Damian's Monastery, Dublin.

Irish Catholic, 1924. 'Colettines In Belfast'. 14 June 1924. *Irish Catholic*, Dublin.

*Irish Catholic Directory*, 1921. Irish Catholic Directory. James Duffy & Co, Dublin.

*Irish Catholic Directory*, 1922. Irish Catholic Directory. James Duffy & Co, Dublin.

Irish News, 1930. 'Poor Clare Colettines'. 20 November 1930. *Irish News*, Belfast.

Johnston, W., 1998. *Deaths in each year of the 'Troubles' 1969–1998*. [Online] Available at http://www.wesleyjohnston.com/users/ireland/past/troubles/deaths_by_year.html [Accessed 28 December 2107].

Johnstone, T. M., 1926. *These Fifty Years. History of Newington Presbyterian Church, Belfast 1876–1926*. The Witness Office, Belfast.

Kenna, G.B., 1922. *Facts and Figures of the Belfast Pogrom, 1920-1922*. O'Connell Publishing, Dublin.

McDermott, J., 2012. *Northern Divisions, The Old IRA and the Belfast Pogroms 1920–1922*. First Edition Publications, Belfast.

MacRory, J., 1922. *Lenten Pastoral*. Cardinal Tomás Ó Fiaich Memorial Library & Archive, Armagh.

McGuigan, B., 2011. *Cyclone My Story*, Virgin Books, London.

McGrath, A. OFM., 2012. *A presentation for the 800th anniversary of the conversion of St Clare.* Unpublished.

McKittrick, D., Kelters, S., Feeney, B. and Thornton, C., 1999. *Lost Lives: The stories of the men, women and children who died as a result of the Northern Ireland troubles.* Mainstream Publishing Company, Edinburgh.

Moloney, E., 1986. 'Loyalist firebrand blamed for riots'. *Irish News*, 14 July 1986. Belfast.

'M.R.', 1973. 'Certainly Not Sport'. *The Protestant Telegraph*, 17 March 1973. Puritan Printing Co. Belfast.

Multimedia Heritage., 2014. *Voices from the North: The Poor Clares.* [DVD]. Multimedia Heritage, Belfast.

Ó Riain, D. OFM., 1996. 'Poor Clare Convent Wins Design Award'. *Franciscan News.* May/June 1996. Irish Franciscan Province OFM, Dublin.

Parkhill, T., 2016. *A Nurse in the Belfast Blitz. The Diary of Emma Duffin 1939–1942.* Northern Ireland War Memorial, Belfast.

Phoenix, E., ed., 2014. 'Death of Cardinal MacRory', *Irish News* [Online] Available at http://www.irishnews.com/opinion/2014/10/16/news/death-of-cardinal-macrory-105213/ [Accessed 21 December 2016]

Poor Clare Nuns, Dublin. St Damian's official website. History. [Online] Available at: www.pccdamians.ie/about-us/history [Accessed 29 May 2016].

Poor Clare Nuns, Dublin. Unpublished journals, newsletters and community correspondence.

Rumsey, P.M.; 2011. *Women of the Church. The religious experience of monastic women.* The Columba Press, Dublin.

Sweeney, J., 2007. *The St. Clare Prayer Book: Listening for God's Leading.* [Kindle Edition] Available at https://www.amazon.com/St-Clare-Prayer-Book-Listening/dp/155725513X [Accessed 16 January 2017].

The News Letter. 1921. 'The King's Speech. I Speak from a Full Heart. Appeal for Conciliation'. *The News Letter,* 23 June 1921, Belfast.

*Thom's Commercial Directory.*, 1925. Alexander Thom, Dublin.

*Thom's Commercial Directory.*, 1928. Alexander Thom, Dublin.

*Thom's Commercial Directory.*, 1930. Alexander Thom, Dublin.

UUP., 1970. *The Facts: The Bullet and the Bomb versus the Better Life.* [Online pamphlet] Ulster Unionist Party, Belfast. Available at: http://cain.ulst.ac.uk/events/crights/docs/uup70/uup70.htm [Accessed 21 March 2017].

# Glossary

Asperges – the sprinkling of holy water.

Benediction – The word comes from a Latin word meaning 'blessing.' It is also a Catholic Church service in which a celebrant, usually a priest and always an ordained member of the Catholic Church, raises a monstrance (see below) to give a blessing. There is usually a time of prayer known as 'exposition' that concludes with Benediction.

Blessed Sacrament – the name Catholics give to the consecrated hosts (which are reserved in a special receptacle for personal prayer and for taking to the sick members of the community)., situated in the main church building.

Breviary - the book which contains the prayers for the Divine Office also known as the Liturgy of the Hours.

Choir – the place of worship within the enclosure reserved to the nuns, especially for the chanting of the Divine Office.

Conventual – relating to the community.

Conventual chapter – the community meeting.

D.G. – Deo Gratias (Latin) meaning thanks be to God.

D.V. – Deo Volente (Latin) meaning God willing.

Discreet – a nun elected by the community to the council which assists the abbess and the vicaress in their governance of the monastery.

Divine Office – also known as the Liturgy of the Hours marking out the different parts of the day for the praying of psalms and Scripture reading.

F.C.C. short for Francis, Clare and Colette.

J.M.J. short for Jesus, Mary and Joseph.

Monstrance – a highly-decorated metal object used to display a large round host which Catholics refer to as the 'Blessed Sacrament'.

Mother – the title given to the superior or leader of the community.

Noviciate – a length of time to live out the religious life in this case as Poor Clare nun without taking any vows.

O.F.M. and OFM – Order of Friars Minor.

O.H.F. – Our Holy Father (St Francis of Assisi).

O.H.M. – Our Holy Mother (St Clare of Assisi).

Postulant – a person, and in the case of the Poor Clares, a woman, seeking admission into the order.

Postulation – elected by 'postulation'. In the constitution of the Poor Clares, a nun may serve as an abbess for two terms. To serve for an additional, this requires permission from Rome to allow her to do so.

Rogation Days – a Christian development of an ancient pagan practice, for the protection from infectious diseases of crops. Fields and crops were sprinkled with Easter water. On the Feast of St. Mark, 25 April, the Litany of the Saints was prayed in Rome. There are minor days in the days leading up to Ascension Thursday.

Rosary – a form of prayer using the Our Father, the Hail Mary and the Glory be to the Father prayers as a way of meditation on the mysteries of Christ and Mary the Mother of Jesus.

Sext – Prayer from the Divine Office at the sixth hour – i.e. between midday and 3.00pm.

S.F.O. – Secular Franciscan Order (lay members of the Franciscan Order).

Tabernacle – the receptacle in a church where the Eucharist is reserved primarily for distribution to the sick but also for adoration/prayer.

Te Deum – an early Christian hymn of praise which takes its name from its first words in Latin 'You God; we praise'.

T.O.S.F. – Third Order of Saint Francis which included lay people who committed themselves to live by a Franciscan spirituality. The name was changed to SFO as above.

Triduum – a three-day series of talks and prayer services.

Vicaress – a nun elected by the community who takes the place of the abbess when she is not available.

# About the author

Fr Martin J Magill was ordained in 1988 in his home Parish of Glenavy and Killead in Mater Dei Church in Crumlin, and qualified as a teacher the following year. He was appointed Parish Priest of St Oliver Plunkett Parish in 2003, having served in the diocesan secretariat, and then as a Curate in the Parish of the Holy Family followed by the Parish of the Nativity in Poleglass. From 2013 until 2016, Fr Magill served as Parish Priest of Sacred Heart, the parish in which the Poor Clares were based. There followed a spell as Administrator of Ballyclare and Ballygowan Parish, his only post outside Belfast since ordination. Well-known in ecumenical circles, Fr Magill returned to the city as Parish Priest of St John the Evangelist Parish in September 2017.

SHANWAY
PRESS

# PARANORMAL
# NORTHAMPTONSHIRE

ANTHONY POULTON-SMITH

AMBERLEY

First published 2019

Amberley Publishing
The Hill, Stroud
Gloucestershire, GL5 4EP

www.amberley-books.com

British Library Cataloguing in Publication Data.
A catalogue record for this book is available from the British Library.

ISBN 978 1 4456 9398 9 (print)
ISBN 978 1 4456 9399 6 (ebook)

Typesetting by Aura Technology and Software Services, India.
Printed in Great Britain.

# Contents

|  | Introduction | 5 |
| 1 | Abington | 6 |
| 2 | Althorp | 10 |
| 3 | Barby | 12 |
| 4 | Barton Seagrave | 14 |
| 5 | Bletchley | 16 |
| 6 | Blisworth | 17 |
| 7 | Boughton | 19 |
| 8 | Brackley | 20 |
| 9 | Braunston | 21 |
| 10 | Brigstock | 22 |
| 11 | Brixworth | 23 |
| 12 | Castle Ashby | 25 |
| 13 | Charwelton | 27 |
| 14 | Clipston | 28 |
| 15 | Clopton | 29 |
| 16 | Corby | 30 |
| 17 | Cosgrove | 31 |
| 18 | Dallington | 32 |
| 19 | Daventry | 33 |
| 20 | Denford | 34 |
| 21 | Duston | 36 |
| 22 | Easton Maudit | 37 |

| | | |
|---|---|---|
| 23 | Far Cotton | 39 |
| 24 | Fotheringhay | 40 |
| 25 | Grafton Regis | 42 |
| 26 | Great Houghton | 43 |
| 27 | Guilsborough | 45 |
| 28 | Harrington | 50 |
| 29 | Higham Ferrers | 52 |
| 30 | Irchester | 53 |
| 31 | Kingsthorpe | 55 |
| 32 | Kislingbury | 57 |
| 33 | Lamport | 59 |
| 34 | Little Billing | 61 |
| 35 | Middleton Cheney | 62 |
| 36 | Milton Malsor | 66 |
| 37 | Naseby | 67 |
| 38 | Northampton | 69 |
| 39 | Passenham | 76 |
| 40 | Potterspury | 77 |
| 41 | Ringstead | 78 |
| 42 | Rockingham | 80 |
| 43 | Rushden | 81 |
| 44 | Rushton | 82 |
| 45 | Salcey | 85 |
| 46 | Slipton | 86 |
| 47 | Teeton | 88 |
| 48 | Weedon Lois | 89 |
| 49 | Weldon | 90 |
| 50 | Welford | 91 |
| 51 | Whittlebury | 92 |
| 52 | Woodford | 93 |
| | Bibliography | 96 |

# Introduction

A few years ago I began writing on the paranormal. I have never seen myself as a ghostly investigator; indeed, it had never crossed my mind to write on such a subject and the opportunity presented itself quite by accident.

Following the publication of an article on walking ancient trackways, over a few days I began to receive calls and emails giving personal ghostly experiences. Never one to overlook a chance, I made notes and duly thanked all those who had taken the trouble to make contact, although at that point I admit I was still perplexed by why the article, which they said had been the reason for singling me out, identified me as someone who wrote on the paranormal.

One week later the mystery was solved when my complimentary copies of the magazine dropped through the door. The editor had changed the title of the article and described the routes as 'Ley Lines'. Instantly I recalled a large proportion of the calls and emails had begun with the words 'I live/lived on a ley line...' and I had the answer. Two quite different ideas of what constitutes a ley had, quite by accident, found something in common – namely me!

When it comes to the paranormal I have an open mind. This is reflected in the stories to follow. Each leaves the decision of whether it is factual or not to the reader. I often hear how these stories are nearly always set during the night and many locations are in or around the local pub or the church. Whether this is related to religion or even indicative of the strength or volume of the drink consumed is for the reader to decide.

Ghosts seem to have no preference for class or culture. Examples of aristocrats to the lowliest servant, from an elderly man or woman to the youngest infant, or the faithful pet to the wildest of mythical creatures can be found here. Some reported being quite horrified by their experiences, although few, if indeed any, of the experiences could ever be considered malevolent. Most I spoke to were simply baffled by events and quite unable to offer a rational or plausible explanation for what they had seen or heard. This is true whether they were believers or sceptics.

Some appeared indifferent, others amused, and few fearful. No matter what these encounters are, be they tricks of the light or the mind, or misinterpretations of the experience, such is irrelevant here. This book is intended solely to record the narratives, both the traditional and the new, which appear here for the first time in print.

To all who have contributed, even in the smallest way, I give my thanks.

CHAPTER ONE

# Abington

## Cabinet Meetings

In September 2002 a lovely antique china cabinet was purchased for Julia Warren by her daughter. Almost immediately problems began for Mrs Warren. Not wishing to appear ungrateful, she tried to ignore the chills and difficulty with the doors but eventually was forced to admit defeat.

The cabinet doors were locked and, as the key was missing, seemingly would remain so. Hardly a good omen for a display cabinet. However, on more than one occasion a cabinet door was found off its hinges. Yet the crunch came when Mrs Warren saw a figure standing alongside the now unwanted gift. She described this woman, very tall and gaunt, wearing clothing from the 1930s and appearing more miserable than anyone Mrs Warren had ever seen.

Thankfully her daughter fully understood and advised her mother to return it to Trends on the Wellingborough Road. Hence one day manager Mark Kypta had a

*Above left*: Formerly Trends on Wellingborough Road.

*Above right*: Wellingborough Road.

visit from Mrs Warren asking him to take the cabinet back. She required no refund, wanting nothing more than to get the cabinet out of her house and so the cabinet was, once again, back at Trends.

This is not the end of the story, for no sooner had the cabinet been returned than it began causing problems for Mark Kypta. Initially he tried to find the previous owner but when that drew a blank he left it in his shop until he could decide upon his next move. It was then that the cabinet began to create problems. On the second occasion the troublesome door was found wide open in the morning, when still no key had been found, he decided it had to go.

Hence, he approached the local press and announced Trends were to auction off the cabinet, with the proceeds going to charity. Did anyone bid on a haunted cabinet? Was a key ever found? Does the cabinet still exist and is its guardian now content in their new home? Presumably, as nothing has been heard, the answer to all three questions must be in the affirmative.

## Manfield Shoe Factory

One of Northamptonshire's most important employers had premises on Wellingborough Road for many years. Born in Bristol in 1819 to a poor family of shoemakers, Philip Manfield was a practising Unitarian. In 1843 he moved to Northampton to manage a new business. Within a year that business had failed, so he turned to the Unitarian Church for help.

With the financial backing of the church he was soon producing shoes again. Initially producing footwear for the poor, his business benefitted from orders from the army. Eventually his business became a national concern, featuring both factories and retailers. It was listed in 1950, by which time ninety-three shops carried the Manfield name in both the United Kingdom and abroad. Active in local politics, Philip Manfield became

*Above*: Manfield Road is a lasting reminder of the Manfield Shoe Company.

*Right*: The former Manfield shoe factory.

mayor for Northampton and later represented the town as MP. His efforts promoting the town were recognised in 1894 when he was knighted by the queen.

In the first weeks of 1986 the management were already struggling to meet targets due to an understaffed night shift. These problems were further compounded by another visitor. The identity of this individual was unknown, but it was disturbing the staff so works manager Martin Hughes brought in a local vicar. Somehow power was cut to the machines. This only affected the night shift and must have been most disturbing for those present when their noisy workplace suddenly and most inexplicably fell silent.

The clergyman apparently had no affect for the local press got hold of the story. When a Mrs Dhami Sisodiya witnessed an apparition in the factory she no longer felt safe working there and left her job. Another experienced member of staff down, by taking it to the local press she made the problem even worse as potential workers were deterred from applying for the night shift vacancies.

# Abington Park

The author had the pleasure of speaking at this venue in 2017. Both before and after the presentation, I spoke to several people about books I was working on. It is as a direct result of those conversations that the following story came.

It is to the east wing of the Abington Park Museum that the finger of suspicion is pointed. Both staff and contractors have reported sensing a presence, a chill, sometimes accompanied by unexplained electrical faults. Another lighting problem seemed to come from an earlier age, a time when candles provided illumination. For the light emanating from under one door appeared to be the flickering of a candle carried past on the other side. Stories did not end there but also spoke of disembodied whispers, a ghostly face at a window, and a misty form at the end of a corridor.

*Above left*: The Northampton crest with a motto meaning 'peace is stronger than a fortress' at Abington Park.

*Above right*: The house at Abington Park now doubles as a museum.

The museum is all that remains of the ruins of the former village of Abington, and the park once the estate's grounds. The enclosure and enlargement of the manor estate saw the end of the village in the seventeenth century. Prior to that the Northamptonshire witch trials resulted in five hangings here. Are any of the sightings the ghosts of Arthur Bill of Raunds, Mary Barber of Stanwick, Agnes Browne and her daughter Agnes of Guilsborough, or Helen Jenkinson of Thrapston? Or maybe the other accused women have returned to the scene of their trial: Katherine Gardiner, Joan Lucas, Alice Harris, Alice Abbott and the three Wilson sisters, all acquitted but their names now tainted for the rest of their lives.

*Above*: The Church of St Peter and St Paul adjoins the house at Abington Park.

*Below left*: Abington Park is clearly man-managed.

*Below right*: Guilsborough.

# CHAPTER TWO

# Althorp

## The Groom and the Clergyman

Althorp House dates from the late seventeenth century and was built by Robert Spencer, 2nd Earl of Sunderland. The family estate, founded a century earlier, was bought from the Catesbys courtesy of a vast fortune amassed from rearing sheep. This initial red-brick Tudor building was radically altered from 1788, most obviously by the tiles encasing the brickwork. The following story takes place fifty years later, some fifty years before the addition of the Great Dining Room, which gave the house its modern appearance.

During the first years of the Victorian era Revd Henry Drury was invited to stay at Althorp. He arrived in the company of Lord and Lady Lyttleton, the daughter of Earl Spencer. As was usual in those times, the guests were treated to a sumptuous meal and after dinner the gentlemen headed off to play billiards. Before long only Lord Lyttleton and Revd Drury were awake and continued with their game until two the next morning.

As sleep came Drury was disturbed by a light shining in his face. He peered through the light to see a man wearing a striped shirt and cloth cap holding a lantern standing at the foot of his bed. He looked for all the world like a stableman and Drury, understandably irritated by this intrusion, ordered him out of his room. The man remained unmoved no matter how much Drury yelled at him, remaining where he was and not speaking a word for several moments. When he did move he went into the dressing room, from which there was no other exit but, despite Drury's protestations, he did not re-emerge. Thinking him drunk the clergyman turned over and went to sleep.

Next morning at breakfast he voiced his disapproval to Lady Lyttleton. At her request he described the man, recalling every detail of this impertinent chap and demanding to be taken to the fellow at once. She replied she could not do so, as the description was that of her father's favourite groom, a man entrusted with making a tour of the house last thing at night to ensure all lights and candles were extinguished who sadly had died two weeks previously.

## Oak Bedroom

A large room, even for Althorp. It has deep red walls, with contrasting bed hangings of a heavy blue velvet. The latter is embroidered with a gold 'S' (for Spencer) motif.

In 1994 Earl Spencer is working in his library. In front of him are press cuttings all dating from the 1850s by the 4th Earl, his great-great-grandfather Frederick, known to all as Fritz. One cutting caught his eye. It concerned a party thrown by 'Fritz' and one guest, the Dean of Lincoln. John Giffard Ward was assigned the Oak Bedroom. Next morning at breakfast he reported how he had been awoken the previous night by a groom carrying a candelabrum. He informed the clergyman it was his task to ensure all was well. A full description was given and the groom was recognised as John Charles, the favourite of John Charles Spencer, the 3rd Earl and brother of Fritz. One of his jobs had been this nightly vigil. Note this is exactly as described in the previous story.

Later that same year, in 1994, the current earl threw a weekend party. When the guests were departing on the Sunday one held back to have a quiet word in private with the earl. The young lady spoke about having her sleep disturbed the previous night by a man wearing a cloak and carrying a candelabrum. She had been given the Oak Bedroom.

The earl asked for her to delay her departure a short while and ran upstairs. Here he sorted out some of the old servants' clothes and soon found the groom's cloak. However, he had a second thought and chose a second cloak to take down for the lady to identify. 'No,' she said. 'That's not quite right, his cloak was longer,' and proceeded to describe the other cloak exactly, which was worn by groom John Charles 140 years earlier.

# CHAPTER THREE

# Barby

## Webb of Intrigue

A village of a little over 2,000 people, Barby stands on the side of a small hill above the Rains Brook. North of the village is a Norman motte and earthworks known as Barby Castle, although it should correctly be referred to as a fortified manor house.

It is 2 on the morning of 3 March 1851 and in the village of Barby the widow Webb's life comes to an end. Having lived in the village for all her sixty-seven years, she was well known, remembered not only for her well above average height but also for her penny-pinching, tight-fisted, miserly lifestyle. Indeed, many of her contemporaries maintained her unnecessarily frugal attitude very much contributed to the death.

Not until late in life had Sarah Webb married. Her husband may have left her a widow a few years earlier, but he left her all his assets, property as well as money. She did not die alone, having been nursed through her final days by her neighbours, Mrs Holding and Mrs Griffin. When it came to her funeral arrangements and last requests, these were handled by a local farmer named Hart, the nephew of Sarah Webb and sole beneficiary in her will.

By the beginning of April Mrs Holding began hearing loud noises coming from the adjoining property: banging on both the wall and the cupboard against said wall accompanied by the sound of furniture dragged across the wooden floor. Significantly these noises were always heard around two o'clock in the morning, the very hour the lady of the house breathed her last just a month before.

Within a fortnight the house had new occupants. A family named Accleton, anxious to find a home, moved in, then the only vacant property in Barby. All three slept in the same room, husband and wife in the large bed with their ten-year-old daughter in a small bed in the corner. Now there were witnesses to the possible source of the noises.

On the very first night they were awoken at that same hour of 2 a.m. by banging on walls and crashing of furniture. Yet their problems only escalated for one night they were woken by their daughter's screams. After quieting her she told them she had seen a tall woman standing by her bed, shaking her head reproachfully. Two hours later this was repeated, although on neither occasion did her parents witness anything. For the next seven nights the girl awoke her parents with her screaming of how the woman had returned.

The family had come to Barby as Mrs Accleton had been raised here – indeed her mother still lived in the village. Hence while Mr Accleton was working away she asked her mother to spend nights in their new home. The mother awoke at the same hour of 2 a.m. to discover a strange and eerie light filling the room, showing her the very familiar figure of Mrs Webb coming toward her. The same luminous glow and figure of the woman was reportedly seen by three others, including the neighbours, the ladies named Holding and Griffin. Furthermore, it was said the lights seemed to rise and disappear into the roof space, accompanied by the most unnerving moans.

The Accletons and their neighbours called in the landlord, Mr Hart, to relieve them of their woes. Sarah Webb's nephew came along and listened with interest for, although he was the sole beneficiary, thus far nothing of the legacy had been found. It was decided to follow the route taken by the lights and investigate the roof space. Aided by the flickering light of a candle, the landlord and his tenant made a thorough search and before long they discovered a small pile that would prove very relevant. Aside from a large amount of cash, they found a bag of gold, a number of deeds and several other documents.

Yet the noises did not cease, nor the torment of the Accleton girl. Still Mr Hart did not rest and continued his investigations, eventually discovering there were several unpaid bills and debts that he settled promptly, and the problems came to an abrupt end.

# CHAPTER FOUR

# Barton Seagrave

## The Ise and Isabel

Lord Latimer of Burton Latimer was known as much for his beautiful daughter as for his wealth and power in the fourteenth century. Lady Isabel Latimer attracted many potential suitors, but the one from Barton Seagrave proved most troublesome.

Lord Segrave's attentions were unwanted and the Lady Isabel made it more than clear he should forget any hopes he had of wooing her successfully. Yet the love-struck lord would not take no for an answer, not even when she pointed out she was already betrothed and very much in love with Hugh Neville. Indeed, Segrave took the law into his own hands and in a fit of pique captured Isabel, imprisoning her in the lowest and foulest dungeons of his castle. Yet still Isabel pushed him away until one stormy and tempestuous night, a rescue attempt was made.

Burton Latimer's welcoming sign.

Hugh Neville, accompanied by the younger Latimer brother, took advantage of the cover afforded by the thunderstorm and managed to release her. Yet even as they made their escape their daring deed was discovered and the enraged Segrave gave chase. By the time they reached the swollen waters of the River Ise the ford was barely worthy of the name. While the Latimer siblings attempted to reach the far bank, Neville turned to face his enemy. A terrific battle ensued, one which resulted in the sad death of Neville. Perhaps he had been distracted by the cries for help from his beloved and her brother as they disappeared beneath the swollen waters of the Ise, never to be seen alive again.

Segrave may have been the only survivor but his days were also numbered. Local stories tell of how the woman he had tormented in life turned to become his tormentor following her drowning. So vehemently did she pursue Segrave to extract her revenge on her captor and killer of her beloved Neville, she in turn drove him into the grave.

The story does not end there. Reports of her figure continuing to cross the ford where she met her end have been repeated for years. It seems ghostly Isabel is reluctant to even get her feet wet, for the figure is said to float over the surface waters of the Ise.

The River Ise in more tranquil mood.

# CHAPTER FIVE

# Bletchley

## Not So Happy New Year

In 1942, with the Second World War already putting a dampener on Christmas and New Year celebrations, John Rollings was awoken. It was quite clear what had roused him from his slumbers, for from beyond the foot of his bed emanated a startlingly bright light.

As his eyes became accustomed to the brilliance, he realised he was looking at a very odd image indeed. In his bedroom a coffin rested on four chairs. The light came from the candles, each in a silver candlestick, at opposite ends of the open coffin, which, to his dismay, held his father. John stepped from the bed but, as he did so, the light was extinguished. This served to disorient him and he resorted to fumbling around for the light switch.

Turning on the light revealed no coffin and no sign in the deep pile of the carpet that anything heavy had been there moments before. He looked at his alarm clock; it was 1.30 a.m. and there was just twenty-two hours and thirty minutes of the old year left and so he returned to his bed and slept. Next morning the whole affair still seemed very real, but already he was beginning to wonder if he had been awake at all.

Three days later he received a letter from Kettering. It told of how his father had asked again and again to see his youngest son, John Rollings. Sadly, they were unable to fulfil his wish and they were writing to express their condolences and report how his father had died most unexpectedly at 1.30 on the morning of 31 December 1942.

# CHAPTER SIX

# Blisworth

## Tunnel Troubles

At 3,000 yards in length this is the third longest navigable tunnel in the United Kingdom and indeed ranks number nine in the world. At its deepest point it is 143 feet below the level of the hill through which it runs, but here the statistics become almost claustrophobic for there is a clearance of just 4 feet 6 inches in parts. It enables traffic along the Grand Union Canal to avoid a circuitous route around this natural obstruction.

Stories of driving the tunnel through the hill differ depending upon the source. What is clear is the tunnel's twelve-year construction was beset with problems and very much delayed. Certainly, a collapse through a problem with sand resulted in the deaths of a dozen or more, with already three years' work behind them, and when nearing completion, it became clear a little adjustment was required as the two were not going to meet, hence the dogleg in the route today.

One can only imagine the number to die within the cold and darkness of the tunnel's depths. Not only the bodies of the navvies, but the passengers, or those leggers lying on the planks and walking the boat through a tunnel where the horse would find no towpath. Are these the source of the fingers of cold, the bone-chilling sounds and the eerie atmosphere many have reported during the seemingly interminable journey through Blisworth Tunnel?

Perhaps the most graphic is the story of the mid-nineteenth-century steamer that entered the northern end and was to collect a carpenter on the way. A wooden channel had been constructed to allow the workmen to continue without being in danger of being hit by a passing boat. This reduced the width so that only one boat at a time could pass this point. When opened users complained of the lack of ventilation within, a factor doubled by the dogleg that prevents the free airflow we would expect. This proved a real problem.

As soon as the workman hopped on board they opened the throttle and allowed the recently stoked furnace to do its work. Unbeknown to them another craft was coming the opposite way, moving well-nigh silently through the darkness, propelled by two leggers. Suddenly realising the danger, the steamer, by far the more manoeuvrable of the two, put the boat into reverse and began to back out. Unfortunately, this did not prevent a collision but, worse still, resulted in great billows of black smoke filling the tunnel in moments.

The steamer emerged first. Two engineers had fallen against the blisteringly hot furnace doors and were horribly burned. The helmsman passed out just as they reached the fresh air, although his plunge into the canal waters revived him quickly and he was able to clamber back on board where he found their passenger, the carpenter, dead on the deck. The other craft emerged shortly after minus the two leggers, who were either drowned or asphyxiated.

Near the point where the accident occurred a new ventilation shaft was added. Here boaters have reported a difficulty in breathing and the cries and gasps of men desperate for breath.

*Above left*: Mouth of Blisworth Tunnel.

*Above right*: Blisworth Tunnel plaque.

*Above left*: The actual diameter of Blisworth Tunnel is revealed by this artefact left over from construction days.

*Above right*: Only powered craft are permitted in a tunnel as long as this for 'legging' would have proven impractical even for the most experienced.

*Left*: The approach to Blisworth Tunnel.

# CHAPTER SEVEN

# Boughton

## Whitehills Hotel

In the late 1970s the hotel was run by Mr and Mrs Barker. The couple were first alerted to problems by their dog Cindy when this normally fearless guard dog refused to place a single paw on the cellar steps.

Husband Dennis described how electrical equipment developed a mind of its own. Lights on the jukebox went out but the records continued to play; room lights turn on and off even though the switch does not move; the tape deck decided to turn itself off halfway through a track; while the hands on the clock were seen to go backwards. However, most of the problems were back at the cellar, where the trap door rattled and banged with nobody near it. Similarly, the cellar's gas and water taps would also turn themselves off or on when no one was around.

Yet all these pale in comparison with what was witnessed by two barmen when performing their cellar duties. Without warning a very green apparition emerged through the cellar wall. It crossed the cellar, passing through barrels empty and full, before disappearing through the opposite wall.

# CHAPTER EIGHT

# Brackley

## Pebble Lane

Shortly before the Second World War the off-licence in Pebble Lane was home to the Clopton family. Mr and Mrs Clopton, together with their son and daughter, all saw a woman in white in one of the bedrooms. This was not the first unexplained event. For some months they had heard odd noises emanating from anywhere in the house. Sometimes these were footsteps crossing an empty room, but most often as if the feet were shuffling across the wooden floor.

These sounds and sights were said to be the memory of the previous occupants. Two sisters lived together, Miss Fanny Sykes for more than fifty years and later joined by her sister, the widowed Mrs Keeler. Fanny had been born sightless and rarely went out, yet was so familiar with her home she could find her way around as well as if she were sighted, albeit a little slower with a shuffling gait. She is thought to have died within these walls.

The Clopton family did not have their ghostly companion for long. Their home, and of course their livelihood, was marked for demolition. It is often thought major changes result in paranormal activity, and there can be no more major change than having your haunt demolished. While it is impossible to know for sure, one cannot help wondering if she found a new home.

# CHAPTER NINE

# Braunston

## Admiral Nelson Inn

Found alongside the canal, the building dating from 1730 predates the waterway. The public house outlived the heyday of the canal but has been associated with a famous name from those days. Even today the name of Fellows, Morton and Clayton can be seen on the side of canal boats. These famous carriers were responsible for ensuring untold millions of tons of goods reached their destinations quickly and safely. Near the end of these glory days, as the railways took over, co-owner and founder Leslie Morton used this building as his office.

Former access points seem to attract attention here. One doorway, bricked up long ago, linked this building to its neighbour and it seems one lady refuses to accept the doorway no longer exists and continues to walk through.

A second figure, this time male and some say a chimney sweep, comes through another doorway that had once led to the chimney. As before the route is no longer used, for the door now blocking access is permanently locked, while the chimney beyond was blocked up long ago.

# CHAPTER TEN

# Brigstock

## Lyveden New Bield

A little-known building and one that merits some background information. It was built by Sir Thomas Tresham, father of Francis of Gunpowder Plot infamy. Religious persecution, dwindling funds and the death of Sir Thomas in 1605 meant the building was never finished. The shell we see today is almost certainly the work of his grandson Lewis. Certainly, the gatehouse had been moved to Fermyn Woods Hall and the staircase shipped to Detroit, USA, to become a part of the Edsel and Eleanor Ford House.

That the building was never finished is pertinent to this story as, although there are clearly two floors, the ceiling and/or floor between the two floors has never existed. Two men, on quite separate occasions, have witnessed a bearded gentleman looking out from the bay windows of the upper floor. What is he standing on?

Not only sights but sounds have been reported. The drums of the regiment known as the Black Watch were heard, although how drumming is associated with a specific regiment is not clear. Perhaps the identity came from the known history of that regiment who, in 1743, were heading to London to be inspected by George II. News filtered through that the king had travelled to Europe to personally lead his troops at the Battle of Dettingen, thus becoming the last ruling monarch to lead British troops into battle, and he would not be in the capital.

Unsurprisingly the regiment turned and headed back to Scotland. This was a personal rebuke to the king and his men soon caught up with them, surrounding them at Lyveden New Bield. They were escorted to London where, following their courts martial, three of their leaders were executed.

*Above left*: A traditional fingerpost directing us to Lyveden New Bield.

*Above right*: The larger and more modern sign is ostensibly for drivers.

# CHAPTER ELEVEN

# Brixworth

## George Inn

An ancient pub with a long history, locals speak of this being commandeered by Oliver Cromwell during the seventeenth century when he used it as a base of operations for his senior troops. It is not hard to see how the former Lord Protector is the first to be blamed for what some of the regulars have experienced.

Between the pub and the adjacent cottage is a passage or walkway. In 1995 landlord Barry Daubney spoke of how locals had seen a figure in period dress walking along this passageway, seemingly without noticing modern visitors. Before anyone suggests the supposed spirit was a result of too many spirits being consumed on the premises, it should be noted that all the witnesses were quite sober. Indeed, none had had a single drink, for this was at seven in the evening and the regulars were making their way into the George Inn.

*Above*: A delightful village sign at Brixworth.

*Right*: The George Inn at Brixworth.

*Above*: Brixworth.

*Left*: The entrance to the passageway at the George Inn.

## Coach & Horses

Perhaps the best-known ghost story in Brixworth is that of the phantom coach and horses, a tale told since the earliest coaching days and oft repeated over the last two centuries. Indeed, locals have come to treat the sightings, or at least the reports, as almost commonplace.

Along the Harborough Road comes the coach and horses, for once not at breakneck speed but a steady trot. Usually sightings are at night, the first glimpse that of the inadequate light of the lamp carried by the coaches. One such encounter saw a mother driving with her daughter along the road. By the time they could discern anything more than the dim light, the beautifully executed emergency stop was not enough to prevent the car and its passengers passing right through the spectral vehicle coming in the opposite direction.

*Above*: The Coach & Horses at Brixworth.

*Left*: The side view of the Coach & Horses better shows the age of the place.

CHAPTER TWELVE

# Castle Ashby

## The Falcon Hotel

For the next tale we need to think back to 1645 and the Battle of Naseby. Wednesday 14 June saw a decisive engagement between Royalist and Parliamentarian forces in the English Civil War. Sir Thomas Fairfax and Oliver Cromwell, leading the Parliamentarians, were engaged by King Charles I and his army. It turned out to be one of the worst decisions the king would make, and he is remembered in history for the results of his bad decisions.

By the end of this rather bad day at the office, the Royalist force of 7,400 had seen 1,000 of them killed on the battlefield and a further 5,000 captured. Many of the latter would be tried (if they were lucky) and subsequently punished. These included his most experienced officers and men, all the artillery and his entire stores of food, clothing, tents, and ordnance removed. Worse still, he also lost his personal baggage, which included papers showing he intended to bring in Irish Catholics and foreign mercenaries to swell the ranks. Parliamentarian forces, by contrast, numbered 14,000 and just 400 of these were killed or wounded.

Visitors to this site will not have seen an inn then but a blacksmiths shop, the workplace of Arthur. When Cromwell's men came along they demanded their horses be shod. Arthur, a staunch Royalist, refused. They hanged him from the walnut tree that still stands in the grounds of the Falcon Hotel.

A modern Castle Ashby sign is older…

...than a seemingly traditional version erected at the millennium.

Since then several have reported the strangest things such as the smell of tobacco smoke when none are smoking, glasses moved on the shelves, a ghostly appearance in one of the rooms, a shove in the back when nobody is around, and the insistent rattling of a locked cellar door, which, when opened, was found to be empty.

In the absence of any rational explanation, the locals blame Arthur the blacksmith.

# CHAPTER THIRTEEN

# Charwelton

## Murder Him, She Wrote

Two centuries have passed since an awful tale unfolded in Charwelton. Those first few days of the year of 1821 at Cherwell Farm saw the death of the owner, Mr Clarke. While getting on in years this was not due to old age but from the blast of a shotgun, dying from the resulting injuries a couple of days later. His agonised last hours at least enabled him to name the man who had pulled the trigger in the nearby barn.

It seems Mrs Clarke had had a lover for some time. An intensive search was launched for Philip Haynes, a much younger man. As many will know the best place to hide an apple tree is in an orchard, hence it should come as no surprise to hear he was eventually discovered, a week after the shot was fired, hiding in the very barn from which the gun was fired together with the murder weapon. Further evidence implicated Mrs Clarke and the many letters, uncovered in Haynes' room, to her lover that begged him to put an end to their marriage. The trial a mere formality, both were hanged on 10 March 1821 and their bodies given over to anatomists for dissection.

Years later, well before the opening of the A361 bypass between Daventry and Banbury, a motorist driving along near the packhorse bridge was horrified as a man suddenly appeared in the road in front of her. A great cloak or coat was over one shoulder and a gun slung across the other, the hood drawn over his head hiding his facial features. Coincidence?

# CHAPTER FOURTEEN

# Clipston

## Bull's Head

By now readers will be noting the number of stories set in pubs and churchyards. Sceptics will have a field day, particularly with those seen in and around public houses, yet remember many of these stories are from a time when venturing out at night meant one of two things – a prayer or a pint. Hence these were the only places where eyes were able to pick out anything amiss. We should balance this by pointing out the lighting was poor at best and the brain is wired to make order out of randomness – thus we see imagery in cloud formations.

Returning to the Bull's Head at Clipston, where we find a couple of reports, one landlord, while getting the bar ready for opening one morning, looked towards the window and beyond to the main road outside. Alongside the window and inside the establishment stood a figure dressed in long white robes. When the landlord averted his gaze for a moment the figure vanished.

A second and invisible figure is said to wander the living quarters upstairs. At the turn of the millennium a young girl living there was found staring at a single point in her bedroom. Alongside her the family's pet cat and dog were also focused on the same point. Thereafter the child would not re-enter the room, neither would the dog nor the cat.

*Above*: Clipston's attractive village sign.

*Left*: The Bull's Head at Clipston.

# CHAPTER FIFTEEN

# Clopton

## Not Cuddly Dudley

One of the most famous people to come to Clopton arrived in 1395. Noblewoman Agnes Hotot married into the Dudley family. Yet before her marriage she achieved fame when her father had been physically too ill to honour his appointment, a duelling challenge. Agnes, determined her father would not lose face, donned the armour herself. When the combatants raced toward each other, their lances poised, she downed her opponent. Victorious, she revealed her identity to the now highly embarrassed knight. A change in the Dudley family crest still marks this achievement.

Five decades earlier, in 1349, the lords of the manor were none other than the Dudley family. A dispute as to the rightful holder of this estate raged between two cousins. In fourteenth-century England it was inevitable that this would escalate to physical violence and a vicious battle ensued. Dudley not just defeated his cousin, but severed head and limbs in the process. Victory proved a bitter taste and guilt overwhelmed him, resulting in his premature aging, a shuffling, stooped gait and early death.

For more than 500 years the villagers repeatedly saw the ghost of Skulking Dudley, as he came to be known, walking the area once occupied by the estate. Most often along the so-called Yew Walk, lined with the trees that would have stood tall in the fourteenth century, although he was also blamed for annoying the livestock in the fields, a door banging, a broken glass or plate, and indeed any unexplained event.

Eventually the locals tired of this former lord of the manor, demanding the Bishop of Peterborough himself perform an exorcism. Not only did he agree he brought along twenty-one clergymen to assist. The sight of twenty-two candles carried along the route used by the troublesome ghost to Skulking Dudley Copse, where the fight took place, and back to be tossed into the old moat around the house appeared to have been successful for no reports of a stooped, skulking figure have surfaced since.

# CHAPTER SIXTEEN

# Corby

## Cold Knights

The Knight's Lodge inn has been here for over three centuries. Over time uncounted numbers will have passed through its doors, be they still evident or bricked up long ago. There are conflicting reports on what has been seen here, for several have seen glimpses of dark shadowy figures while others report the movement of long white flowing robes. These figures tend to disappear through walls no longer fitted with doors. In both cases, not only because of the length of the attire but because of former ownership by the Cistercian monks of Pipewell Abbey, men of the church have been cited as responsible.

Yet there is a general agreement when it comes to unexplained sounds. Consensus of opinion is that the Knight's Lodge is an awfully noisy place – noisy when speaking of those with no apparent source. For example, an original staircase is said to harbour the sounds of rustling skirts, giggles or barely heard whispers.

Such sounds are normally drowned out by the inevitable background sounds of an open public house and only heard at the quietest moments. This is not true of the heating. Cold spots in the pub are well known, most inexplicably near the former hearth, although such has also been felt at random spots around this former hunting lodge (hence the name) almost as if the cold spot passed through the individual.

In recent years the landlord and his wife together witnessed a monk walk through the bar downstairs during one of the quieter moments. Meanwhile, once more seen by both, a woman in long flowing robes walked through the upstairs accommodation area. Tradition has it that this place is haunted by a woman weeping for her lost child.

*Above*: The Knight's Lodge at Corby.

*Left*: The sign hanging outside the Knight's Lodge at Corby.

# CHAPTER SEVENTEEN

# Cosgrove

## A Shepherd's Story

A humble shepherd counted himself a lucky young man. He had won the heart of the local beauty, a daughter of a prosperous local family. Yet her family refused to allow their courtship to continue and the man of the house decided he would put an end to his daughter's plans.

The devious man had the young lad charged with sheep stealing. Of course, he was innocent but that did not prevent the young man being found guilty. Seen as a serious crime, his sentence saw him transported to the by now well-established penal colonies of Australia. However, the plan backfired. In a frenzy of grief at the injustice, the daughter threw herself into the mill race and drowned.

Around the time of the full moon and in the area around the now long-gone watermill, she is said to wander the region, unable to rest and still pining for her lost love.

Cosgrove no longer has its mill.

# CHAPTER EIGHTEEN

# Dallington

## Church of St Mary the Virgin

Built in the twelfth century near the site of the earlier Saxon church, this Grade II listed building has a couple of ghost stories. The first concerns the seemingly obligatory Grey Lady, the colour a reflection of her indistinct appearance. Two friends saw this woman passing near the church sometime during the 1950s.

The second is more intriguing, a tale from the first decade of the twentieth century. Two young girls went out for a walk and returned home through the churchyard. One opened the door and entered the church but soon came rushing out. Her friend, wondering who or what had frightened her so, also entered the old building and immediately saw the reason.

Both girls later spoke of the church being full of people kneeling in prayer. Yet this was no normal congregation, for they could see right through them – describing these individuals as 'translucent just like bubbles'. No record of any previous or subsequent sighting has ever been reported.

## Sound Problems

In 1988 the residents of a council property in Dallington were experiencing noise problems. Yet these were not coming from the neighbours but emanating from within their own four walls. The problem was that they had no idea who or what was responsible.

It began when Glenn Pendleton and Denise Reynolds, having retired for the night, heard footsteps along the landing passing their bedroom door. On investigating they found nobody there and the house securely locked. Next the doorbell started ringing at odd times, when clearly there was nobody about.

The final straw came when, while they listened to the sound of child-like music coming from one of the (empty) bedrooms, someone brushed past Denise, giving her an electric-like shock. They packed their bags and left, refusing to return.

# CHAPTER NINETEEN

# Daventry

## Viscount Stafford

It is June 1645 and England is gripped by civil war. To Daventry comes Charles I with his Royalist army, prepared to do battle with the Parliamentarians led by Oliver Cromwell. The king makes for the Wheatsheaf, the finest lodgings available and still fit for a king, where he would meet an old acquaintance. He never expected to see the man for he had signed Viscount Stafford's death warrant five years earlier. Stafford had suggested raising an Irish army to assist in putting down the rebels. Considered an act of treason, he was beheaded.

Charles will have been more than a little surprised to discover his visitor that night. Maybe he thought it a dream for he ignored Stafford's advice not to engage Cromwell as it was a battle he could not win. It should be noted this warning came not once but three times and he did express his concern to the generals, but was dissuaded from changing his plans by the commanders including Prince Rupert.

History records this as a mistake for on 14 June one of the most famous battles on English soil saw the Royalists routed at the Battle of Naseby. Interesting to note Stafford visited thrice but not once did he mention his own execution, nor warn him of his own impending execution and removal of his head.

# CHAPTER TWENTY

# Denford

## The Cock and the Blacksmith

For many centuries blacksmith and innkeeper worked hand in hand, seeing to the needs of both rider and horse. Yet the advent of the twentieth century put an end to this long partnership, as the invention of the motor car made the blacksmith's art virtually obsolete. At Denford the blacksmith's old shop has been incorporated into the body of the pub and with it has come the former proprietor.

There are several reports of his appearance in the bar, where the forge once burned fiercely, still wearing the tell-tale apron that marked him out as the metal worker of yesteryear. It seems he is quite unable to leave his place of work. Yet he is not alone for two others have been reported here. A lady in wholly white attire is seen by those coming to and from the ladies' toilet. She is also blamed for locking the cubicle doors when no one is in residence, while a yet more mischievous character plays havoc in the kitchen by removing vital pieces of equipment exactly when they are needed, only to return them the next day.

Denford.

*Above left and right*: River Nene at Denford.

*Below left and right*: Cock Inn at Denford.

# CHAPTER TWENTY-ONE

# Duston

## The Grantham Family and Troubles from Thomas

A title that could fit as the latest episode of *Downton Abbey*, it is really the story of a family and their uninvited visitor. Correctly the location of this story is the new development of New Duston.

Here in the late 1970s and early 1980s the Granthams endured eight years of torment. Their ghost was nicknamed 'Thomas' by the females of the house. The father was the only male and he considered the idea ridiculous and called them all 'potty' – a result of Thomas only ever appearing to the ladies. This was not restricted to those living here, for their friend Amanda Britten came to feed their cat while they were away. As the cat began to eat a strange and eerie knocking sound came from upstairs and the hungry feline left its food and shot out of the door.

Felines and friends apart, the family were subjected to an array of unexplained phenomena over their eight years at the property. Apart from ornaments falling from shelves of their own accord, a weird tapping and footsteps on the stairs, nineteen-year-old daughter Louise Grantham recorded some music on a cassette tape, yet when she replayed the tape the music could hardly be heard for a man's voice shouting over the top.

*Above left*: Modern development at New Duston.

*Above right*: A new sign at Old Duston.

# CHAPTER TWENTY-TWO

# Easton Maudit

## Francis Tolson

Easton Maudit is a seemingly unremarkable village that has little history prior to the late sixteenth century. The vicarage has seemingly always been the focus of interest here, for Dr Samuel Johnson, David Garrick and Oliver Goldsmith were regular guests of the vicar, as is evidenced by the plaque in the church showing the very pew these great men of their day would have used.

Yet it is another resident at the vicarage that intrigues us here. Revd Francis Tolson served as vicar for thirteen years until his death in 1745. He was buried in the church but apparently corners were cut, which seems to have interfered with the good vicar's hopes of finding eternal peace. At the time bodies were required to be wrapped in a woollen cloth prior to burial but, for reasons unknown, Revd Tolson was unwrapped at burial.

He is said to wander the vicarage garden, returning to the pond that had been among his favourite places to sit and think in life. Villagers, thinking this was not a good omen, sought help from the church and it came in the form of twelve clergymen. Together they performed the necessary rituals culminating in thirteen lighted candles being placed in the pond. Twelve for the living clergymen and one for Tolson, each light preventing the men of God from returning from the afterlife until the candles had burned out completely. This was, of course, impossible as the lighted candles could never burn underwater.

Entering Easton Maudit there is no sign of the problems of the eighteenth century.

*Above*: Francis Tolson would not have seen this modern sign.

*Left*: The Church of St Peter and St Paul at Easton Maudit.

# CHAPTER TWENTY-THREE

# Far Cotton

## The Blonde Lady Vanishes

In February 1996 Alison Clark drove home after her shift as a cleaner. The day is clear and visibility is good, it being shortly before midday. Passing the Double Four public house, she negotiated the roundabout and climbed Southwood Hill. Then her troubles began.

Ahead of her the vehicle in front was already pulling away up the hill, while to the right was a telephone box. Suddenly she was aware of a woman standing alongside the phone box and, almost immediately, saw her step out right in front of her car. Slamming on the brakes, Alison expected the worst but, when there was no sound of an impact, she looked around to see the woman walking off up Southwood Hill.

Determined to give the woman a piece of her mind and teach her how to cross the road, Alison drove after her and pulled up alongside. The woman was described as in her early forties, had blonde-grey hair worn in a ponytail, wore black flat shoes, a matching shoulder bag, and a long black coat over what looked like a sixties-style outfit.

Sharon called out and, when there was no response, pulled over and got out of the car. When just a foot away Sharon cried out once more but, rather than respond, she simply vanished into thin air.

*Above left*: A modern housing development now occupies the site of the former Double Four public house.

*Above right*: The road at Far Cotton near where the lady vanishes.

# CHAPTER TWENTY-FOUR

# Fotheringhay

## Church of St Mary and All Saints

Sometimes stories are told based on a theory. At some point a tale is told to explain the inexplicable and, when told and retold, is perceived as an oral history. Such a tale can be traced to this church in Fotheringhay, although those who first coined the narrative could not possibly have known what would transpire in the twenty-first century.

Reports of funeral music in an empty church are blamed on how Richard III was not buried at his place of birth, unlike his father Richard Plantagenet and mother Cecily Neville. For many years it was believed the mutilated corpse of the defeated king had been buried at Greyfriars in Leicestershire but later exhumed and thrown into the River Soar at King Richard's Bridge. Others speak of his ghost walking near the church, further evidence of the former king not being given a decent burial.

Neighbouring Leicestershire has hit the headlines all over the world in recent times. Famously the skeleton has been uncovered, identified and reburied in Leicester Cathedral. Now we are certain the body had not been moved in the sixteenth century or later. There have been no reports from the church at Fotheringhay of late either. Yet, one can only think if the unexplained sounds and sights persist, the explanation will be the same – King Richard has not been laid to rest alongside his parents at the place of his birth.

A famous place name in history.

*Above*: The Church of St Mary and All Saints at Fotheringhay.

*Below left*: Fotheringhay's church is now closed and a danger to the public. A warning from its ghost?

*Below right*: All that remains of Fotheringhay Castle.

# CHAPTER TWENTY-FIVE

# Grafton Regis

## The Manor

The year is 1643 and, as with several other stories in this book, we are in the middle of the English Civil War. On 21 December Parliamentarian forces began a siege of Grafton Regis Manor House. Unlike many siege stories this does not herald a narrative of a staunch defence where those cut off from the rest of the world suffer terribly as disease takes hold and starvation results in them resorting to eating their horses, the dogs and even the rats responsible for spreading all manner of diseases. Here the defenders gave up on Christmas Eve and watched as their home burned to the ground on Christmas Day.

Moving forward exactly 300 years, to 22 December 1943, and six Irish labourers are bedding down for the night in a field on this site. Not only is this one of the shortest days of the year but the nation is at war, so not a light would be allowed to break the gloom. It is not difficult imagine that they would be more than a little concerned to hear the sound of men fighting, the pounding of horses' hooves above the general sounds of a battle fought with swords, muskets, bows and arrows.

Not quite what we would normally expect of a manor house at Grafton Regis.

# CHAPTER TWENTY-SIX

# Great Houghton

## After Hours

Several stories here, all of which seem to suggest this place is and has always been one where mirth and merriment are found. Perhaps this is due to a quirk of British licencing laws harping back to the early post-war years. Normal hours saw pubs shut up shop at 10 p.m., this being the case across the boundary in Northampton. Yet here, quite literally a short step over that border, at the Old Cherry Tree another thirty legal minutes awaited the thirsty. Furthermore, the landlord would also extend the hours illegally by retiring to the cellar, so no light revealed the lock-in to the outside world.

Just such an after-hours session was apparently in full swing when the landlord's son wandered out to the old stables, the cellar being accessed through here, for he noted a tell-tale light from under the door and the sound of conversation. Yet he decided against joining them but did help himself to a drink and settled down to read the newspaper.

Eventually he drained his glass and folded the newspaper, then went to wish the crowd a fond goodnight. To his great surprise he discovered the cellar in darkness and nobody about. On questioning his parents, it emerged there had been no lock-in that night and both had been sleeping in their bed for some time.

An attractive sign hangs outside the Old Cherry Tree.

*Above*: The Old Cherry Tree, a thatched public house.

*Below left*: Great Houghton, home to the Old Cherry Tree public house.

*Below right*: The Old Cherry Tree public house gave its name to the lane.

# CHAPTER TWENTY-SEVEN

# Guilsborough

## The Perambulations of John Harris

Tower House had been home to, and was indeed built by, John Harris. At the time of his death, early in the twentieth century, he was instantly recognisable if only by his posture, for the passage of time meant he walked almost doubled over.

In 1927 local newspapers reported he could still be seen walking through his former home. All who knew him in life confirmed the description as that of the long-dead former owner. Although now more than two decades after his internment in the churchyard, he still follows a well-trodden and predictable route through Tower House, beginning in the high tower that gave the building its name, although this no longer contains the clock for which it was constructed.

Beginning in the tower, he comes through a bedroom, before passing along a corridor to descend the stairs. Reaching the door at the bottom of the flight he exits to the garden, thereafter crossing to where his workshop once stood. This is where he could once be found almost every day, John having been the village carpenter.

Proud of his woodworking skills, he left nothing to chance and even produced his own coffin many years before he would occupy it. For convenience, and particularly so should he die in his sleep, he stored the casket underneath his own bed. His last will and testament requested burial in the very garden where he spent so much time. However, this request was refused and he lies alongside his wife in the local churchyard.

This refusal to adhere to his wishes has been cited as why later residents of the house have reported seeing the man walking through his beloved home and garden. Furthermore, footsteps have been heard plodding slowly through the house and across the garden, while from the area where the workshop once stood the sound of someone sawing wood emanates.

Another refuted this story. In 1927 this was home to the well-respected Mrs Williams, mother to a well-known solicitor and known as a strong and forthright individual. When asked to confirm the reports she retorted, in her words, 'All my eye and Betty Martin!', adding she slept in that very bedroom near the tower and had never seen or heard a thing.

Yet a maid, employed at Tower House for many years, disagreed. Annie Winkless once slept in that very same bedroom, albeit she refused to spend a single night more there after being kept awake by noises such as the shuffling of feet, unexplained banging of doors and sawing from the garden workshop. Then she had worked for Colonel Foster. He and others in the house also heard noises but none would dare investigate the room or workshop.

Others corroborate Annie's story. Oliver Scott, whose mother was the cook, saw the shadow of a bent man crossing the rear courtyard but no figure there to cast the shadow. While taking a well-earned break and enjoying a drink of tea, parlour maid Mrs de Vos felt a hand on her shoulder but turned to see nobody near her.

Villagers were keen to come forward and give their version, many saying they would never be convinced to spend a single night in the house, and especially the tower. Mrs Collins worked there and often heard noises, a Mrs Harrop also heard him in his old bedroom, but former cook Mrs Perkins heard and saw nothing. However, there is a second part to this story...

## Mrs John Harris

Sometimes referred to as the Vanishing Lady, this figure is seen anywhere between Nortoft Hill and its descent to the village of Guilsborough below. She died shortly before her husband and reports began coming in shortly after his burial.

Miss Marchant, the village nurse, reported seeing a white figure coming down the slope in front of her at one o'clock in the afternoon. This prompted her assistant, Phyllis Masters, to come forward and say how she, too, had seen almost the same thing just four weeks earlier at eight in the evening while the light was still quite excellent. The only differences in their reports were that Miss Marchant described the figure as wearing a white dress, while Miss Masters said she wore an apron.

Phyllis' older sister Dorothy had been walking with her friend Gladys Tarry when they saw a tall figure in white pass in front of them before turning off. They said she walked with the aid of a stick, this leading to the connection with Mrs Harris. They searched with the aid of a torch but could find nothing.

Villagers maintained sighting this figure is a portent of bad news. This is likely due to the mother of the Masters' sisters falling ill shortly after Dorothy's later sighting. While Mrs Masters was hospitalised, she did not suffer unduly and was released, fully recovered, a short time later.

## John Croxford

Perhaps this could be considered a third John in Guilsborough that continues to make waves in the town long after they have passed on from this world. This tale begins in the year 1764 when four men – Thomas Seamark (thirty-five), Benjamin Deacon (twenty-three), Richard Butlin (twenty) and John Croxford (twenty-five) – are brought before the bench to answer the charge of murder.

In the summer of 1764 the court heard how, just weeks before, a Scotsman travelled to Guilsborough where he happened to call at the house of a shepherd by the name of Seamark. This was also where the four men would meet and all four were present that day. He never emerged alive. Robbed of his money and goods, the four men murdered him in cold blood before bundling him into the oven piece by piece to destroy the evidence.

Yet there were witnesses. On the floor above, overhearing the events below and peering through the cracks in the floorboards, was Anne Seamark, the wife of the householder, and one of their children. One can only wonder at just how the horrors of what they saw – a knife taken to the throat and, when that failed to prevent him thrashing about, stabbed through the skull – affected the mind of that child, for that boy was but nine or ten years of age. Anne Seamark also witnessed them stripping the body and, after burying the corpse, unearthed it and began attempting to incinerate the pieces. The bones, however, refused to be consumed by the flames and these had to be reburied, later to be used as evidence.

To his credit the child gave evidence to the court, bringing a verdict of guilty and the sentence of death for the murder of an unknown person – a second sad result of that day being the victim's name would never be known. Indeed, it was only through the evidence of Anne Seamark that it was discovered that the victim, whom she had seen selling his wares at a neighbouring house, was known to have hailed from Scotland.

Their execution was carried out on 4 August 1764, courtesy of the hangman's noose. As was the norm at the time, Croxton's lifeless body was put on display near the scene of their crime – a warning to others that such atrocities would not be tolerated and punishment would be the severest permissible. Other corpses were delivered to a surgeon for dissection to further medical knowledge. Yet despite the clear evidence against them all four delivered similar words to the crowd before being despatched. All most vehemently protested their innocence, each speaking to the assembly and telling of how they could expect their offended God to wreak the heaviest penalties on those present for allowing such a miscarriage of justice.

We turn next to the chaplain of Northampton Gaol, who recorded the events of that day. Having performed his role as man of God for the condemned, a role they are said to have had shown little interest in, he noted how their pleas of innocence at the gallows, veritable curses, seemed to affect the crowd, with many showing concern and beginning to question the verdict. Of course, this was their intention – these were superstitious people and any chance of upsetting God would have meant a rethink for the majority.

Yet as their bodies hanged by chains from the gibbet on Hollowell Heath, as close to the spot where the dreadful deed took place, the chaplain received a sharp reminder of the sentence. A pious man, he would always find time to read the scriptures and had returned to his office for that very purpose that evening, locking the door behind him.

Eight days had passed since the sentence and would likely have been well-nigh forgotten. While reading from the Bible he was suddenly aware of a figure standing to his right. Initial surprise turned to fear when he realised that the individual's features were those of someone who was wearing a featureless mask. He later wrote that he knew at once that this was an apparition but noted he soon saw it did not represent evil.

The figure addressed the chaplain, saying he meant no harm and had the permission of God to come to speak to him that day. Settling back, the chaplain composed himself and prepared for the wonders to be revealed by the messenger from the Lord. As the double-wick oil lamp illuminated the room, his hopes rather evaporated as his visitor revealed his identity as one of the prisoners executed on the 4th. When asked his name the reply had come 'John Croxford' before he continued to explain something of the events on the day of the murder and the executions.

Firstly, he named Seamark as the ringleader and main perpetrator of the crime. He went on to tell of how the four had taken a blood oath never to confess and, should it come to it, each would die for the other. Macabrely they had not sworn the oath on their own blood but by dipping their fingers in the still-warm blood of their victim and licking them clean. Their allegiance held that the witnesses, being not only related to the leader but one of tender years, would not be believed, nor would Butlin be considered a potential murderer, for he had only recently joined them and yet was still comparatively young. It seemed they thought the worst they could ever expect would be transportation to the penal colonies.

Astonishingly he then notes the figure is said to have claimed the wife and son's testimony, although absolutely correct in everything they said, should have been dismissed as circumstantial and unreliable as they had not included how they had taken the oath. Furthermore, when asked as to their behaviour in court, the response that they were the worse for drink, alcohol being brought to them when incarcerated awaiting trial.

Upon being asked as to the identity of their victim, the figure told the chaplain that two of them had initially tackled the man but, on discovering him to be very strong, summoned help from the others. As to a motive he who claimed to be Croxford replied that they had not needed the money but had set about him for mischief and a habit of wantonness.

The chaplain also records how the victim's gold ring was buried near to where the murder had taken place. A ring on which they discovered was engraved HANGED HE'LL BE STEALS FROM ME 1745. Hence, they had not attempted to steal the ring, being wary of such bad omens. It was at this point in the conversation that the lamp flickered and distracted the chaplain and, when he looked back, the figure had vanished. Next morning at an early hour the chaplain records that he went straight to the spot where the ring was buried, quickly uncovered it and found that very inscription in the gold.

Several points should be raised here. First, the entire account, aside from the records from the court case, is from the record of the chaplain. The court case does question why neither Anne Seamark and her son failed to report this crime immediately, who replied that they were in fear of their lives as they had threatened her with the knife to her throat. Their son, whose terror would normally have been explained away, seems to have been something of a chip off his father's proverbial block for the local schoolmaster reported that he had seen several instances of bullying by the lad and, in one instance, saw him aim a kick at another boy while threatening to 'Do for him as his father had done for Scottie'.

In the chaplain's record, even if we accept the visitation story as true, it is impossible to believe he managed to recover the ring the next morning. Furthermore, should we really consider the story of the engraving to be true? Coincidences happen all the time and the message may well have been on that gold ring. However, why would the owner want to put such a dire warning and yet only have it applicable to one year – i.e. 1745?

Creaton.

*Above and right*:
Hollowell.

# CHAPTER TWENTY-EIGHT

# Harrington

## Lady Jane

The Stanhope family had held the manor house here since the seventeenth century. Inherited by the Tollemache family after the marriage of Sir John Tollemache and Elizabeth Stanhope, it was known for its gardens. These gardens are central to our story, as we shall see.

An error was made by one gardener employed by the Stanhopes due to him not following orders. The error is not recorded but had clearly incensed the young Lady Jane Stanhope, for she picked up his spade and proceeded to beat him over the head with it repeatedly. He died before the realisation of what she had done filled her with remorse. For the rest of her life she was a different person. Barely sane, she walked the estate and, even though long dead, reports suggest her ghost still wanders these lands. Beware seeking her grief-stricken memory for the legend warns anyone seeing her will be so affected by her misery they, too, will lose the will to live and fade away.

Little remains of this history today. Once immaculate gardens have given way to agriculture, and the house was demolished in the eighteenth century, while the only reminder of the once-powerful Stanhope or Tollemache families is in the name of the local pub, the Tollemache Arms.

Harrington.

Over the years this bridge has taken the railway across on the A6003, just north of the junction. The A43 has seen numerous sightings of a ghostly monk. This apparition seems to be the bane of motorists, although perhaps this is due to the area being a virtual no-go for pedestrians.

Most drivers report the figure appearing in front of their car, shimmering as if in a heat haze. This is worth noting as one driver spoke of his vehicle catching fire as it passed here while he was still at the wheel. Yet others have reported the ghostly sight of the monk joining them in the vehicle, seated in the back seat.

It should be noted that this is not far from Pipewell Abbey, a home for Cistercian monks established by William Butevilain in 1143. Indeed, the whole of Pipewell still surrounds the area of the abbey, which closed as part of the Dissolution of the Monasteries in 1538. Nothing of the abbey or subsequent manor house remains today.

One explanation for the wandering monk is to be found in the nearby hamlets of Great Newton and Great Oakley, not forgetting Barford itself. None of these sites had a resident priest and monks would cross the fields to lead services as required. While this may be one explanation, it does not apply to Pipewell itself for while Pipewell today can boast the county's smallest church, this was not built until 1881.

*Above and right*: Tollemache Arms at Harrington.

# CHAPTER TWENTY-NINE

# Higham Ferrers

## The Griffin

If you are looking for a place to find a haunting, where better to start than a Grade II listed seventeenth-century building with a licence to sell alcohol. Something of its history as a coaching inn is revealed simply by looking at the front of this place, where access to the rear stables could be had through the arch on the left.

During the seventies successive landlords reported the actions of 'Nick, the thieving ghost'. Now while 'Nick' is a clever name, the accusation of theft is a little strong for the items were later found elsewhere. Nick did seem to have a strange taste in items, for among those sought were a pair of spectacles, several T-shirts, a chef's apron and, of all things, a thermometer. Nick also seemed to be fond of music, particularly the song 'Summertime', which blasted out of a tape recorder in the early hours that had certainly been disconnected earlier.

Under private ownership since 1991, several customers have reported seeing the image of a young lady wearing blue trousers and gold-buckled shoes seated at the fireplace. This appears to coincide with each refurbishment. It has been suggested that she was the victim of some unwanted attentions when the inn was occupied by Parliamentarian soldiers. The same source has given her the name of 'Erica'.

*Above left*: The Griffin at Higham Ferrers.

*Above right*: Higham Ferrers.

# CHAPTER THIRTY

# Irchester

## Menace in Milton Road

It is 1929 and for some time the Townsend family have heard an assortment of weird noises in the darkest hours of night. Awake in bed strange wailing, moaning and odd cries could be heard throughout their home. Nothing could ever be found to explain the quite unsettling noises, so they continued.

That summer both the parents and their three children had certainly earned their holiday in the sun. Meanwhile they left the care of the house with the three members of the Rogers family. Nothing untoward happened the first night but on the stroke of midnight on Sunday the peace and quiet was broken by an increasingly insistent rattling of the front door. Initially they put it down to the wind outside but eventually Mr Rogers was forced to investigate. Yet when he came downstairs and threw open the front door, expecting to find the Townsends having returned early, he found nobody there.

Little Irchester.

*Above and left*: Milton Road at Little Irchester.

Nothing changed when he returned to bed. The door rattling became ever louder and before long moans and groans mingled with the noise from the front door. Later that night a nerve-jangling scream forced them to relocate downstairs. This hardly helped as the locked front door suddenly flung itself wide open, slammed shut and later found locked again, with footsteps running away outside.

When the Townsends did return they were hardly surprised by what they heard. The two families joined forces and were determined to sit an all-night vigil to solve the mystery. On the second night their attention turned to the back door when it began rattling alarmingly. Yet when opened the enclosed yard was empty. Almost immediately there came a banging of fists on the front door but, once again, when opened there was nobody there.

This torture continued until Mrs Townsend decided enough was enough and the family moved out.

# CHAPTER THIRTY-ONE

# Kingsthorpe

## Photography Problems

Alan Coare contacted the author and spoke of his own experiences. Living in a securely controlled community with access limited to those with the code, the residents have their own library. Several of those using the library that day saw a woman come along the passageway, enter through the door and walk between the shelves. As none recognised this woman in the blue dress with highly distinctive long grey hair, they approached to ask what she was doing. A thorough search of a very small library showed how, despite there being but one way in or out except for the alarmed fire door, she had vanished.

Mr Coare also told of a problem he had hanging pictures. Mrs Coare sadly died some years before and, when he thought himself ready, he had been keeping company with another lady. Having two photographs of her framed, he hung these on the wall above the sofa. Next morning when he came into his living room both framed photographs were on the sofa. Indeed, it seemed impossible they had fallen (the hooks were still in situ), appearing to have been placed there.

Over the next two weeks or so he replaced the pictures only to find them back on the sofa resting against the cushions the next morning. It was now that his children

*Above left and right*: Kingsthorpe.

St David's at Kingsthorpe.

paid a visit and swore they could not only smell cigarette smoke but also their mother's perfume. Smoking was banned here and, although his wife had been a heavy smoker, he only moved here after her death.

When his children voiced what he had not, Mr Coare replaced the photographs but added a framed picture of his late wife, too. Since then four years have passed and nothing has been noted.

## Cyclist

George Dobbs is walking his dog. Heading north along the A508 towards the Fox & Hounds public house, they pass the cemetery gates. It is the winter of 1940. Conditions are awful. With the temperature already well below freezing, the ruts in the snow created by passing traffic earlier in the day were already hard.

From the opposite direction he noticed a cyclist. The rider was having problems with traction. As the car approached from behind, its headlights seemingly showed a headless cyclist but, being a rational man, George dismissed it as the angle of illumination. Yet the car did not overtake but drove straight through both bicycle and rider. How could he not have seen him? A thorough search revealed no sign of a body or the machine.

On reaching the pub, the now trembling and visibly shaken Mr Dobbs told of his experience to other regulars. He was amazed to hear a retired gravedigger relate how, when he worked there in 1915, a cyclist had been hit by a passing vehicle at that very spot. On a snowy and very cold night a cyclist was decapitated in an accident.

## St David's Church

Building work, refurbishment or sometimes just decorating is often the catalyst for paranormal activity. One such example is this church in Kingsthorpe.

Although much of the work had been completed without incident, when it came to the installation of the new church organ things changed. Imagine the surprise when, as they brought in the new instrument, they noted three figures standing a couple of feet off the ground. Later investigations discovered this would have been the height of the floor earlier in the history of the church.

# CHAPTER THIRTY-TWO

# Kislingbury

## Oh Brother!

Born and bred in Kislingbury, in later years Mr and Mrs Watling moved to a neighbouring village to enjoy their twilight years. Every Tuesday afternoon she returned to visit her daughter where, over the obligatory cup of tea, they would catch up on local gossip.

One afternoon they saw an old acquaintance, Mr Hardy. They watched him open the gate and walk along the neighbouring path. Mrs Watling commented on how he had lost weight since she had last seen him. That had been a couple of months previously, when she learned that his sister, also a long-time friend, had moved in next door to her daughter.

Later that afternoon Mrs Watling left to catch her bus. Seen to the gate by her daughter, she saw the neighbour looking somewhat distressed. Being polite,

Kislingbury welcomes us.

she avoided asking what was wrong but opened the conversation by enquiring after her brother: 'We saw him coming up the path earlier'.

'No. That's not possible,' replied the neighbour. 'I've just had the telegram telling me of John's sudden death this afternoon.' Had Mrs Watling witnessed the recently departed John Hardy on his journey from this world?

The River Nene at Kislingbury.

# CHAPTER THIRTY-THREE

# Lamport

## Something is Afoot

Whether these two reports are connected remains to be seen, yet both are so close it would seem worthwhile putting the two together, along with the tenuous link of both featuring men of God. The first concerns the monk who is said to stand at the level crossing holding a light source. Several thought the figure to be flagging them down and approached to find a man in a brown monk's habit, who then slips away.

Nearby stands the old rectory, a building dating from 1730 that reused fittings from the nearby Hanging Houghton manor house. When a rector brought back a relic that he purchased in a Northampton, he could never have envisaged the resulting problems. In the twenty-first century to hear of a man of the cloth purchasing a mummified human foot in a box sounds, at the very least, unusual. However, such oddities were once deemed most desirable.

Hanging Houghton.

Manor Road, Hanging Houghton.

After showing his prized possession to as many as he could, the foot was locked away securely in the attic. Soon after his daughter Amy began experiencing some horrendous nightmares, dreaming of priests amputating her foot. When one such traumatic experience awoke her, she sought comfort from her mother. On opening the door, she discovered her father's cherished box. It was partly open, with the foot partially showing as if it had been trying to escape.

## Level Crossing

Since restructuring of the railways courtesy of the so-called Beeching Report in 1963, this part of the network has seen several odd reports. In the eighties a lorry driver was convinced he had run over a monk holding a lamp on the crossing. He had had no time to stop as the figure stepped in front of his vehicle.

A similar story occurred twenty years earlier, this time a husband and wife witnessing the figure descending the steps to the nearby signal box and stepping out in front of their car. Both occupants were convinced they had hit him but there was no sign of anyone until the lady noticed a figure running along the tracks and into the distance.

Research revealed a similar report from a Victorian railway crew. Although travelling on the rails not the road, they also spoke of how they had hit a similarly attired figure at the level crossing a century before, again leaving no trace.

# CHAPTER THIRTY-FOUR

# Little Billing

## Soaked to the Skin

Before the First World War, then known as the Great War, a strange occurrence in the church at Little Billing perplexed the rector. During Sunday service, he noticed a young man standing near the door, apart from the rest of the congregation. There was nothing untoward about his appearance other than he was quite clearing soaked to the skin and the rector naturally thought this was the reason why he had not sat in the pews. Yet when he went to find the individual later, no sign could be found. Not only had he vanished but no tell-tale sign of his very damp appearance remained on the stone floor of the church.

In the years following the Second World War the wife of the then vicar spoke of a very similar experience. While arranging the flowers in the church she noticed a figure nearby. Again, this young man appeared to have been soaked through – no surprise as it was raining heavily. She told him to go through to the house and warm himself by the kitchen fire. She would be through in a moment and make him a hot drink. Seconds later he had disappeared and, once again, there was no sign of any wet area on the floor where such should have been.

Other reports of a rather wet figure have been recorded over the last century, one of which suggested the figure was female. Although the tales have latterly suggested this to be someone who had drowned, no record of such a death near here can be found.

# CHAPTER THIRTY-FIVE

# Middleton Cheney

## The Snob and Ghost

For many years there had been stories of footsteps being heard along the floor of the upper floor when nobody should be there and, on investigation, shown to be empty. Nothing was ever seen, or at least no reports of a sighting recorded, yet persistently the blame was levelled at a shoemaker, a former resident who committed suicide in an upstairs room.

However, no shoe had been made here for around 150 years. Recently this has been a residential property but even now reports of unexplained footsteps continue. Furthermore, an unconfirmed story of a head carved in stone and wearing a crown being discovered in an upstairs room has seen a revival of interest in the story. Subsequent research showed this had once been home to father and son John and James Braginton, both of whom were among the many in the county earning their living making footwear.

In between this had been licensed premises that was known unofficially as 'The Nest' until an official name was demanded by the owners. While this story goes some way to explaining the latter part of the old pub's name, the former reveals local knowledge for a 'snob' in this context would not refer to an aloof individual but was local dialect for a shoemaker.

Middleton Cheney welcomes us.

## Girl in Curls

During the first half of the twentieth century a group of old cottages were to be found in Braggingtons Lane. What seems unbelievable to us today is that there was just one entrance and exit, via a door at the rear, and a floor of earth. No surprise that these cottages were due for demolition soon after the inhabitants moved to what must have seemed luxurious new homes in The Avenue.

Yet prior to moving, one young girl had a regular visitor to tell of. As she started to make her way up the cold narrow stairs on a winter evening, she saw a girl of around seven or eight years of age sitting on the upper steps reading a book. She wore dark clothes under an apron of white, topped by her golden hair in ringlets. Just as the girl looked up and smiled, the daughter of the house called out to her mother that she could see a ghost. Her mother did not appreciate such 'silly tales' and told her to get straight to bed.

In the ensuing weeks and months, the girl saw the visitor with the golden ringlets several times. Indeed, years later she could still see the friendly face smiling at her and

The Avenue at Middleton Cheney.

The Avenue at Middleton Cheney is hardly the tree-lined route its name suggests.

would recognise her instantly should she ever return. Of course, she could never be seen in the cottages for they had been demolished. Yet it is thought the large property on the same site is still troubled by patches of unexplained cold in one room of their home and a succession of occupants have spoken of feeling ill at ease.

One story as to the possible identity of the ghostly girl concerns the old well, still found in one corner of the latterly built properties. Down this well the girl is said to have fallen, the result of an innocent children's game that went tragically wrong. Her body never retrieved.

## Mrs Waters

After a particularly busy evening, the landlord of the Dolphin is enjoying a quiet drink with a friend. As they talk, he watches an old lady in dark attire enter through the then front door. He nods a greeting, yet she ignores him and walks past. His friend, who has not seen the woman, did say he felt very cold moments before.

A few nights later the landlord mentions the experience to a group of regulars. They are not surprised and even know the identity of the individual, who had long been a regular at the pub. Prior to the landlord's arrival, Mrs Waters would, in their words, 'sit alongside the window supping her way through a crate of Guinness'.

Note how this phrase dates the episode. Today public houses have the famous Irish stout on tap and yet, for many years, the only way to enjoy a Guinness would have been by taking the top off a bottle – as is referred to indirectly by mention of the crate.

Dolphin Inn at Middleton Cheney.

# Typing Error

Once the rectory and latterly a nursing home, a new employee understandably questioned the story of the ghostly typewriter, which was related shortly after her arrival. Hearing how a famous writer and former rector once worked at the rectory and how he had committed suicide, she thought she would research the story.

The writer was easy enough to find. This turned out to be William Ralph Churton, a prolific writer and brilliant scholar whose career is well documented in *The Dictionary of National Biography*. Yet, he was not the rector but the third son of Revd Ralph Churton. Furthermore, he did not commit suicide but died after developing tuberculosis on 29 August 1828.

However, the biggest problem with this story is pointing to the typist who died in 1828. This is forty years before the first commercially successful typewriter was produced. We should also point out how 'successful' is subjective as the typewriter's inventors – namely Christopher Sholes, Frank Hall, Carlos Glidden and Samuel Soule – somewhat lose their credibility when we learn how Sholes quickly distanced himself from the invention, refusing to recommend or even use it.

*Above left*: Rectory Lane at Middleton Cheney has hardly changed.

*Above right*: Cheney House is now a care home.

From the exterior Cheney House looks much the same as the day it was built.

# CHAPTER THIRTY-SIX

# Milton Malsor

## Ghost Walk

As if oblivious to the modern village and housing developments, monks from long ago continue to walk around the village. No reports of anything inside any properties thus far but outside is a different matter.

First seen emerging from a driveway of one house, they cross the road and walk alongside the walled footpath before turning left into a second building. Here they walk through a doorway that has been bricked up. Is this a reminder of a route taken in an earlier age?

*Above left*: Malzor Lane in Milton Malsor is the centre of the earliest village.

*Above right*: The wall at Milton Malsor where the unidentified individuals were seen apparently oblivious to the modern street layout.

*Left*: Note how the stones in this wall at Milton Malsor show that access has been allowed and blocked at various stages in its existence.

# CHAPTER THIRTY-SEVEN

# Naseby

## Battle of Naseby

A well-known and oft-repeated tale speaks of the battle being replayed in the skies above the battle site. This was said to happen on the anniversary of the battle, 14 June, since the original in 1645, with reports continuing right up to the present time.

For the author this casts doubt on the validity of the reported sightings. In 1752 Britain adopted the Gregorian calendar and dropped the former Julian calendar. This, somewhat famously, proved highly unpopular as it meant 2 September 1752 was followed by 14 September 1752 and an uproar ensued as many felt they had been robbed of eleven days of their lives. What this means is the Battle of Naseby was fought on 14 June in the Gregorian calendar but would have been at an earlier date in the Julian calendar.

Naseby is one of the most famous battles in English history.

It would be highly improbable for a seventeenth-century soldier, even as a ghost subsequently, to have foreseen the change in the date more than a century later and managed to convince every other ghost to appear and re-enact the battle according to the corrected calendar.

*Left*: The Obelisk monument at Naseby.

*Below*: Fairfax's view of the Battle of Naseby is recreated by the platform.

# CHAPTER THIRTY-EIGHT

# Northampton

## A Close Shave

During those first uncertain years after the Second World War when housing was at a premium, thousands of prefabricated houses appeared in towns and cities all over the country. Northampton was no different, and one such house was home to the Hutchings family.

Father Donald, mother Grace and son Adam were living here when it became apparent things were far from normal. Footsteps were heard where nobody walked, doors opened and closed of their own volition and electric lights switched themselves on and off. When sounds of an intruder were heard coming from the boy's room, it came as a shock to find him sound asleep and completely alone.

In April 1955 the family's size was increased by one with the birth of a daughter, Ruth. When her mum and dad went out to the cinema, granny jumped at the chance to babysit. However, when the parents returned they found the terrified elderly woman sitting outside on the doorstep with a child cradled in each arm. Thereafter she refused to babysit and was reluctant to come to the home in broad daylight even when other adults were present.

Yet the most interesting story comes from when the children's uncle, who was serving in the Royal Navy, came to visit during his leave. While in the bathroom and halfway through a shave, he saw someone walk through that bathroom, someone 'not quite there'. He instantly fled, not just from the bathroom but from the building and still only half-shaven! He vowed never to return to the place, even having his personal belongings brought out to him.

## Old Black Dog

Standing alongside, and somewhat overshadowed by, St Peter's Church is this seventeenth-century public house. With Northampton Castle opposite, the stories of tunnels to the church and the castle are inevitable but unproven. Closer examination reveals that this Grade II listed stone-built building has its own quiet charm. Perhaps this is the reason that several individuals are reluctant to leave, despite their lives ending many years ago.

It is not clear just when 'Old' was officially added, although other changes of name have been recorded. Originally this was the Plasterers Arms. After that building burned down in 1675 it was rebuilt, eventually being named the Black Dog in 1720. With the arrival of the railway the inn played host to the railway workers, making the change to the Railway Tavern predictable if unpopular. Soon afterwards it reverted to the Black Dog.

Reports of lights turning themselves on and off, severe chills and inexplicable sounds have mostly been attributed to the notorious events in the area during the late nineteenth century. At the time the pub was under the ownership of one Andrew McRae. His association with the lovely Anne Pritchard was common knowledge, with their affair resulting in a child. In 1892 both were murdered by McRae, although just what sparked this heinous act has never been clarified.

As if taking their lives was not terrible enough, he then proceeded to butcher the bodies. His brother, who sold bacon at the local market, had a copper boiler in which he prepared the meat for sale. It was in here that he dropped Anne's head and limbs, her torso being discovered in a large bag bearing the name of the brother's meat firm. Within hours Andrew McRae was arrested for both murders and charged to appear before the court on Christmas Eve 1892. Found guilty, McRae was hanged on 10 January 1893, the last murderer ever to be executed at Northampton.

Back at the pub, perhaps the misty woman seen on the staircase is Anne Pritchard. Is the perceived dark outline of a man with a black dog her murderer?

In later years a paranormal investigator reported picking up a sense of the black dog, saying it had been beheaded and linked to witchcraft, going on to suggest that this was where witches convened in the early sixteenth century. She was adamant the ghost was not that of McRae, who, or so she maintained, was abroad in Dychurch Lane, near Fish Street. This is thought to be the site of the murder.

## Theatre Royal

Over the years several stories have emerged from this venue. Indeed, there have been suggestions of more than staff members, paying customers and cast appearing here almost since the day the doors first opened on 5 May 1884 with Shakespeare's *Twelfth Night*.

The building has been renovated and refurbished many times over the next 130 years. The first time was in 1887 following a fire, and since the 1960s regular upgrades have been cited as the reason for the appearance of a strange figure. One of these appearances occurred in daylight.

It is March 1992 and Rachel Danville, then twenty-two, and Andrea McGee, aged sixteen, are sitting in the theatre café enjoying what is considered a well-earned cup of coffee. Suddenly their attention is drawn to the sound of the rustle of a dress. Looking up they see a bluish-grey figure, a woman with a walking stick, bent over and gliding, rather than walking, right past them and through the café. The girls were understandably petrified by the experience and thereafter refused to be alone during their coffee break.

Six years later the stories of the appearance of this figure were retold when, during rehearsals for a production entitled *The Turn of the Screw*, props were moved around when there was nobody to move them. Lights turning themselves on and off and doors banging when securely locked were quite baffling, especially for the staff and particularly stage manager Joss Matzen. The play is a ghost story written about two children and their new governess, who takes the position following the mysterious death of her predecessor.

Every morning the rehearsal room was laid out to enable the cast to rehearse their parts without interfering with the performance currently playing to the public. Joss then made sure the door was locked securely before the cast arrived. Yet when returning with the actors just thirty minutes later, he found all the props, including cups, a table, chairs and books, had been moved. Joss had the only key and that locked door was the only entrance.

It seems every place has its Grey Lady and Northampton is no exception, for this was the name given to the Theatre Royal's entity. Over the years she has been observed walking the corridors and aisles, while different travelling companies have reported her appearing in their midst while on stage, albeit never in front of an audience.

This hooded woman never speaks and has been said to walk through locked stage doors and through the green room. The earlier description as bluish-grey fits with mentions of the grey lady wearing a blue cloak with a hood. However, she appears somewhat different to other witnesses, who have said she is aged between forty and forty-five and is tall for a woman – unlike the bent old woman with a stick.

Stage carpenter Bryan Douglas said in an interview in March 1989 that he had seen the hooded woman on three different occasions. The first time had been in the green room, when she had walked past him and ascended to the room above. One staircase, one door, and yet when he investigated the room had been quite empty.

His next experience came when locking the stage door in Swan Street. He saw a figure cross the road to that now locked door and approached her to see if he could help. She did not break stride as she walked straight through that securely fastened door and, despite a thorough search, he could find no trace of the woman or indeed of anyone within.

Guildhall Road in Northampton.

Guildhall Road in Northampton.

To discover more about what was happening, theatre staff allowed a psychic to conduct enquiries. However, far from clarifying the position, they only served to complicate it further. One Saturday in 1989 a local reporter and the psychic locked themselves in the building after the evening performance. Initially they discovered nothing but eventually they came to a blank wall of breeze blocks very close to where the carpenter's workshop had once stood, just off the side of the stage.

The psychic reported sensing the area as it had once looked before the wall or indeed the building had been constructed. He saw a well in a garden with lots of open spaces. He could smell burning and thought it the distinctive odour of a blacksmith's forge. The lady wandering the theatre lived here, he claimed. In her early forties he described her as slim, a woman of elegance and well above average height for a lady. She is a sad, very lonely widow and had been disturbed when the nearby Derngate Centre had been built as this was where a burial ground had once been. Perhaps it had held the remains of her late husband?

Perhaps the spirits took them back too far, for their scene was very different from the modern theatre. A smell of burning was reported, not wood but probably a forge. There is no proof there was ever a blacksmith on this site and there are no records of any burials here either. There is nothing to suggest that there never could have been though.

## Staks

This shop on Gold Street had a visitor in 1996 that worried some of the staff. Unfortunately, although their presence was known, they could never find enough of their uninvited guest to throw him out! Here they stock cane and straw items

No mention of the paranormal on the county sign.

and non-traditional furniture, trendy stuff before anyone had really heard of a certain Swedish chain.

Staff were already troubled before the sighting. Locked doors flung open by unseen hands proved enough of a mystery, but when objects began to fly across the room staff began to fear for their safety. It seems the visitor became increasingly frustrated at being ignored and the objects became progressively heavier. What began with candles and wooden bowls soon became vases and picture frames, then a heavy plinth, and finally the furniture took to moving across the room of its own volition.

However, the crunch came when a figure was seen walking up the stairs. All that could really be seen, because of the layout of the shop, was the lower half of this individual. Perhaps it should be said that a pair of blue jeans was seen climbing the staircase. They were all that was visible, albeit not visible for long. Thinking they had an intruder, the staff rushed around to intervene but there was nobody there.

A thorough search upstairs was undertaken and yet, with the stairs the only exit, there was nobody there.

## Thornton's

Of the many retail outlets in the modern Grosvenor Shopping Centre, our attention turns to the well-known chocolatier – Thornton's. In the spring of 1996 manager Gaynor and her two co-workers were convinced that they were not alone in the shop. All three of the girls described a presence, a distinct cold feeling whenever 'he' walked past.

Initially staff members were concerned about their visitor and undertook some research to try to ascertain his identity. A visit to the local library revealed this was once the site of a thirteenth-century monastery built for French monks. Having discovered they were occupying a site that had previously been home to men who had dedicated their lives to God, the girl's fears were alleviated – and perhaps reasonably so.

However, less understandably, the girls also announced that their resident spirit was either Richard of Devon or Richard of Illingsworth. Just how they made the connection is unknown.

# The Friary

The Grosvenor Shopping Centre is built over the site of the former Greyfriars Friary. Destroyed in the Dissolution of the Monasteries in 1539, there may still be evidence of the former inhabitants more than 600 years after they are said to have left.

Six centuries and six individuals, five wearing grey habits, which suggests Greyfriars, and the sixth wearing white. All were seated and reading quietly when seen by cleaners working at night.

# Cock Lane

No good looking at a map of Northampton today as you will not find Cock Lane. This name was used some 300 years ago, taken from the Cock Inn public house, and had previously been known as St Michael's Lane. The change to first Wood Street and latterly its modern name may have been due to the notoriety the place gained during the eighteenth century.

While there are some versions that put the location as the cellars of the Cock Inn, it seems most lead to the cellars of the old saddler's business. The story concerns an apprentice, a young lad who seemed to incur the wrath of his employer more often than most. Overworked, poorly paid, with an even worse diet, they were the target for every bad-tempered employer. To find apprentices with the marks of severe injuries was not uncommon, and in this example the attack proved fatal. The killer tried to cover his tracks, dumping the poor lad's body in a convenient local pit but this was not the last to be heard from the victim. Shortly afterwards attention was called to the cellar when an awful wailing could be heard. Later a nearby timber yard played host to the same ghostly figure, and other reports said he was also to be seen in the sawmill.

Oddly there is no written record of the murder until comparatively recently. Hence, we have no idea of the identity of either the murderer or victim, nor if the killer was ever brought to justice.

# Cromwell Cottages

During the 1970s workers at a nearby garage told of several separate encounters. Both proprietors and mechanics have seen either a strange mist in a corner of the main building, or what they described as the appearance of a 'Cromwellian soldier'.

One man, when working overtime on a Sunday, was so frightened by the image that he clocked off two hours early and went home!

At the cottage itself there stood a well. A figure was seen here, albeit briefly, before disappearing down the well shaft. Historical records suggested this was a replay of a real event, although the poor chap in this narrative was thrown down this well.

## Ennerdale Road

Formerly a large building stood here, built in 1891 and listed as a mental asylum. By 1907 it was home to a launderette. Yet years later, almost ninety years after construction, a family had made it their home.

At 7.30 in the evening the lady of the house let her dogs out for their evening exercise. Flash and Owen normally charged around that garden, keen to take advantage of every second outdoors, but on this occasion their initial exuberance quickly evaporated. Before too long their mistress noted the unusual actions of her dogs and, seeing that they were both fixed on a point out toward the rear of the garden, followed their gaze.

Standing looking out across the fields beyond the end of their garden was a woman. Wearing Victorian attire of pure white, she stood underneath the apple tree near the pond. Looking closer she noted the apple tree could be seen through the woman; furthermore she also noticed her face had no features. Some years later, having moved to a smaller home, she met with those who had purchased their old home and listened to how, just a few nights earlier, they had seen a woman on the first-floor landing matching the same description.

## Hazelrigg House

In the decade nearly always labelled as 'swinging', the resident of Hazelrigg House, one of the oldest properties in the town, heard a rather loud banging coming from the house next door. While neighbours do sometimes have to make some noise, this continued for over an hour. Yet what troubled him more than anything was the adjoining property had been empty for some time.

A bungalow in the neighbouring garden had previously been sublet and the owner of Hazelrigg had spoken to him on several occasions. The tenant had never felt at ease in the property for twice he had witnessed a soldier, a Parliamentarian, seemingly climbing out of the ground and walking past the old stables before disappearing over the rise. When this was mentioned to his landlord all he had to say was the corner where the ghost emerged had only been uncovered the previous year and found to contain a well.

# CHAPTER THIRTY-NINE

# Passenham

## The Rectory

Undoubtedly the most prominent and important building in Passenham is the church dedicated to St Guthlac. Correctly St Guthlac of Crowland, maybe not the best-known Anglo-Saxon to be canonised, he hailed from Lincolnshire. Having fought in the army of Aethelred of Mercia, he joined Repton Abbey as a monk aged just twenty-four, then left to live the life of a hermit in Crowland. Here he heard and understood the *strimulentes loquelas* or 'sibilant speech' of the demons who haunted him in his cell.

However, it is the nearby rectory that interests us and particularly the so-called 'Haunted Bedroom'. For years it has been shunned by residents and returning guests and although one resident had been warned by the previous occupant of its reputation when purchasing the house, he still set this room aside for his adult daughter when she came to stay with him. Her children and their nurse were allocated the nursery next door.

For two nights the daughter got not a wink of sleep, always aware of a presence in the room and the sense of others unseen walking about throughout the night. These feelings were echoed by the nurse, who, bedding down with the children in the adjacent room, also felt the room occupied by persons unseen. Thankfully the children seemed oblivious to all this activity and slept soundly both nights but the nurse vowed never to spend another night in that awful place.

A couple of years later the owner began much-needed repairs, which included the relaying of the floor in the dining room, which was directly below both the infamous bedroom and the neighbouring nursery. Work was held up while the relevant authorities were summoned to oversee the removal of seven skeletons found beneath the old floor.

# CHAPTER FORTY

# Potterspury

## Coach and Horses

One late autumnal evening in the 1950s the residents of Potterspury House were somewhat taken aback when what should have been a quiet evening turned out to be anything but serene.

Legends of the ghostly chariot had been heard for many years but tucked away in the house this was dismissed as superstitious nonsense by the owner and employee, breeders of dogs. The first they knew of it was the sound of galloping hooves and of wheels crunching the gravel along the path leading to the house. Outside the dogs were barking wildly and the faithful companion inside stood rigid, its hair bristling as it stared ahead.

It seems the occupants were spared the last part of the sequence of events, perhaps put off by the cacophony of barking dogs. It is held that the driver of the chariot, a woman, dismounts and walks up to the kitchen door and knocks loudly seven times. At the seventh bang on the door both she and her transport promptly vanish.

*Above left*: The village of Potterspury.

*Above right*: The former Potterspury House is now a restaurant.

# CHAPTER FORTY-ONE

# Ringstead

## Lydia Atley

Buried in the churchyard, as evidenced by the parish registers, is Sarah Ann Atley, daughter of Lydia Atley. She was buried on 19 June 1849, aged just six months. Infant mortality being what it was in the middle of the nineteenth century, such tragedies were all too commonplace. Yet, a more telling piece of information is found just ten days earlier, for on that day young Sarah had been baptised. This is most unusual. Normally infants would be baptised within a matter of days or even hours after their birth. A clue to the reasons is found elsewhere.

In Thrapston Workhouse in March 1846, the same Lydia Atley gave birth to a son, Henry. There is some evidence to suggest the father was baker James Wilkinson. Henry appears on the census of 1851 as in the care of one Elizabeth Major,

Ringstead.

another former Ringstead resident. Both girls had a history of producing illegitimate children and, as neither have a job or career listed against their names, it takes little understanding to see what they were forced to do just to feed themselves and their children.

That Henry was in the care of Elizabeth in the spring of 1851 is certain as, not only does the census state such, but we know Lydia died in July of 1850. Her body, once again pregnant, was found in the orchard near the churchyard where her daughter had been buried the previous year. Known to be keeping company with William Ball, many pointed the finger at this butcher from Ringstead but no evidence could be found to bring about a conviction.

The sad story of Lydia continues. For the last 150 years a mysterious figure has been seen near the orchard where she breathed her last. Occasionally she is seen making her way towards the churchyard, presumably to visit the grave of her daughter Sarah. Yet, she always turns back just before reaching it.

Church at
Ringstead.

# CHAPTER FORTY-TWO

# Rockingham

## Dickensian Ghosts

Charles Dickens would visit here regularly during the nineteenth century, a guest of Mr Richard and his wife. While here he penned much of the novel *Bleak House*, describing much of what he saw as the setting for events in the village he named Chesney Wold at the home of his character Lady Deadlock.

He also wrote of a personal experience during his stay. Once, from the vantage point in his room, he looked through the window to the grounds below and saw a ghostly figure walk between the yew hedge, planted during Tudor times, and disappear at the iron gate leading to the Wild Garden. He maintained that he saw a Parliamentarian, a memory of the route they took when taking the castle during the English Civil War.

# CHAPTER FORTY-THREE

# Rushden

## Newton Road

During the 1980s a family resident in Newton Road had had enough. For weeks they had been plagued by an invisible and most unwelcome guest.

They informed the press how this infuriating and frightening presence had pulled down the curtains in an empty room, how the bedclothes had similarly been removed shortly after the bed had been made and, once again, while the room was empty. They also spoke of how a torch, made heavy by the batteries inside it, flew across the kitchen, thankfully without doing any damage.

No explanation was ever offered for these manifestations nor did we ever hear of any follow-up and perhaps these events were short-lived.

# CHAPTER FORTY-FOUR

# Rushton

## The Monk

For at least thirty years there have been reports of a figure in a habit seen to the east of Rushton. The road between Kettering and Corby (the A6003), where it crosses the railway line, is thought to be the haunt of a bearded man of God.

*Left*: Rushton – does the monk still roam here?

*Below*: The bearded man of God was reported here, where the railway now crosses via the bridge.

Did the monk come from the church at Rushton?

Once here was a hamlet known as Barford, although this place was abandoned many years ago. Around this time monks were resident at nearby Pipewell Abbey, one being charged with seeing to religious instruction in the hamlet. It seems this monk has a penchant for modern vehicles. Just south of the railway bridge is Grange Road – the name of which tells us it was associated with lands held by the church – which heads east to Geddington. Many drivers travelling along this country lane have reported a mysterious figure, not in the lane but suddenly materialising in the front passenger seat. Not all could be considered to have an overly active imagination, for two drivers who reported seeing the bearded monk in their rear-view mirrors were police officers. Both members of the force reported the incident in 1984, firstly by a police constable and then by a sergeant.

## Rider at Rushton Hall

Rushton Hall has seen much change since the Tresham family's ownership since the fifteenth century. Later it passed to the Cockayne, Hope and Clarke-Thomas families before being sold off and used as first a school and currently an impressive hotel.

Around the hall, the 30 acres of grounds have seen several reports of a horse and rider. Accompanied by a hunting dog, he roams the grounds. Although what he is looking for is unclear, there are stories of how he is only ever seen at points where bodies were uncovered during the hall's renovation periods.

*Above*: Rushton Hall is now a hotel.

*Left*: Rushton Hall's gatehouse.

## Thornhill Arms

When staff and customers at this establishment spoke later of what they had witnessed they were naturally quite sceptical. Yet subsequently they heard just how many were present at the time they were forced to reconsider. All present saw a woman from a different era, wearing a long dress and cloak. The apparition floated rather than walked past an area between the main doorway and entrance to the toilets.

Meanwhile in the living quarters the family dog refused to walk through the area of the landing at the top of the stairs, no matter how much they pulled and pushed the pooch. Similarly, downstairs in the cellar the inexplicable was reported. For example, the key in the lock turned with no one touching it. On another occasion these same doors slammed shut of their own volition, while a light bulb located firmly in its socket vanished without apparent cause.

The Thornhill Arms has changed little, at least from the outside.

# CHAPTER FORTY-FIVE

# Salcey

## Foreboding Forest

Salcey consists of two focal points. The first is Salcey Lawn, the ancestral home of the Fitzroys, an illegitimate line descended from Charles II. We also find Salcey Forest, and together they formed an important hunting chase.

There are three quite separate reports from here, although two could be seen to be related. One describes thundering hooves and the clatter of wheels described as reminiscent of a coach and horses at full gallop being heard. A second speaks of Charles II and his famous lover, Nell Gwynne. The two are said to be seeking the other for a rendezvous, although never together. It must be said this seems a little odd for secrecy was pointless, as their affair better known than any of the king's many liaisons and it may be a case of mistaken identity.

The third apparition is somewhat mysterious, for the hooded figure in the long cloak is always hidden. Some have said this is a monk, an obvious explanation for such an image, yet another suggestion may be of greater relevance. As already noted there is no connection between this place and Nell Gwynne, yet there is a link to Barbara Palmer, another of the king's mistresses and through whom the Fitzroy line was created. It is known that she was as faithful to the king as he was to her and had taken at least one other lover. Justifiably or not the king's jealousy meant an end to their relationship through the death of his rival and was widely believed to be on the orders of Charles II.

*Above left*: Salcey Forest in Northamptonshire.

*Above right*: The forest at Salcey looks far more daunting on a dark and miserable day and even when there is shade from the leaves.

# CHAPTER FORTY-SIX

# Slipton

## Samuel Pepys

Named after the famous diarist, although he made no entries to substantiate the reported events here, all we have is an oral history. In recent years, and a reaction to entice customers back to the traditional pub, the premises markets itself as a restaurant. Often such radical changes during refurbishment is the reason that resident spirits make their objections known. Yet when speaking to the proprietors they could recall nothing untoward either during or since the rebuilding work.

Nearly fifty years ago the sound of shuffling feet moving about in the room above the bar, a room found to be empty, reminded the then licence holders of a member of the family who had stayed in that room for a couple of nights and spoke of the woman in the blue dress standing at the foot of the bed before fading away. Earlier residents discovered ornaments thrown from the mantelpiece and a rag doll torn to shreds in the same room where others had reported a ghostly appearance.

Slipton.

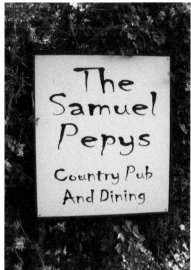

*Above left*: Slipton Lane.

*Above right*: The Samuel Pepys sign at Slipton.

*Below*: The Samuel Pepys at Slipton.

# CHAPTER FORTY-SEVEN

# Teeton

## Pail Face

Shortly after the end of the Second World War, Mrs Leatherland was milking her cow. No automated milking processes here; this was the traditional method seated on a milking stool and filling a pail. This was a typical metal bucket, although great care and attention had been paid to ensure it was clean and highly polished.

As the container began to fill with the still-warm milk, Mrs Leatherland saw a face staring back at her. This could not have been a reflection as the image was above the level of the liquid and a mirror image would have appeared to be an equal distance below the surface as the real image is above it. Furthermore, it was not her face staring back at her and there was nobody else present. Yet she did recognise the individual, as indeed would many people, for this was that of Sir Robert Fossett, the famous circus owner and Mrs Leatherland's brother.

She called out to the family to come and see and many witnessed the image of their relative. All recognised the image, it matching that of a portrait of the man. Yet this was no isolated occurrence, his face appearing again and again over the following weeks. She scrubbed and cleaned using a variety of traditional products, but the image persisted.

A few weeks after the image first appeared Sir Robert Fossett died. However, the picture in the milk persisted and was seen by a number of reliable witnesses, including the local press. All would recognise Sir Robert for he and his father before him had been noted bareback horse riders even before their name was used for the circus. Eventually Mrs Leatherland resorted to disposing of the receptacle. Has it been recycled and melted down, or is it rusting away in a Northamptonshire field with the image still staring out from within?

# CHAPTER FORTY-EIGHT

# Weedon Lois

## Weston Hall

This home of the Sitwell family was built in the late seventeenth century and listed Grade II in 1985. During his time here, Sir Sacheverell Sitwell wrote many of his 130 published books, so clearly none of the reported incidents troubled him in his work.

Within the walls of Weston Hall lives a lady. She is said to manifest herself in several ways, including the sound of her heels as she trips down the corridor towards her favourite room. Others have glimpsed her as she swoops along, dressed in the bonnet and voluminous skirts typical of the latter half of the eighteenth century. When she is visible so is a black cat, which follows her along the corridor. From inside her room come the sounds of a harpsichord, playing this instrument said to have been the favourite pastime of Mary Heber. She was the granddaughter of Bishop Reginald Heber, Bishop of Calcutta, until his early death at the age of forty-two.

Her painting still hangs in the hall, which is now open to the public. Visitors should keep an eye on the portrait for several people working here have spoken of the eyes of the portrait following them as they walk past.

# CHAPTER FORTY-NINE

# Weldon

## A Cock and Nun Story

Currently still an independent village, its growth will seemingly see it eventually indistinguishable from its bigger neighbour Corby. Two stories are told of this place, both explaining the same phenomenon – a blood stain.

The first suggests a murder. A nun was killed by a person or persons unknown, her body removed and hidden, never to be found. Yet evidence remained in the form of the blood stain on the floor of a long-gone house, which, no matter how hard they scrubbed and cleaned, could never be removed. A white ghostly figure is said to walk here, perhaps still looking for her corpse or perhaps hunting her murderer.

An alternative story suggests that this is not the ghost of a nun, but the image of an old man. He is also said to have killed. Awoken so many times long before dawn had been broken by the crowing of a rooster, when he opened his eyes only to see the ghostly galliformes at the foot of the bed he leapt into action. As the bird attempted to make good its escape by fleeing downstairs, close behind followed the man. With an effort belying his years, the enraged fellow finally caught the creature. After wringing its neck, he hung it by a line, tethering it by the feet from a beam.

When the bird was taken down for plucking, a pool of blood had stained the floor and, as above, no amount of elbow grease could remove it. However, the old man had the last laugh for the dressed bird ended up in the pot and hours later, filling the old man's belly.

# CHAPTER FIFTY

# Welford

## Sulby Hall

This estate is now home to a stud farm, as the hall itself was demolished in 1949. However, Wheler Lodge is still standing and this is the location for our story where all manner of noises have been reported both inside the building and from the garden. Bells and bangs, clatters and cries, doors that slam, footsteps, strange tapping and eerie lights all resulted in an exorcism.

At the time it was home to a Mrs Bretherton. She temporarily turned her home over to the family of Major Biddulph, who, as Roman Catholics, summoned the priest from Husbands Bosworth, one Father Petres. Together they sat up all night, fortified by glasses of whisky in preference to communal wine. When dawn broke the men gave up their vigil and decided to retire. As with all good stories, just when everything seems fine, this is when trouble begins.

Reaching the bottom of the stairs it felt as if they were being held and had to force themselves to move away and take a seat to recover. Next time they were able to get to their respective rooms and prepare for bed. As he prepared to pray the priest suddenly felt his knees buckle beneath him and his vision blurred. He climbed into bed but was thrown out. Then, having got beneath the sheets, he found the bed rocking and bouncing him around. He resorted to prayer and discovered that this at long last brought peace and sleep.

When he awoke he had a throbbing pain in his head, his eyes hurt, his throat was parched and, worst of all, he tasted sulphur, which all convinced him that he had been visited by none other than the very Devil himself. With bloodshot eyes, an awful headache and shaking hands he arose and visited every room in the house, sprinkling holy water and offering up prayer after prayer. Not another complaint was ever heard from Wheler Lodge.

Welford is on the very border with Leicestershire.

# CHAPTER FIFTY-ONE

# Whittlebury

## Sir Richard

What remains of Whittlebury Forest, a medieval royal hunting forest, is several areas denoted Sites of Special Scientific Interest. Within the borders can be found hazel coppices, silver birch, aspen, ash, beech and pedunculated oaks. These areas are also noted for the vast carpets of bluebells in spring, along with woodland indicator species such as yellow rattle and lesser celandine.

Some of the ancient trees will have been mature specimens when Sir Richard roamed the forest, heartbroken at being shunned by his true love. A similar tale tells of a young knight who was teased and ridiculed by the beautiful woman he adored. So pained and humiliated was the knight that he took his own life. She will forever walk the woodland until she is forgiven by her former suitor. There is also the tale of the headless horseman who rides along the trackways through the forest, galloping along accompanied by his equally ghostly dog.

It seems there may be some crossover between the three stories. Perhaps a clue to this is found in later reports of a group staying in a house to investigate the reports. Some felt and heard nothing, but others spoke of hearing the hooves of a horse at the gallop and of the air being moved as if by something passing nearby them at pace.

# CHAPTER FIFTY-TWO

# Woodford

## St Mary the Virgin

In 1866 the thirteenth-century Church of St Mary the Virgin was undergoing much needed repairs. One piece of masonry in the stone archway of the nave was in a particularly bad state. Removing a wooden supporting beam allowed the broken stone to be taken away, revealing a hidden recess lay behind.

Reaching inside the builder pulled out what he believed to be an old bird's nest, hence he simply allowed it to fall to the floor. This turned out to be the badly decayed remains of a small wicker basket, which disintegrated as it hit the floor, revealing a small bundle of coarse cloth. Hoping to find treasure within they quickly unwrapped the bundle, only to find it contained a mummified human heart.

Such 'relics' were much prized in the Middle Ages for these were considered the source of miracles, which in turn led to pilgrims, and ultimately money. Presumably it had been hidden here to protect it during the Dissolution of the Monasteries by Henry VIII. However, this did not reveal the original owner of the heart, what connected it to Woodford and thus why it was brought here.

These discoveries were as difficult to keep secret in the nineteenth century as they are today. Thus very soon the whole village was asking the same questions concerning this heart. Two villagers heard of the discovery and these women were very keen to tell their stories to anyone who would listen.

Both ladies had volunteered their time to take care of the church interior. One had been arranging some flowers when she saw a figure in the habit of a monk approach the altar, where he knelt to pray. She managed to summon the courage to run from the church and return with a priest. However, by the time they returned the figure had vanished.

The second had been dusting pews near the back of the church when she saw a figure answering the same description, this time approaching her from the direction of the altar. Unlike the other, the second woman remained rooted to the spot until he vanished before her very eyes. Interestingly his disappearance was exactly beneath the arch where the recess was later recovered by the stonemasons working here in 1866. For both women this was sufficient explanation. The heart belonged to the monk, although this did not answer the question of who this figure may have been.

One suggestion of this being the heart of a knight who had fought in the Holy Land on one of the Crusades was to be expected. Returning with the body of a fallen comrade would have proven impossible, but a heart would easily fit into a pouch or bag and much easier to preserve. Yet this did not explain who and surely did not fit the image of the monk.

*Above and left*: Woodford.

One researcher came up with the most plausible reason, at least for the discovery of the heart. Among the documents of the Duke of Buccleuch was a note regarding the death of one Roger de Kirketon. This man had married the daughter of Lord Robert Mauf and, on his death in 1280, his body was interred at the place of his death in Norfolk, while his heart had been brought to the church at Woodford. It seems this was ordered by his brother, an officer of Peterborough Cathedral named as 'W de Wod'.

During the 1960s two boys were cycling around the area. They stopped off in Woodford to take photographs both inside and outside the church. When developed the inside images included the sight of a ghostly knight. Scrutinised by photographic experts these images, dismissed as forgeries by the press, could not be proven to be anything but genuine.

*Right and below*: Church at Woodford.

# Bibliography

Ball, David, *Ringstead People* (http://ringstead.squarespace.com/)

Codd, Daniel, *Mysterious Northamptonshire* (Kidderminster: Breedon Books Publishing, 2009)

Gould, Jack, *Gothick Northamptonshire* (Princes Risborough: Shire Publications, 1992)

Hill, Peter, *Folklore of Northamptonshire* (Stroud: The History Press, 2009)

Houghton, John, *Eccentrics & Villains, Hauntings and Heroes* (Dunstable: The Book Castle, 1994)

Lee, Dr F. G., *Glimpses of the Supernatural* (CreateSpace, 2017)

O'Donnell, Elliott, *Byways of Ghost Land* (London: Forgotten Books, Reprinted 2017)

O'Donnell, Elliott, *Haunted Houses of Britain* (Glasgow: Andesite Press, Reprinted 2017)

Pipe, Marian, *Tales of Old Northamptonshire* (Newbury: Countryside Books, 1990)

Priest, Dorothy, *Haunted Inns of Northamptonshire* (Wellingborough: W. D. Wharton, 2007)

Sherwood, Simon, *Haunted Northamptonshire* (London: Black Shuck Press, 2013)

*Chronicle and Echo*
*Northampton Chronicle*
*Northampton Independent*
*Northamptonshire Life*
*Northampton Life Magazine*
*Northampton Mercury and Herald*

Middleton Cheney History Society